ALDO ROSSI

ARCHITECTURE
1981–1991

EDITED BY MORRIS ADJMI
INTRODUCTION BY DIANE GHIRARDO
TEXT AND AFTERWORD BY KAREN STEIN
ESSAY BY ALDO ROSSI

PRINCETON ARCHITECTURAL PRESS

Book Design
Studio di Architettura, New York

Layout/Graphics
Lisa Mahar-Keplinger

Associate editor
Stefanie Lew

Published in the United States of America by
Princeton Architectural Press, Inc.
37 East 7th Street
New York, New York 10003
212.995.9620

Printed and bound in Canada by Friesen Printers.

Library of Congress Cataloging-in-Publication Data
Rossi, Aldo, 1931–
Aldo Rossi : architecture, 1981–1991 / Morris Adjmi, editor ; introduction by Diane Ghirardo ; text and afterword by Karen Stein ; essay by Aldo Rossi.
304 p. 9 x 12 in.
Includes bibliographical references.
ISBN 1-878271-15-6 (cloth) : $60.00.
ISBN 1-878271-16-4 (paper) : $40.00.
1. Rossi, Aldo, 1931– —Themes, motives.
2. Architecture, Postmodern—Themes, motives.
I. Adjmi, Morris. II. Ghirardo, Diane.
III. Rossi, Aldo. IV. Stein, Karen. V. Title.
NA1123.R616A4 1991
720'.92—dc20   91-27398 CIP

Cover photo: Barbara Burg and Oliver Schuh

Acknowledgements

Since I am by nature a bit shy, it fascinates me that a group of my American friends believed it would be useful to publish a collection of my projects, and that they managed, with considerable effort, to do so.

I wish first to thank Kevin Lippert of Princeton Architectural Press for having assumed the risk of such a project, and Stefanie Lew for her editorial assistance. Thanks also to Morris Adjmi, editor of this volume, for having the patience, but especially the impatience, to put the book together. Along with him, thanks are due to Ghego Da Pozzo and Max Scheurer, who work with me every day, collaborating on the book and on my projects.

But above all, I must thank three American women. Lisa Mahar-Keplinger who worked day after day with grace and intelligence on the book, and responded to my tediousness and occasional brusqueness with her enigmatic smile.

Karen Stein, whom I sometimes call Barbara because she seems to have emerged from a Venetian painting, wrote a lovely essay. Karen has frequently and beautifully introduced my work in America. I fondly admire her.

And last, Diane Ghirardo. My dear Diane, what can I say to you? Texas highways and the most incredible American universities, and your Italian face, and even Rome, which I do not love, but which you manage to Americanize enough for me to like—or is it the reverse? I want to thank everyone without asking the time. As in Byron's *Manfred*, the time is always "an hour before sunset."

CONTENTS

PART ONE

A NEW INTERNATIONAL STYLE
THE THEATER OF SHADOWS

A NEW INTERNATIONAL STYLE

MORRIS ADJMI

The projects in this volume cover Aldo Rossi's work during the decade 1981–1991, a period that witnessed not only a progressive increase in the number of projects from one year to the next, but also their globalization, with buildings in Europe, Asia, and America. The work in the past ten years has built on the foundations laid in earlier projects both in terms of theory and built form.

The success and dispersion of this architecture can be seen as the realization of one of the dreams of the Modern Movement, the hope for an international style with a specific aesthetic image. There are, however, fundamental differences between the work of "modern" architects and that of Aldo, and for this reason I prefer to use the phrase a "new International Style." Until 1981, when Aldo Rossi was awarded first prize for the Friedrichstadt housing project in Berlin by the IBA, almost all his projects were located in Italy, specifically in the northern and Lombardy regions. These projects have a strong typological and morphological sense that relates to the sense of place, a principle he expounded in *The Architecture of City*. The buildings share more with the indigenous or "anonymous" architectures of those regions than with a modern ideal. Gallaratese (1969) has more in common with the traditional apartment houses in Milan than with the nearby contemporary constructions in the city's *periferia*. At the same time, the project is more than a study of type or vernacular architecture—Gallaratese would have been impossible without the conscience of the Modern Movement. In terms of scale, materials, and structure, Gallaratese is a modern building.

The idea of a "new International Style" comes from a specific attitude about architectural design as well as from the changes that are reconstituting the world as a global village. It is an architecture that has regional and global components—one that is inseparably universal and inherently specific.

Rather than approaching each project as an imposition of some ideal image or utopian solution, Aldo tries to understand the specifics of the site and the cultural spirit of the city and country. This is not to say that his work is without personal identity; rather, the projects share common themes and forms. This idea is best seen in a comparison of the Friedrichstadt housing project in Berlin (1981) and the Vialba apartment building in Milan (1985). Both projects are similar in size and program. Even though the plans are almost identical—including the famous Filarete column at the corner—the impression of the two buildings is very different. It would be impossible to exchange their locations. Friedrichstadt is *Berliner*. Vialba is *Milanese*. Aldo explained this attitude in his acceptance of the Pritzker Prize:

I have never believed that any profession could be disjointed from culture...I am fascinated by the possibility of building in different places and countries. It is as if all the cultures of these diverse countries make up my architecture and come together to form a whole— a unity that has the capacity to recompose the fragments of those things that were originally lost. Like many architects today, I am working in many places around the world—in Italy, Germany, England, America, and Japan. This is a sign of a new architecture that supersedes style and personal character, a universal architecture.

When we first presented the Il Palazzo project to the client, he was extremely happy to have an Italian building. We thought the building was Japanese. In fact, it is both and more. It is the Baptistery in Parma, a turn-of-the-century cast-iron building of New York's SoHo, and a collage of the way we experience the city and the world today. Years ago, I expressed the idea that Aldo works like a Pop artist. He uses the city as his palette. Everything is a potential source: high and low, classical and vulgar. The poetry in Aldo's work comes from his ability to carefully blend these artifacts and experiences into a coherent whole. In looking at the projects collected in this book, I think that view is even more valid today.

THE THEATER OF SHADOWS

DIANE GHIRARDO

In 1978, Aldo Rossi designed a simple box with a steel skeleton topped by a pediment and a clock (bottom). He devised this Teatrino Scientifico (Little Scientific Theater) as a machine with which to study architectural elements. Like all theaters and projects, he later wrote, its sole purpose was to be "a tool, an instrument, a useful space where definitive action could occur."[1] Upon this miniature stage, Rossi orchestrated endless recombinations of the elemental stereometries so fundamental to his work, something akin to five-finger exercises for larger designs. Having elaborated a theory of architecture in *The Architecture of the City* (1966), he rendered his ideas about buildings in this Teatrino Scientifico and at once encapsulated a microcosm of the themes that continue to inform his projects.

The conception of architecture as a theater or stage of the world dates back to classical antiquity and stubbornly recurs through the subsequent millennia. Stage performance expressed civic ideology in classical Greek theater, and Roman theaters articulated the relationship between theater and public life in the architecturally defined *scaenae frons* with projecting columns and niches on a palace facade.[2] By the late sixteenth century, theaters began to detach from ecclesiastical and courtly constraints to become distinct urban structures once again, in which the treatment of interiors often replicated an idealized but recognizable urban public space.[3] Explicit references to architecture and theater surface in the Prologue to Palladio's Fourth Book and also in his Teatro Olimpico in Vicenza, in Serlio's Second Book, and later in Karl Friedrich Schinkel's presentation drawings of his theater project in Berlin. By the nineteenth century, when Carlo Francesco Barabino designed the Teatro Carlo Felice for Genoa, operatic and other stage productions demanded that the architecturally elaborated *scaenae frons* of antiquity give way to constantly changing pictorial backdrops stretched on canvas frames.

Heir to this legacy, Rossi consistently explores the conception of architecture as the stage of life. In the Carlo Felice Theater in Genoa, he evoked the ancient bonds between city and theater, reality and representation, in both interior and exterior for the reconstruction of a theater which by 1981 was a double casualty: first of Allied bombs during World War II, then of two ill-fated post-war reconstruction attempts. Barabino's orientation of the building responded to the complicated urban context,

with the pronaos opening on Piazza Mazzini and the expanse of Piazza de Ferrari beyond, while the rusticated masonry portico faced a busy thoroughfare. Only the portico and pronaos remained following the massive destruction caused by repeated bombings during World War II, and both post-war restoration proposals envisioned retaining the double entrance.[4] Rossi also elected to reconstruct the building's exterior much as it had been before World War II with the original pronaos and the masonry portico. Barabino could not have anticipated that another typical nineteenth-century bourgeois urban structure, the Galleria Mazzini, would be erected as a shopping arcade on the theater's eastern flank. Rossi acknowledged this important urban structure by opening a passageway, in effect a covered piazza, from the pronaos to the slightly off-axis entrance to the Galleria.

The three screens of trabeated colonnades lead into the covered walkway and theater and also mediate urban vistas: every view out from the interior passageway is architecturally framed, a constant reminder that Carlo Felice constitutes a nodal point in a complex matrix of public, private, and commercial zones. As in its antique Roman prototypes, the interior passage is elevated above street level and articulates the junction between public and private spheres. Two axes intersect in the interior piazza, one terminating at the stage inside the theater and another connecting Galleria Mazzini and Piazza Mazzini. Together they emphasize the double role of thoroughfare and theater forecourt, and in each case, one is led into a cityscape, either the real one of Genoa or the simulated one inside the theater.

At the level of the street, colonnades, porticos, and the interior piazza denote the architectural and hence civic importance of the theater; from the air or elevated vantage points elsewhere in the surroundings, the enormous flytower, Rossi's imposing addition to the mass of Barabino's original theater, dominates. The robust presence of its massive marble-framed copper cornice firmly anchors the surrounding neoclassical buildings and its burnished molding powerfully projects raking shadows across the smooth plaster facing below.

Rossi's commission in Genoa bears an uncanny similarity to that of Karl Schinkel for the Schauspielhaus in Berlin in 1818. Both envisioned the reconstruction of a destroyed theater using the same colonnade and foundations, but increasing the interior volume, and both architects responded to complex urban settings. Schinkel emphasized the connection between theater and context in an urban panorama featuring the Schauspielhaus (top) and its surroundings depicted on the stage decoration, while Rossi went a step further in linking city and theater by articulating the proscenium and lateral walls with replicas of typical elevations found in Genoese piazzas and indeed, as the ideal settings for antique Roman comedies.[5] The marble revetted facades, with shuttered windows and pearwood and marble balconies, merge with proscenium arch and lateral walls to unify audience and actors, stage and auditorium, by a continuous but subtly differentiated urban enclosure. As with the architecture of stages themselves, Rossi here offers an architecture of illusion, explicitly summoning the fabricated world of the cityscape into the fantasy world of the spectacle, where events of public import are to be recounted.

Although Rossi parallels an architecture as the theater of urban life with that of the stage at Carlo Felice, the *topos* consistently reappears in his work. In the Casa Aurora in Turin, the interior *teatrino* repeats on a small scale the Casa's grand entrance elevation of massive white columns topped by a green steel I-beam lintel (bottom). The unfenestrated expanse of brick in the corner elevation on Corso Emilia and Corso Giulio Cesare in its smaller replica in the *teatrino* is perforated by five windows in the unfaced brick proscenium. In reality, the stage itself backs up against the sheer brick wall of the angled corner entrance. In the Schauspielhaus the curtain with the image of the theater reminded the opening night audience of their urban situation by foregrounding Schinkel's design as they readied for the performance. Rossi also prominently repeats his grand facade, but in the architectural forms themselves rather than in an impermanent medium, as if to demonstrate that however the staged events may alter, the urban surround remains constant. Fashion showings will always be enclosed in an architectural setting, an anamnesis of the building's public presence. By endowing the *teatrino* with an explicitly public architectural character, he underscores the relationship with civic life even in this exclusive domain, and at the same time, the role of architecture as the stage of urban life.

Nowhere are Rossi's *topoi* more effectively deployed than in the Hotel Il Palazzo, Fukuoka. In a repetition of a favorite motif, Rossi subverts the private character of the El Dorado bar by endowing it with a luminous replica of the exterior elevation on one full wall. Outside, the waterfront elevation soars above the surrounding townscape with the polychrome rhythms of rich red travertine columns, red tile wall, horizontal bands of deep green copper lintels, all recessed between unfaced brick side walls. Rossi decided to treat the waterfront elevation as an unfenestrated *scaenae frons* in a deliberate rejection of the facile *parti* of hotel rooms overlooking water. Instead, private rooms enjoy oblique views, while only the public space of the raised piazza offers a privileged moment to pause and enjoy a panoramic vista over the harbor. Like its interior monochrome replica, the east facade is presented as a theatrical backdrop, where Rossi masterfully orchestrates yet another conflation of civic piazza and theater.

Visitors ascend a broad flight of stairs framed by polished terra-cotta rampart-like lateral projections to a large piazza paved with blocks of Roman travertine—at once a piazza and a Roman theater stripped of historical detail. The stage gives off on either side to side wings (*versurae*); the columnar screen of the *scaenae frons* is pierced by three doors on the ground level and articulated by tiers of columns pressed between base and architrave and topped by a projecting copper cornice and attic: altogether a denuded and extended echo of Roman theaters such as that of Sabratha, Libya.

For an architect who responds kinetically to such urban settings, designing a town hall in an open field entirely free of an urban setting represents a significant challenge. The deceptively named Venetian community of Borgoricco's most distinct buildings, dispersed among a scattering of farmhouses in the ancient Roman road pattern, were schools, church, and a wildly decorated Egyptianate restaurant, Il Faraone. Absent an immediate urban context, Rossi chose a proximate one—the Venetian rural villa. Eschewing an abstract arrangement of forms, he imaginatively transformed the rural building type into a new civic configuration. The lateral wings, with trabeated porticos framing a palatial forecourt and giving off to the administrative offices, recall the villa type, itself a variation on an even more ancient rural vernacular. But Rossi broke the typology with the civic spaces compressed between thin perpendicular brick walls that rise through the full height of the central volume. Shallow bronze barrel vaults cascade down to a recessed I-beam lintel held aloft by narrow deep piers and two massive concrete columns. Marking the central section as containing the most representative, collective spaces, this civic variation on the villa type becomes a focal point for a community dispersed through the Venetian hinterland.

The various functions—office spaces, council hall, meeting rooms, library, museum—each receive distinct volumetric articulation on the exterior, something Rossi emphasizes not just through forms, but by playing off recesses, solids, and voids to achieve maximum visual differentiation. This delicate tension between parts and whole is sustained by the brick walls, which at once divide, frame, and emphasize the diverse volumes.

The social significance which Rossi emphasizes within his buildings mirrors his approach to the civic setting outside—a link rendered explicit in a presentation drawing for Carlo Felice (top), which echoes Schinkel's tactic of putting the theater itself

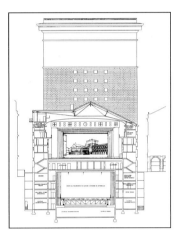

on stage. In a section cut through to reveal the proscenium, Rossi depicted the theater in its urban context and reduced to miniature scale, much as Schinkel had done. Exactly the reverse operation holds in a drawing of the Casa Aurora (page 10) where the theater—itself a replica of the exterior elevation—is magnified to urban dimensions on the corner facade. A similar manipulation of scales appears repeatedly in Rossi's drawings, where coffee pots swell to the size of skyscrapers and buildings shrink to the dimension of domestic furnishings. More than simple playfulness with forms and objects, this device testifies to Rossi's fundamental conviction that however inextricably public and private realms are connected, nested endlessly one within the other, we chiefly experience the city in its public spaces and civic architecture. Rossi finds the stage as the setting for the reenactment of human dramas alluring precisely in its function as a microcosm of full-scale urban settings, where human dramas are not re-

enacted but lived for the first time—so too in his stage designs for theatrical productions, which also reproduce cityscapes. Just as the empty stage awaits the performance, so the city depends upon our participation to bring it to life, for all of which architecture serves as the necessary backdrop. Again and again Rossi returns to this theme in his buildings, such as in the Hotel Il Palazzo in Fukuoka, where the

interior El Dorado bar reproduces the urban elevation of the hotel, and also in his drawings. In the Casa Aurora drawing, the privileged view of the *teatrino* depicted at the urban scale is mediated by a square, four-light window—by architecture, in other words. And unlike the static figures in De Chirico's paintings, Rossi's are always in motion, gesturing, striding, leaning: tiny figures emerge from brightly lit windows, doors or porticos, or frolic in an urban scene.

In yet another reversal, Rossi shuffles the scenic backdrops outlined by Sebastiano Serlio in the sixteenth century as the ideal settings for the three classic types of plays. For comedies, Serlio described images of typical urban backdrops for the lives of average citizens, including an inn, a church, a loggia, and a brothel. For tragedies, which involved great personages, strange adventures, and murders, the stately houses of aristocrats were necessary, austere palatial elevations with classical orders and pristine geometries; and for satires, involving rude and rustic country folk, bucolic settings where nature itself is put on stage were indicated. Rossi upsets all these categories. The compact, highly differentiated volumes of the town hall at Borgoricco, echoing the disparate backdrops of the comic scene, are introduced as the only rupture into a bucolic setting. Hotel Il Palazzo's pedigree is aristocratic, fitting for the grand tradition of tragic drama, but Rossi inserts it as an alien element into a classic comic setting—in fact, almost a red-light district—of jumbled houses and markets. Carlo Felice carries the comic into the heart of tragedy in the palatial neoclassical building, a theme reiterated in the model and section with the image of the theater on the stage. The old distinctions between social and dramatic venues crumble precisely in the city, or in the town hall as its symbolic center, and for Rossi, architecture is the armature upon which new relationships can be freely reassembled.

With these strategies, Rossi seeks not to poise his buildings uneasily in some fictive realm between public and private, but rather to heighten the awareness of the indissoluble interpenetration of the two. More precisely, Rossi's major public buildings seem to many critics to confirm the historically defined public–private polarity and all of the tensions with which it is riven with uncanny precision, but in fact he employs strategies that render them stunningly transparent, as he so compellingly reveals in the Casa Aurora drawing. Weaving a narrative of the interlocked spiral of public and private worlds is perhaps easier to accomplish in literature, as in the works of Jorge Luis Borges, than would seem possible in architecture. Rossi manages to carry it off while avoiding the twin risks of producing buildings that are either anonymous insertions in the urban environment, or empty monuments of indeterminate location.

The fluid interplay of interior and exterior elements extends to the repetition of motifs, forms, and details in drawings and projects. The elegant terracotta cornice lining the rectangular, double-height volume of the Teatrino in the Casa Aurora marks the point of transition between the floors, recalls an identical one on the exterior, and also serves as a stable architectural counterpoint to the evanescence of the fashions displayed on the stage below. Other motifs recur throughout Rossi's *œuvre*, such as those paradigmatically employed in the Monument to the Partisans at Segrate: an equilateral triangle formed of rectangular slabs perched atop a

massive concrete cylinder and sliding off of a sarcophagus-like volume. A much smaller, shallower version of the triangle spills water into a cubic receptacle in the De Amicis School in Broni; others appear in drawings of a theater, in a fountain for the civic center in Perugia, in the pediments of the beach cabins endlessly redrawn by Rossi, and again as a fountain in the Via Croce Rossa monument in Milan. A massive, monolithic cylinder—identified for Rossi with Filarete's column (top) in the unfinished Ca'del Duca in Venice—is among the most persistent *topoi* of all. From its early presence in the Segrate monument to a more recent appearance, doubled, in Carlo Felice, the column has journeyed through hundreds of drawings and the majority of the built works (bottom). It has stood alone, doubled, supported lintels, framed passages, interrupted sequences of piers and marked corners in his designs for well over a quarter of a century. Like his other recurring motifs, the column denotes some of Rossi's deepest beliefs about architecture. In *A Scientific Autobiography*, he remarked on Filarete's column as both a relic and a fundamental element of architecture.[6] These two features, combined with its absolute formal purity, render the column at once singular and repeatable, not locked into associations with specific historical eras, but an architectural element whose primitive character transcends simplistic periodizations. These and

Rossi's other elemental forms persist and retain their integrity beyond trends, embodying an entire historical trajectory from a preclassical past to today.

Perhaps one of the most remarkable things about the persistence of Rossi's *topoi* is his uncanny ability to invent endlessly with them, generating new configurations and combinations with none appearing twice in quite the same way. Elements such as the cylinder or the stacked tower in their recombinant forms in drawings and projects attenuate the delicate tension ideally always present in architecture between stasis and change. In his earlier work Rossi registered these tensions through the repetition of crisp stereometric forms—cube, cone, rotunda, prism—usually strung together by narrow corridors, pergolas, or raised walkways. Especially before 1980, his buildings were almost entirely free of historical detailing, thus conveying the strikingly archaic simplicity of the forms. In the last decade, as the programs have become more complex, Rossi has begun to articulate surfaces by drawing from an ever wider palette of details and sources. Technical necessities such as drain pipes as well as purely structural elements are deployed to accentuate rhythms in the Casa Aurora. Green I-beams both frame the stone colonnade and are held aloft as lintels, conveying the structural purity of architecture's most primitive form of construction, trabeation, and the machined elegance of the steel members. With ever greater frequency, Rossi has incorporated neoclassical elements into his projects—the interior elevation in the funerary chapel at Guissano, the cornices at Carlo Felice, Casa Aurora, and the Museum of German History in Berlin. Like the I-beams, Rossi's cornices modulate the surfaces of his buildings, enlivening them with deep recesses and bold projections, thereby achieving in the architecture the deep shadows and play of light and dark so unfailingly present in his drawings.

In these repetitions of his *topoi*, Rossi accomplishes more than simple gestures from one project to another. Instead, as with the elemental geometries of his forms, he reaches toward a universal essence of architecture—even a fictional one—beyond the particular expression of a single building. It is no accident, then, that he now employs neoclassical references which likewise harbor universalizing tendencies. Like his simple stereometric volumes, the neoclassical elements at once resist time and reveal its inevitable passage. Although Rossi explicitly manifests his preoccupation with time by insistently inserting timepieces into his drawings and projects, including an early plan to top Carlo Felice's proscenium arch with a clock, more subtle indications suffuse every drawing and building. He chose copper roofs and cornices for the town hall at Borgoricco, Carlo Felice, and Perugia precisely in anticipation of the transformation that time works on the material, and the Persian red travertine columns at Fukuoka for the remarkable chromatic transformations they undergo in the rain. Deeply recessed porticos and windows, pergolas designed to be engulfed by vines, lamp standards planned to be smothered by foliage in the Via Croce Rossa monument—with these and many other devices Rossi yokes the transformative power of time to the timelessness of his architecture forms.

At the level of simple, direct experience, one absorbs this kinetically passing through Rossi's buildings: the long high corridors of the San Cataldo Cemetery in Modena punctuated by shafts of sunlight; the vertiginous industrial stairs and passageways in the columbarium with its small square vistas on the surrounding cemetery; the rhythmic sequence of solids and voids, light and shadow along the Casa Aurora's deep portico. The brilliant cone of light in Carlo Felice, where atmospheric and temporal changes are most powerfully registered, alerts one to Rossi's passion for shadows as a melancholic undertow to the waves of Mediterranean sun. Insistently recorded in hundreds of drawings, this fascination loops back to the most enduring drama of everyday life—time's passage minutely marked by the shadows of and on buildings until they are consumed by darkness, over and over again. So essential is Rossi's grasp of the insistence of time and the transience of human activity that he bypasses the banal narratives that vitiate so many other architectures: for him, the orchestration of human dramas occurs elsewhere, and architecture is but record and backdrop.

The modest Via Croce Rossa monument in Milan (1990) most succinctly evinces Rossi's view of architecture's role. Via Croce Rossa was formerly the intersection of several major thoroughfares in the heart of Milan, like the ancient *trivium*, or intersection, where Romans erected altars or shrines to divinities. Since Via Croce Rossa itself dates back to Roman antiquity, Rossi appropriately sites his monument here, as part of a new piazza. From Via Montenapoleone, colonnades of alternating mulberry trees and green lamp standards with granite benches in the intercolumniations mark the approach to the monument, a cube open on one side by a steep flight of stairs and a viewing platform. Here one can peer through a bronze-framed aperture to glimpse fragments of Milan and its Duomo, much as Rossi peered out as a child from the San Carlone in

Arona. The richly polychromed Candoglia marble—from the same quarry as the marble of the Duomo—indicates that the complex is destined to participate in civic life much as the Duomo does, though on a smaller scale. The monument endows a district bereft of public spaces with a small urban theater for the rituals of everyday life, where workers, tourists and shoppers linger and rest, where fashions can be photographed, where friends can meet—the setting for a potentially unlimited array of random and organized activities. Like the Duomo, it challenges the notion of the city as a center of consumption available only to those with money; instead it expands the field of uses and legitimate users of civic space to embrace everyone. Decisively rejecting both pedestrian re-creations of historic styles and the frantic search for novelty, Rossi's powerfully archaic vision of architecture reinscribes it back in the city. For Rossi, architecture should be evident only to spark imagination or memories, not to orchestrate and determine events. The fixed scene is important precisely because it remains fixed while spectacles and spectators pass before it. And this is what Rossi meant when he wrote, "In order to be significant, architecture must be forgotten."[7]

NOTES

[1] Aldo Rossi, *A Scientific Autobiography*, translated by Lawrence Venuti (Cambridge, MA: MIT Press, 1981), 33.

[2] John J. Winkler and Froma I. Zeitlin, eds. *Nothing to do with Dionysos? Athenian Drama in its Social Context* (Princeton, NJ: Princeton University Press, 1989).

[3] Kurt W. Forster, "Stagecraft and Statecraft: The Architectural Integration of Public Life and Theatrical Spectacle in Scamozzi's Theater at Sabbioneta," *Oppositions* 9 (Summer 1977), 63-87.

[4] Paolo Chessa designed the first restoration proposal, and Carlo Scarpa the second.

[5] Karl Friedrich Schinkel, *Sammlung Architektonischer Entwurfe* (Berlin, 1966; reprint New York: Princeton Architectural Press, 1989), plate 14.

[6] Rossi, 6.

[7] Ibid., 45.

PART TWO

BUILDINGS AND PROJECTS

CEMETERY OF SAN CATALDO

MODENA, ITALY
1971

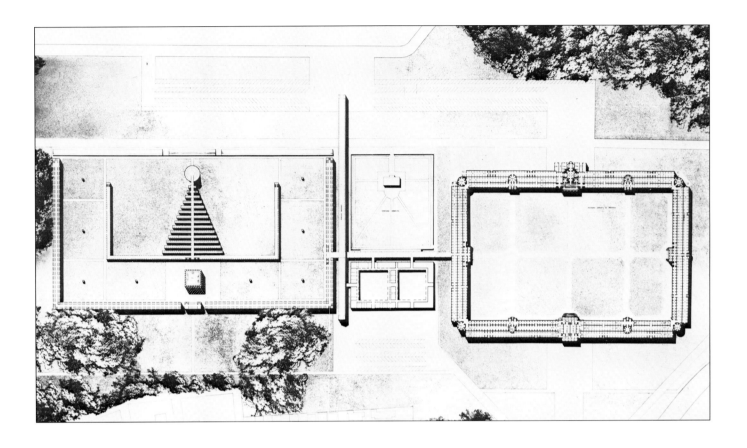

It has been over twenty years since Aldo Rossi and Gianni Braghieri's entry in the competition to extend the San Cataldo Cemetery in Modena was awarded first prize. With approximately two-thirds of their scheme for a city for the dead now built, the project has grown alongside, though not necessarily apace with, Rossi's own architectural practice.

When unveiled, the scheme for San Cataldo was seen as a startling metaphor for the urban theories Rossi presented in his 1966 book *The Architecture of the City*. Since then, it has also become a touchstone for his own professional development. Visible in this early project are the overlay of stark forms and the mundane rituals of daily life that continue to imbue Rossi's work with emotion. The project consists of a colonnade that separates the new San Cataldo from the Jewish burial ground and adjacent 1858 cemetery by Andrea Costa. The colonnade is both path and shelter for the grounds keepers and flower vendors who work there. Above the colonnade is a gable-topped pavilion lined with niches for ashes—suspending above the living the remains of the dead, who provide a source of livelihood for those that tend their remains.

Ossuaries form concentric C-shapes (incomplete) around tapering rows of bone repositories (unbuilt), which resemble a skeleton in plan. A path bisecting the site connects a red cube—a giant

ossuary—with a mass grave capped by a brick chimney (unbuilt). Rossi's matter-of-fact presentation—cinerary urns in what appear to be industrial sheds, caskets of decaying bones in a roofless red "house" swept by wind, and a factory chimney, adjacent to a plot segregated for Jews, that unintentionally, conjures the death camps of World War II—has an unsettling, yet cathartic directness. Rossi brings to bear his Catholic upbringing and his own contemplation of mortality, giving an underlying message of life as episodic and fleeting, with cemeteries as the physical link to the dead.

Rossi's fluency with themes notoriously difficult to capture in built form is in part the result of a single incident, a professional and personal turning point: only a few months before he and Braghieri submitted their entry to the Modena competition, Rossi had a serious car accident. Afterwards, lying immobilized in his hospital bed, he was painfully aware of his bones and their displacement. "I saw the structure of the body as a series of fractures to be reassembled," he wrote in his journal, published in 1981 as *A Scientific Autobiography*. By process of association, the discomfort confirmed his theory of architecture as a sum of parts arranged in a logical framework. This incident, which, his journal entry says caused his "youth to reach its end," became the proving ground of a mature architectural practice.

View of the ossuary

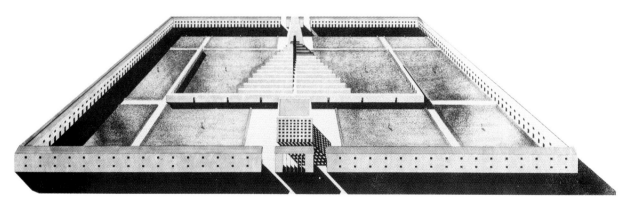

Perspective from the competition submittal

View of the ossuary next to the gabled columbarium

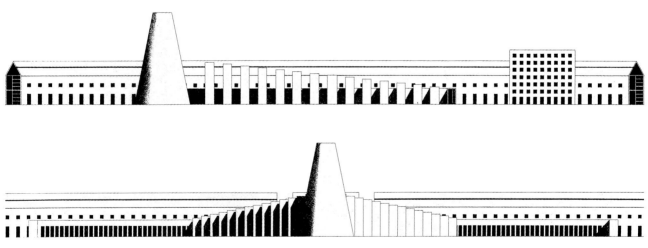

North and west elevations

View showing family tombs near the columbarium

View of the columbarium from the Jewish cemetery

APARTMENT HOUSE

BERLIN, GERMANY
1981

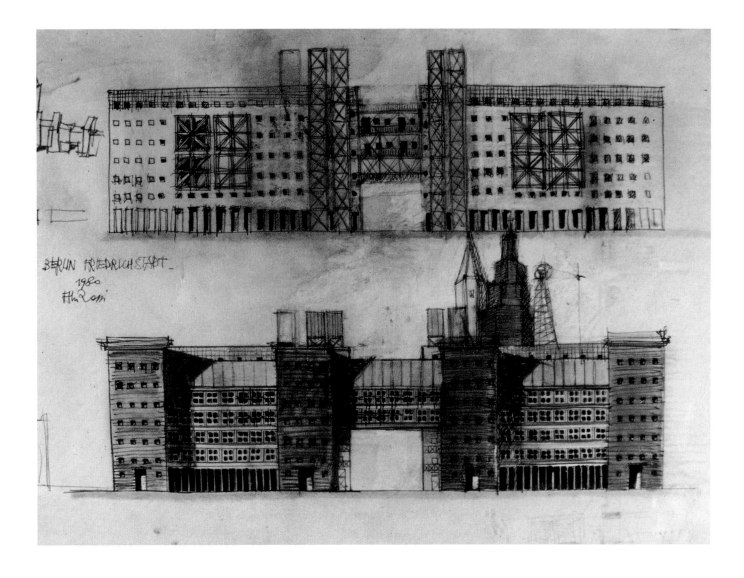

Rossi's design of the Südliche Friedrichstadt complex in Berlin was his first major commission outside of Italy. He was one of a group of prominent international architects invited to participate in the International Building Exhibition (IBA), an ambitious urban renewal plan to rebuild areas destroyed during World War II. Architects were asked to compete for select parcels; Rossi and his team were awarded a site in a southern district of the city.

The principal aim of the project was to "respect the alignment of the street," a course of action Rossi felt would correct the failure of the city's typical Modernist housing blocks, which split sites into awkward front and back yards. Although Rossi's vision of Berlin is largely shaped by his admiration of the architecture of Karl Friedrich Schinkel (an influence that reappears in future Berlin projects) he realized that Schinkel's buildings were not the proper models for Friedrichstadt because they "are intended for a city of

monuments…they do not represent systematic, continuous building," which was the focus of Rossi's proposal.

The first phase of the project—roughly 270,000 square feet—was completed in 1988. Where possible, existing buildings were either incorporated into Rossi's new streetfront building or allowed to remain in the center, which was remade into a garden court visible from the street. The "systematic, continuous building" and the permeable streetfront were not seen as mutually exclusive by Rossi, who punctuated his building with large portals to permit movement and views back and forth. The metal and glass skin is enlivened by square openings at two scales: windows are small squares while four balconies make giant squares. Steep gables top glass and steel elevator cages. As if to articulate IBA's commitment to rebuilding Berlin, Rossi marked the corners along Wilhelmstrasse emphatically with giant white columns.

View of the west elevation along Wilhelmstrasse

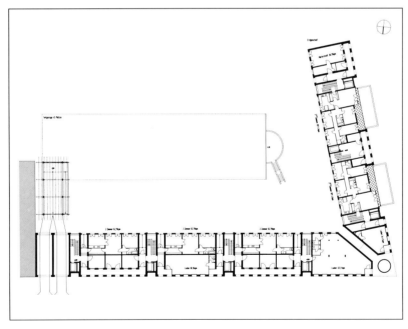

Ground floor plan

View of the building from the courtyard

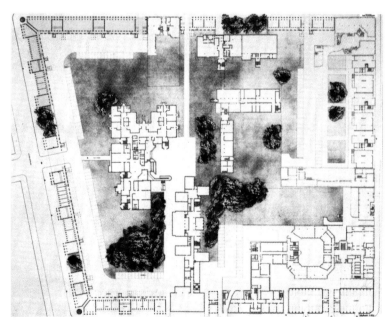

Site plan

Detail of courtyard facade

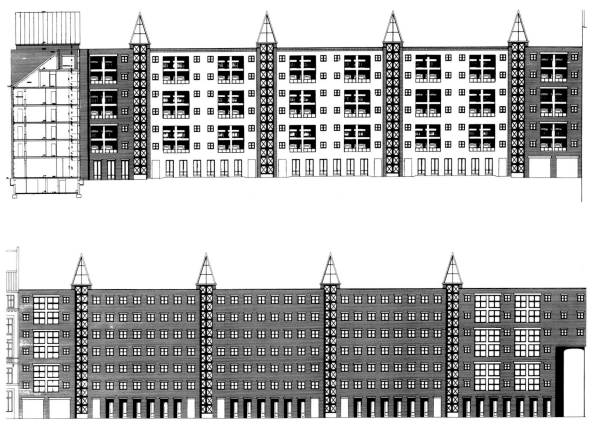

Longitudinal section and north elevation

FUNERARY CHAPEL

GUISSANO, ITALY
1981

Rossi's design of a funerary chapel and tomb in the northern Italian town of Giussano is, by his own admission, an important project, possibly because in this private commission he chose to reveal the most about himself. For the second time in his career, Rossi was asked to contemplate the requirements both practical and philosophical of a burial place (the first such project is the ongoing expansion of the San Cataldo cemetery in Modena). For Rossi, the additional challenge here was to make an appropriate symbol of the achievements of the founder of a wood furniture company.

For the family chapel, Rossi made a rectangular prism of handmade brick set atop a stone plinth—a virtually windowless detached row house. Wrapping the top are pieces of a classical cornice in what is at once an assessment of the limited life of architectural styles—"It is impossible to recreate ancient forms," says Rossi—and of people—"Life itself is a fragment."

Inside the chapel is a twenty-foot-high screen, or *retablo*, modeled on Andrea Palladio's Porta Borsari in Verona, that leans against a wall painted a baby blue called "Celeste della Madonna" (Heavenly Light of the Madonna). Louvers in the glass roof's steel trusses admit natural light into the space, but are hidden from view on the exterior by the brick parapet. The trusses would seem more at home in an industrial shed, but here they conjure a vacant factory, one abandoned since the proprietor's death. Light filters through the roof, enveloping the wood altarpiece (meticulously built by factory carpenter Amedeo Vigano) in an otherworldly blue haze. A cutout in the chapel floor, protected by wood balusters (also made by Vigano), reveals the underground tomb, which can be reached by a sheltered staircase that descends along the side of the chapel. Dominated by a giant cross, the dark chamber lined with blue Brazilian marble is used by family members for prayer and meditation.

View of the chapel from the northwest

View of the chapel from the southwest

View to the skylight from ground level

Interior view of the chapel

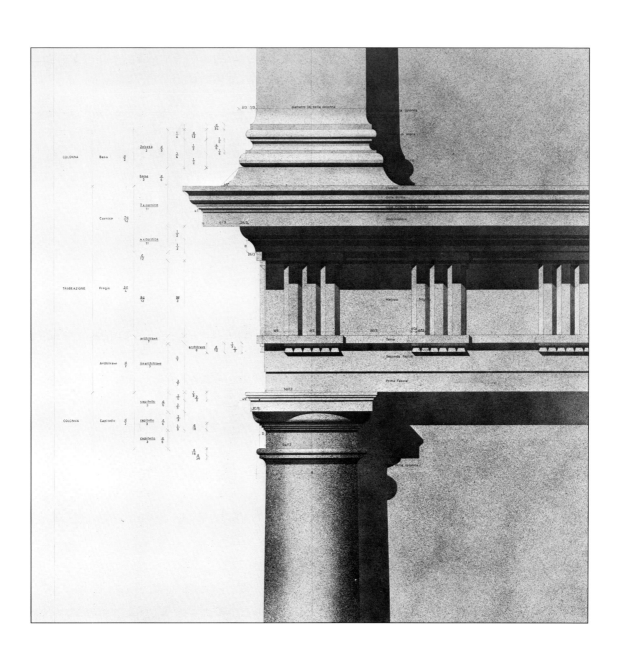

Interior of the tomb from and looking towards the entrance

CIVIC CENTER

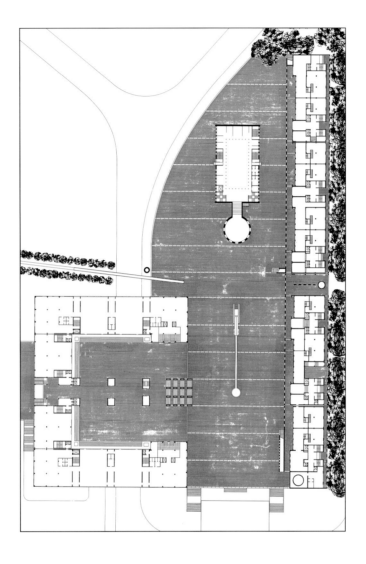

Rossi's scheme for Perugia's civic center comprises 850,000 square feet of new construction, including the Palazzo Regionale (completed), a fountain (completed), offices (under construction) and a theater (unbuilt), set atop a shared base, which accommodates underground parking. Centro Direzionale, a joint venture of pasta manufacturer Buitoni and the city of Perugia, is located on the site of a former industrial complex in the Fontivegge district, between the city's historic heart and its postwar business center.

Rossi's proposal for Umbria's capital combines historic building types and forms with modern functions. Rossi conceived the Palazzo Regionale in the tradition of the Italian *broletto*—a public edifice usually arcaded at the ground level. The structure is a roughly square block bisected by a toplit galleria with an arcade. It integrates the massive masonry corners typical of a sixteenth-century palazzo with

the glass-and-steel expanses of an up-to-date office building. On one side of the Palazzo Regionale is the only remaining evidence of the site's previous incarnation: a smokestack, which Rossi has made the focal point of an avenue leading into the complex.

Between the Palazzo Regionale and the linear office block is a theater with a conical entrance tower set into the sloped piazza. Facing the theater is a monumental fountain, a larger version of the geometric shapes Rossi designed for Segrate's city hall square in 1965. Water from the fountain flows through a channel in the brick and stone piazza into a round basin on axis with the Palazzo Regionale's public galleria. The office building steps down the length of the inclined piazza; its rusticated base, protruding pairs of chimneys, and overlay of two scales of window sizes make the structure look like an amalgam of old-fashioned apartment houses.

View of the Palazzo Regionale from the east

East elevation of the Palazzo Regionale

View of the fountain and the Palazzo Regionale

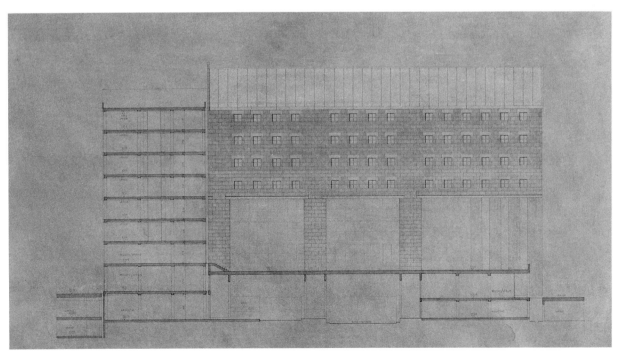

Longitudinal section

View of the civic center in context

Early sketch showing the project with the fountain and unbuilt theater

CARLO FELICE THEATER

GENOA, ITALY
1983

Genoa's Municipal Opera House has had a rich and varied, if somewhat troubled past—elements of which are brought into powerful relief in Rossi and Ignazio Gardella's Carlo Felice Theater, completed in 1990. The subject of decades-long political squabbles, the original neoclassic hall by Carlo Barabino was finished in 1828. During World War II, the building was repeatedly bombed, leaving only the side portico and marble pronaos facing Genoa's central square, Piazza Ferrari. Beginning in the late 1940s, several attempts were made to rebuild the opera house. In 1949, Paolo Chessa won a competition to do so, but his scheme became the subject of a law suit when the Ministry of Public Works rejected it for failing to meet Ministry standards. In 1963, Carlo Scarpa was hired by the city council. He submitted two projects, one hotly-debated proposal in 1969, and another in 1978, which was underway when he died suddenly later that year.

In 1981, the city council decided to start over, and staged a two-phase competition. Seven teams participated. The winning entry by Rossi and Gardella solved the architectural dilemma that had been plaguing the project for some thirty years—how to incorporate the physical remains of the 1828 structure and the technological demands of a twentieth-century opera house into a visually coherent whole.

The new Carlo Felice Theater retains the footprint of the original opera house. The partially damaged Doric columns of the pronaos and the side portico were restored and a portion of the original theater was recreated according to Barabino's drawings. The performance hall spans a passage that connects Piazza Ferrari with the covered Galleria Mazzini, a smaller, more somber version of

Milan's Galleria, making real the public thoroughfare that had been proposed by both Chessa and Scarpa. Rossi conceived the 2,000-seat auditorium as the square of a small Italian town: marble facades with windows, wood shutters, and marble balconies flank terraced rows of seating and the proscenium; the thickness of the marble cladding and the supporting walls is varied to control high-frequency sound reflection.

A cone-shaped light well dominates the public foyer, piercing the roof as a steel and glass spire—-a hybrid of the port city's lighthouses and its new crop of post-war skyscrapers. A squat, copper cornice-capped tower contains the backstage, and is a state-of-the art version of Barabino's innovative "fly tower" that allowed scenery to be raised rather than folded, accommodating four independent performance platforms that can be rotated into place from storage underground. Above the backstage are four floors of rehearsal and mechanical rooms; the transition is expressed on the exterior of the tower in the change from grayish-blue rusticated plaster to parchment-colored smooth plaster typical of Genoa.

Rossi likens the careful interweaving of old and new in the Carlo Felice Theater to surgery, emphasizing that this particular operation required more than the repair of damages. Says Rossi: "Once the individual pieces were restored they had to be put together to form a new whole. They were not fragments but large chipped, damaged pieces. Architectural wounds are as fascinating as human wounds: they are inwardness and outwardness at the same time, they are life mingling with death, we are sorry to close them up, leaving scars behind....This was how I saw the wounded body of Genoa's theater and this was perhaps the emotion that carried me through the work."

Il Teatro Felice.

Quando passavo per Genova vedevo il
Pronao del Carlo Felice emergere sopra
le rovine / ma non mi riferivo alle
rovine stesse del teatro quanto a una rovina
più generale della città e dell'architettura.

Questo Pronao portava l'angelo (forse lo
stesso angelo sterminatore di Buñuel)
bello nella sua serena mutilazione.
Forse nessun Teatro Italico aveva e ha
questo superbo profondamente richiamato
l'ingresso del Principe - E non permetto
destinato a un principe ma per questo
suo Pronao di architetti con le piante del
teatro per svolgersi alla città e per
stare come a picco sopra i vicoli che
scendono al mare, contorti e/o pendenti,
e stare come in un'acropoli di bianca
pietra greca.
Lasciamo ai filologi le differenze non
La Scala, con il Regio con tutti i teatri
d'opera italiana : entrare un filo che
li lega ma che io non vedo.
Genova è ... una bellezza sgraziata
è anche spiazzata con questo teatro / nel
era difficile prevedere come operazione
chirurgica che non ingrandiva il restauro
perché tornati i singoli pezzi questi
si dovevano ricomporre in un corpo
nuovo.

È non erano frammenti, ma pezzi

preziosi schiappiati e feriti.
Le tante dell'architettura sono affascinanti
come quelle degli uomini / per quel
loro essere esterno e interno e anche
vita e morte, con il dispiacere di
chiuderle e i segni del raggiungimento.

Così vedevo questo corpo ferito del teatro
genovese dove è forse l'emozione che
è poi rimasta in tutto lo svolgimento
dell'opera

Altri parleranno delle vicende del teatro
e così io potrei parlare della fortuna
di aver lavorato con Ignazio Gardella
e con altri bravi architetti.

Ma non mi è stato chiesto uno scritto
di omaggio o di tecnici, ma un
parlare ai questo teatro, o di questo
progetto.
E i progetti nascono dove questo nucleo
che via via si conforme / come si
conformavano il pronao e le Torri
scenica come se fossero inconciliabili
nella loro superba autonomia.
Ma lentamente formavano la
città / se pure una nuova piazza
aperta nella galleria Mazzini (bellissimo
e misteriosamente genovese) mentre
le torri formano uno skyline

di triste ricostruzione.

Così si formavano interno ed esterno e
terminava come una sintesi necessaria
le torri fare che attraversando i
piani dei foyer portava la luce del
cielo all'interno del teatro e la luce
interna, l'intimità del teatro, nelle notti
genovesi.

Abbiamo lavorato molto a questo teatro
sino all'avvicinamento e alla costruzione
della sala - The Torre le costruivano il teatro
offre all'architetto una strana serenità,
e infine l'interno ...
della realtà ...

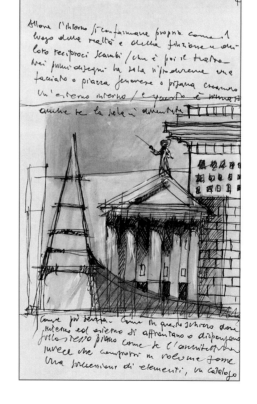

Allora l'interno si conformare proprio come il
luogo della realtà e della finzione e dei
loro reciproci scambi / che è poi il teatro
Nei primi disegni la sala riproduce una
facciata o piazza genovese o piazza creando
un esterno interno / e questo è rimasto
anche se la sala è ...

Come più scritto - Come in questo schizzo dove
interno ed esterno si affrontano o dispongono
sullo stesso piano come se l'architettura
invece che comporsi in volume fosse
una successione di elementi, un catalogo

5

di forme note e ignote
In altri disegni emergeva la torre animata e
c'è occhio luminoso al posto dell'orologio.
Infiniti sono gli elementi del teatro di
Genova e nulla esso etensiverentè lui
penghna di fierno niuolupporti

per proporre ancora nuove dimensioni e
sconcertare l'ordine come, se c'ordine in
architettura fosse solo la ripetizione e
non la ricerca di ciò che intravediamo e
partire dalla stessa dimensione.
Così, a dispetto di altre storie, mi piace
chiamare il carlo felice, il teatro felice
anche se poi ogni teatro come troppa mi
banonenione un un teatro felice.

PianoRenzi, NY luglio 80

47

ORDO·GENVENSIS·SATAGENTE·HECTORE·IENNEO·REGIO·GVBERNATORE·CONSVLVIT
NE·VRBI·TOT·INSIGNIBVS·MONVMENTIS·INSTRVCTAE·THEATRVM·SPECTABILIVS·DEESSET
MDCCCXXVII
RECE·CAROLO·FELICI·DVCE·NOSTRO

48

View of the theater in context, and plans of the main foyer with stage and the secondary foyer with hall

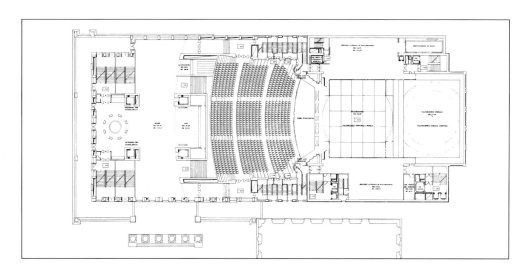

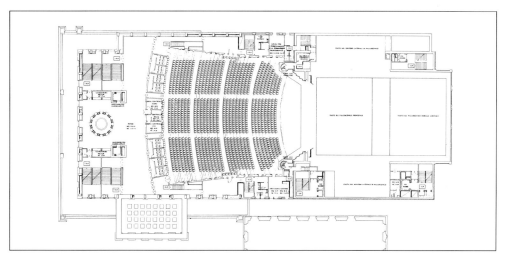

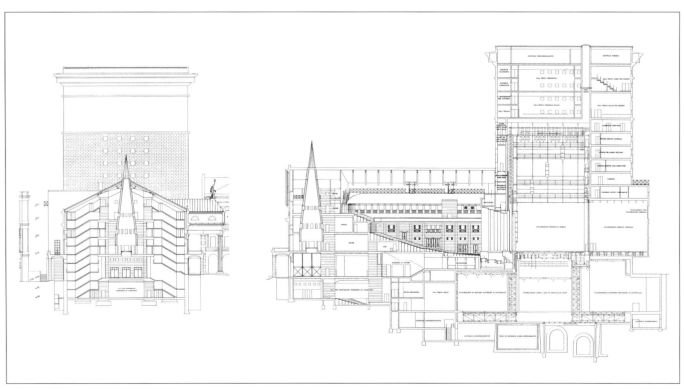

Cross-section and longitudinal section

Perspective from the competition submittal

View of the stage from the balcony

Side elevation of the theater

View inside the lantern

View of the lantern from the main foyer

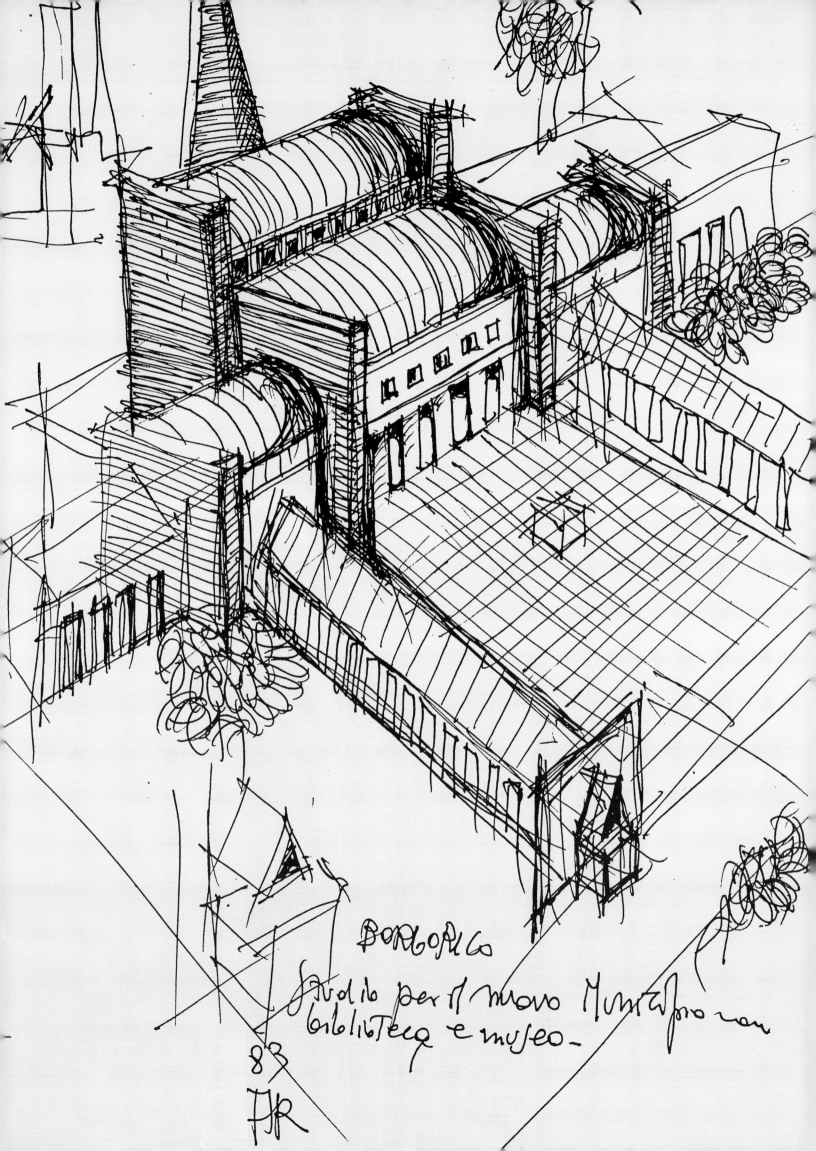

BORGOALGO

Studio per il nuovo Museo-?-?-
biblioteca e museo-

83

FJR

TOWN HALL

BORGORICCO, ITALY
1983

Borgoricco is one of a string of small Veneto towns neatly arranged according to axial Roman town planning principles; its north to south *cardo* and east to west *decumanus* continue on into the horizon. Situated at the outskirts of Mestre, the port city that serves as gateway to the islands of Venice, Borgoricco is both recognizable as a type and without its own public identity. In fact, before local authorities commissioned Rossi to supply civic presence, Borgoricco's "town hall" consisted of a motley suite of offices above the local lending library.

For this design, Rossi took his cues from both ancient planning precepts and villas of the region. The 20,000-square-foot building consists of a central block and two parallel wings arranged in a U-shape, creating a paved courtyard setback along the *decumanus*. Following the typical plan for a villa of the Veneto, the central block contains the public functions: a grand foyer, offices for local

dignitaries, exhibition space, and a library. Offices for municipal functionaries are arranged in double-loaded corridors behind porticos on either side of the courtyard. Upstairs are a grand magistral meeting hall whose curved wood beams resemble a rib cage, and rooms for archival storage.

The outstretched arms of the U-shaped building give a welcoming presence to the copper barrel-vaulted "head" and *marmorino*— stucco infused with marble powder—coated surfaces of the building's front. The rigorous symmetry is continued on the brick and concrete rear, where an exhaust chimney reinforces the axis of the lintel-spanned entrance.

Due to limited public coffers, construction was carried out in stages. For several years during the late 1980s, the building was at once under construction and abandoned—a surreal symbol of Borgoricco's, and Rossi's, progress.

South elevation and principal entrance

Southeast endwall with fountain

View from the northwest

View of the entry forecourt

BERLIN TIERGARTEN AR 81

APARTMENT HOUSE

BERLIN, GERMANY
1983

Rossi's second apartment building in Berlin was designed in 1983. The volume of this five-story structure is symmetrical to the former Norwegian embassy, located across the street. Appearing at first glance to be an old-fashioned Germanic apartment house, Rossi's Rauchstrasse building has some distinctly Italian touches. Individual apartments are arranged around a central corridor emanating from a square shaped stair tower that looks like a lighthouse, forming a stacked series of inner courtyards, or loggias, lit from above by windows in the iron cupola. The dark Berlinesque brick of the facade is enlivened by stripes of yellow ceramic tile that roughly indicate floor and ceiling heights. Recessed in the facades are square openings alternately filled with windows framed by green painted metal lintels, and balconies. The L-shape configuration along the streetfront forms a semi-enclosed yard and transforms the building's open corner entrance into a three-dimensional cross-section of the entire complex.

progetto per torre a Buenos Aires 1984

TECHINT OFFICE TOWER

BUENOS AIRES, ARGENTINA
1984

A tower is often considered the ultimate architectural commission, more for its sheer size and promise of posterity than for the opportunity it provides for artistic invention. Happily for Rossi, his first tower project, an entry to the Peugeot skyscraper competition, was for a site in Buenos Aires, giving him the chance to explore new territory. In 1984, Rossi designed a smaller structure for Buenos Aires as the headquarters of Techint, a financial institution.

Rossi saw the Argentine capital as a composite of Latin American and European cultures, with an architecture of truly international style, whose only unifying characteristic was "discord." The neighborhood of Techint's site was a motley assortment: Santa Catalina, a church and convent, occupied the adjacent property along Avenida Viamonte, while on the opposite side of the street stood a tower of the local university. The nearby Avenida Reconquista embodied the port-of-call aspect of the city, with rows of shops, bars, and brothels.

Rossi embraced the constraints imposed by the city, which required the building's main volume to begin at a height of 42 feet, so that new construction would not block views of Santa Catalina. This stipulation was integral to the project not only because it caused the structure to be raised on metal scaffolds, with elevators clustered in the middle, but also because it made Rossi take a closer look at the church and convent. What he found was a self-contained compound in a state of transition. Santa Catalina's mixed architectural lineage—its Spanish Colonial courtyard, Baroque bell tower, and what Rossi interpreted as its overriding Piedmontese severity— was further confused since it had been turned into a museum. In its eclectic assemblage, Santa Catalina became Rossi's model.

Rossi proposed a fourteen-story block made with three sections. The central portion has a shaft that changes from grey stone to a plaster finish about three-quarters of the way up. It is capped by a stepped pyramid of pink stone, which contains the cooling system. The side pieces of prefabricated concrete have barrel-vaulted roofs. There is a sheltered courtyard along Avenida Cordoba which is dominated by a fountain—water pours from a nine-foot equilateral triangle into a pool paved with turquoise tiles—and another courtyard along Avenida Viamonte that continues the streetfront perimeter wall of Santa Catalina.

Casa Aurora

Turin, Italy
1984

Casa Aurora, loosely translated as the "House of Dawn," is the corporate headquarters of the Turin-based conglomerate, Gruppo Finanziario Tessile (GFT), named for the Aurora pen company, which formerly occupied the site. In 1984, the venerable apparel manufacturer, parent company to such designer labels as Giorgio Armani, Emanuel Ungaro, and Valentino, asked Rossi to build a new office building adjacent to its manufacturing facility. Dedicated in June 1987, the 75,000-square-foot building occupies a prominent city corner, which Rossi marked unceremoniously in a manner reminiscent of Le Corbusier's Villa Schwob—with a blank brick expanse propped up by two massive columns and a green steel I-beam. This portal leads to a bank, which leases ground-floor commercial space. Entrances to the GFT offices are in keeping with the secretive nature of the fashion business, behind smaller, also blank, brick walls positioned more discreetly at the ends of the L-shaped office block. Narrow stone porticos line the outside of the building as stripped-down versions of the arcaded avenues of downtown Turin. The taut facades of stone panels, brick, and steel-framed windows are enlivened by domestic-scale dormers along the roof line.

In this building, Rossi further explores themes that appeared in earlier projects. The giant corner column that acts as a hinge to two wings of the Friedrichstadt housing complex is doubled here to outline the entrance. Similarly, Rossi's signature steel lintels appear more outwardly decorative, used alternately as brackets for the stone colonnades, a frame for the bank entrance, and inside, in a scaled-down version of the double-column exterior corner, as the seeming curtain rod for the stage's "curtain wall."

Partial view of the Via Emilia elevation

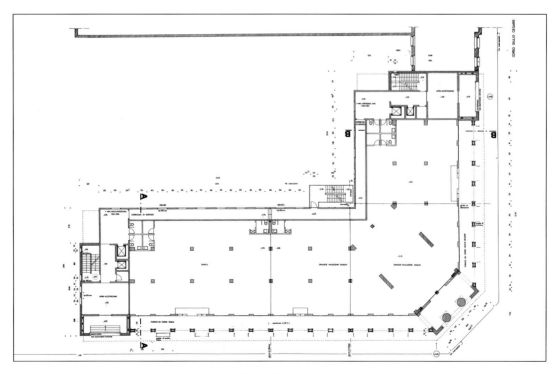

Ground floor plan

View inside the west portico along Via Emilia

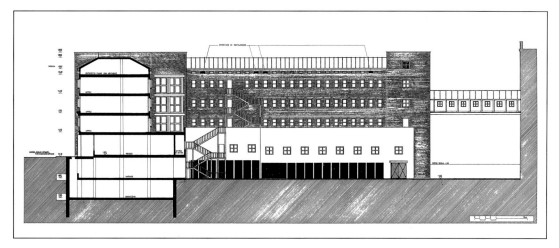

Longitudinal section

View showing guard house and bridge to existing building

Interior of the theater

VIALBA LOW-COST HOUSING

MILAN, ITALY
1985

Sponsored by the city of Milan, this low-cost housing complex is located on the outskirts of town in an area known as Vialba. The C-shaped structure is on the corner of Via Arsia, which runs north-south, and Via Zoagli, which runs east-west; it has nine floors and 196 units.

Recalling his Friedrichstadt apartment building in Berlin, Rossi marked the intersection of the two streets with a giant column that hinges two wings of the building. Here too the structure is pushed up against the sidewalk to maximize the area of the semi-enclosed courtyard behind. The long facade is divided into 46-foot-wide protruding stucco towers alternating with 20-foot-wide recessed stairwells; the corners are brick. Entrances to the building are located in the back and lead to a communal corridor overlooking the courtyard.

View of the courtyard
Site and ground floor plans

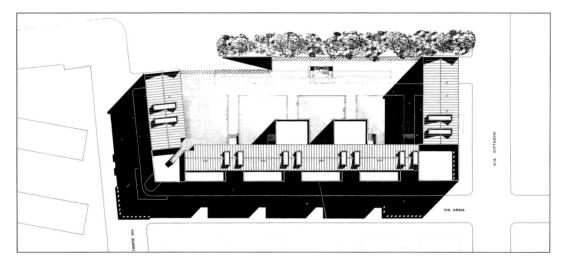

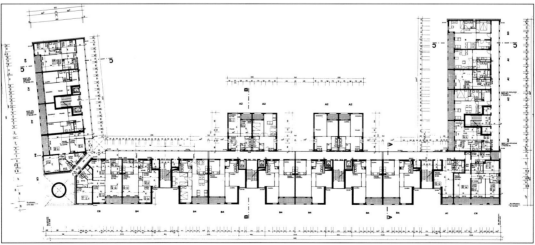

Detail of courtyard elevations
Courtyard and Via Arsia elevations

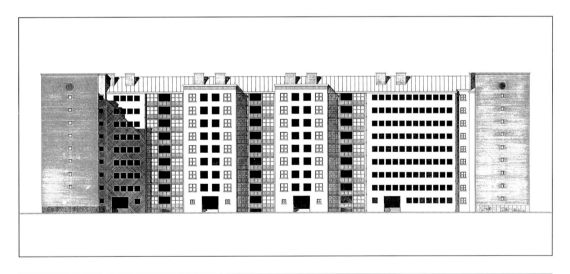

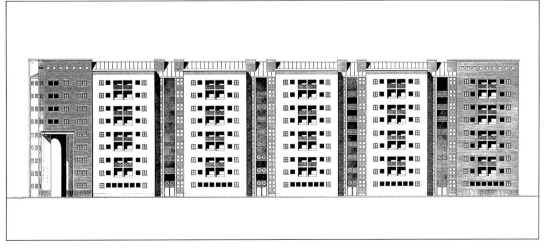

LOW-COST HOUSING

VENICE, ITALY
1985

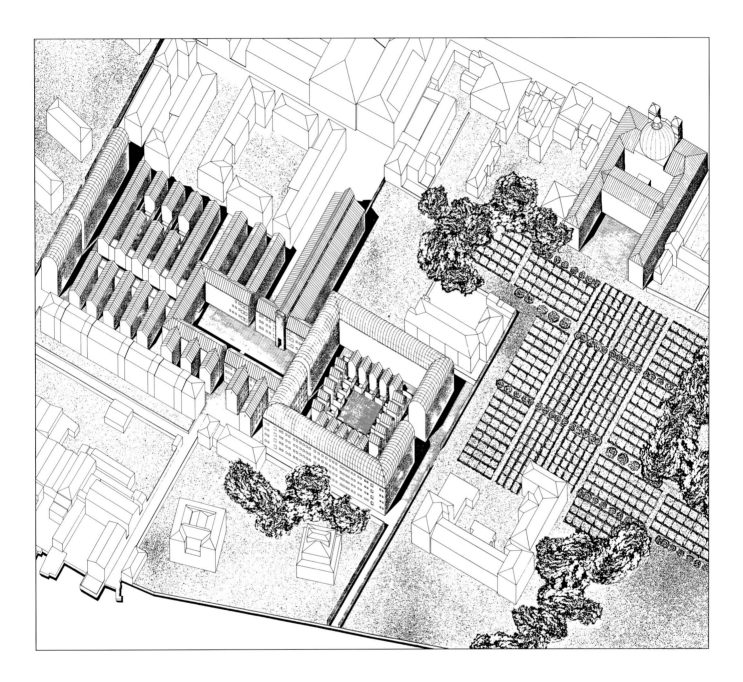

This project originated as an entry to an invited competition to rebuild the Campo di Marte section of the Giudecca, an island of Venice. Adjacent to the competition site is the sixteenth-century church of Santa Maria della Presentazione, known as Le Zitelle, attributed to Andrea Palladio. Coincidentally, Rossi had done a never-realized scheme for the adaptive re-use of Le Zitelle in 1982, whose dome and twin side towers figured prominently in his design of the Teatro del Mondo for the Venice Biennale of 1979.
For the Campo di Marte competition, Le Zitelle continued to be inspirational, but this time more for its rigorous symmetry and scale than for the actual arrangement of its forms. Rossi grouped the program requirements into a series of public squares that connect to a garden behind Le Zitelle. A four-story square apartment block surrounds two-story structures and leads to two successively narrower rectangular courtyards lined with four-story T-shaped buildings. An increase in degrees of privacy occurs in the transition from communal piazzas to alleys to residential units creating a mix that is particularly Venetian.

Centro Torri Shopping Center

Parma, Italy
1985

Rossi's design for one of the largest shopping centers in northern Italy was based on the idea of making a vertical mark on the flat terrain of Parma and the surrounding Po valley.

Rossi proposed a series of interconnecting, free-span market halls punctuated by 50-foot-high hollow towers—the towers, he felt, were needed to add interest to the vast, otherwise uninterrupted volume of the required leasable area. His client, the Cooperativa Emiliane, initially dismissed the towers as decorative and functionally useless. But Rossi convinced the consortium of agricultural producers that his plan held a potentially lucrative purpose: the towers along the edge of the complex would be left unfinished on one side— forming a U-shaped section—to hold billboards and giant product endorsements. As they now stand, the brick towers announce the shopping center's name Centro Torri, or Towers Center, in the Emilian tradition of hand-set, high-gloss blue, yellow, and white ceramic tile that is legible from the nearby highway. These ruddy brick sentries flank the main hall of the shopping center, which is topped by a copper gable roof. Shops and cafés are clustered in a rectangle around a skylight galleria. By making the name "Centro Torri" an essential part of his scheme, Rossi intentionally invokes traditional civic monuments, whose names, like town hall and even church, are inscribed in stone on their facades. Rossi's new city monument celebrates the late twentieth-century rituals of commercialism.

View of the west elevation

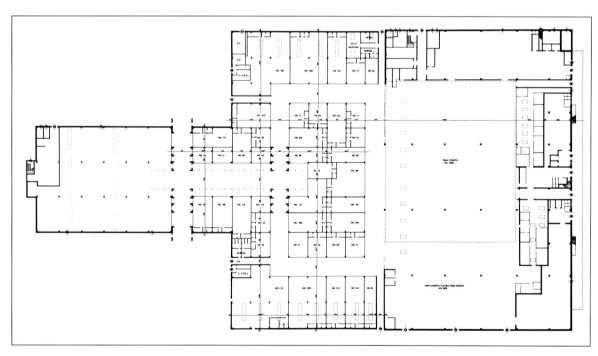

Ground floor plan

View of the towers and covered gallery

Study for glazed tile

View of the towers from the roof

Interior view of the skylit galleria

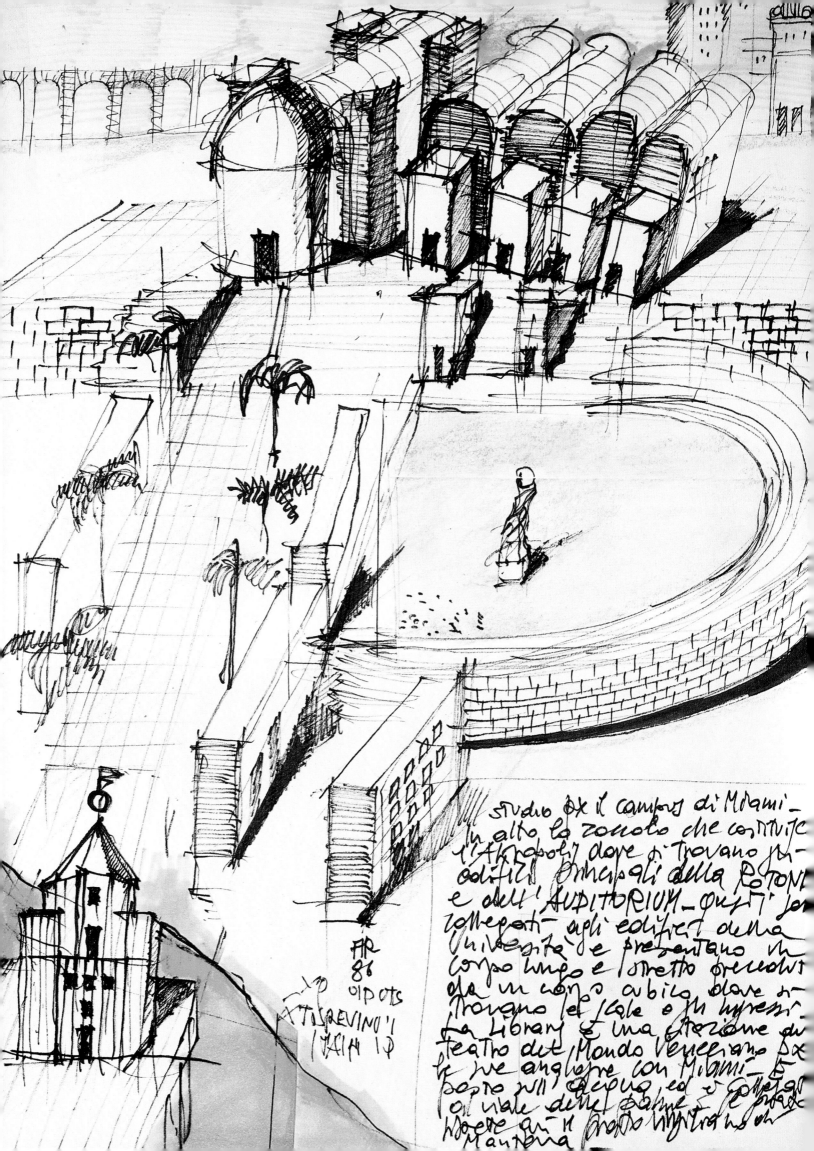

studio pX il campus di Miami.
In alto la zonolo che costituisce
l'Akropoli dove si trovano gli
edifici principali della ROTONDA
e dell'AUDITORIUM questi sono
collegati agli edifici della
Università e presentano un
corpo lungo e stretto preceduti
da un corpo cubico dove si
trovano le scale e gli ingressi
a Librari e una citazione del
teatro del Mondo Veneziano px
le sue anglogie con Miami
posto sull'acqua ed è collegato
al viale delle palme

AR
86
13 OIDOTS
TORREVINO'I
JAIM 1D

SCHOOL OF ARCHITECTURE

UNIVERSITY OF MIAMI, FLORIDA
1986

Rossi dubbed his design for the new architecture school at the University of Miami the "Acropolis in Miami"—emphasizing his plan to make a monumental focus for a scattered campus. For Rossi, the most memorable feature of the site is a nearby lake, which he sought to connect to his project.

His proposal consists of a group of interconnected volumes set atop a stone plinth—a raised, outdoor gathering spot that contains an underground parking garage. The structures are clustered together like a miniature town: a rotunda and adjacent auditorium for lectures and public gatherings, and five identical barrel-vaulted pavilions with administrative offices, classrooms, and a library.

The School of Architecture's existing buildings are incorporated in what Rossi calls the "Avenue of the Palm Trees," which connects the "Acropolis" with the lake. These buildings will be re-clad with new stone stair towers and metal balconies. An *allée* of palms leads to the Ziff Tower, a later addition to the scheme, with stacked cube-, sphere-, and cone-shaped seminar rooms, an excerpt of Rossi's 1982 proposal for Milan's Palazzo Congressi.

Rossi's original plan included a wood castle—his Teatro del Mondo reincarnate—permanently moored in the lake, revealing his tendency not only to quote from his own work, but also to make connections or "analogies" from past to present, and from one place to another. The Ziff Tower makes references of a different sort: to the pure geometric shapes of Etienne-Louis Boullée, whose essay on the sublime aspect of architecture Rossi translated into Italian.

The commission, Rossi's first in the United States, led to his partnership with Morris Adjmi and the opening of a New York City outpost of Studio di Architettura in 1986.

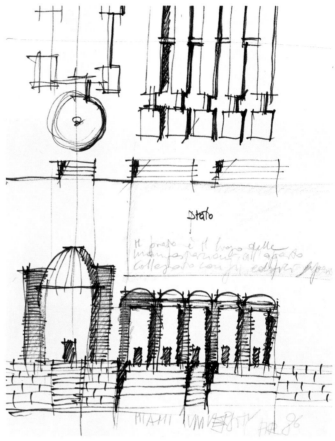

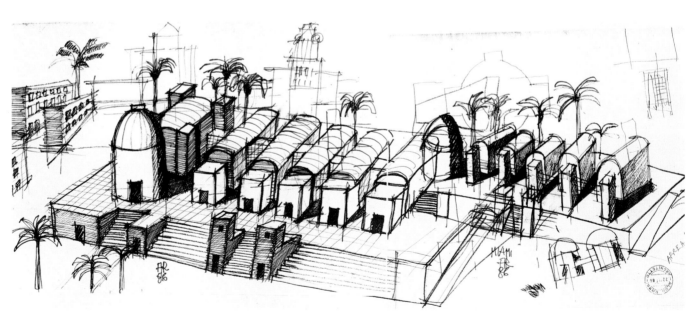

Early sketches for the school showing the Ziff tower and acropolis

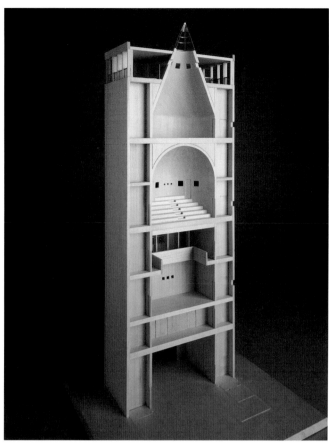

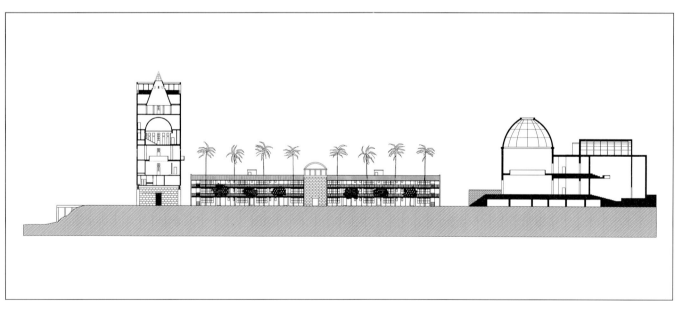

Ziff tower model, views of front facade and section
Site section

85

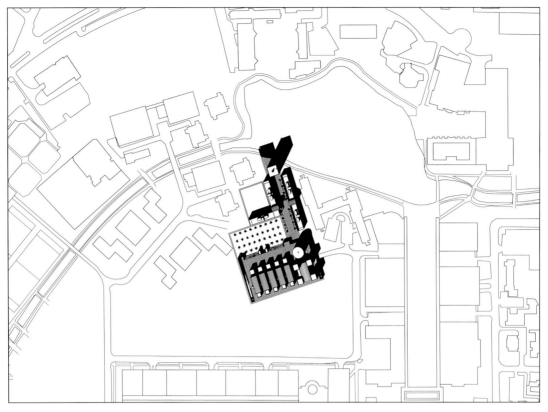

Site plan

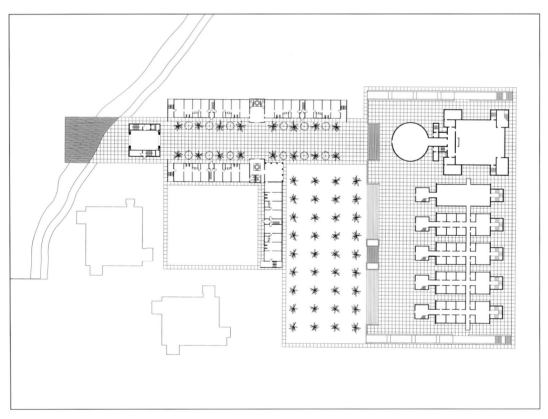

Piazza level plan

SECONDARY SCHOOL

CANTÙ, ITALY
1986

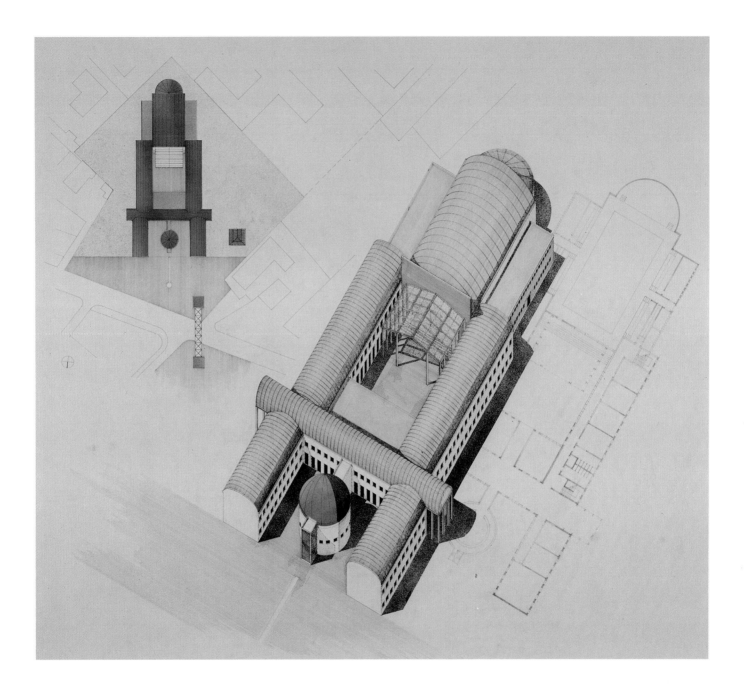

This project for a secondary school in the northern Italian town of Cantù includes classrooms, lecture halls, and a gymnasium that doubles as an auditorium. The volume of the building is spread around two courtyards, one semi-enclosed and one completely enclosed, that step down an irregularly shaped sloped site, in a more insular version of his 1972 school in Fagnano Olona. Rossi's proposal includes a bridge over adjacent Via Manzoni that connects a parking lot with the triangular paved plaza in front of the building.

The first of the two courtyards is C-shaped and dominated by the metal cupola of the planetarium. The lecture halls and the library are housed in the two-story side wings. Connecting the planetarium to the rest of the school is an arcaded gallery that runs from east to west. Perpendicular to the gallery are two two-story rows of classrooms, which form the perimeter of the lower courtyard. The courtyard is partially screened by a glass and steel canopy, which marks the main entrance to the gym. Attached to one end of the 60-foot by 97-foot gym is an apse containing a stage that allows the space to be used for school performances.

BICOCCA AREA DEVELOPMENT

MILAN, ITALY
1986

Bicocca is a district of mostly abandoned industrial buildings located along the eastern edge of Milan. In 1986 the city and manufacturer Pirelli sponsored an invited competition to physically restructure the area as a way of examining possible methods of instigating economic recovery. Rossi's entry proposes a new, self-sufficient—both architecturally and financially—city center, illustrating his long-standing thesis that the historic mono-centric city is no longer able to sustain the demands of contemporary life. In order to offset the perceptible isolation of Bicocca from the rest of Milan, Rossi makes an existing regional railroad station the literal focus of the project. The renovated station is connected by the continuation of a major city traffic artery to the public square of a proposed office *broletto,* or arcaded civic structure. Behind the *broletto* is Rossi's scheme for a new Pirelli tower, destined to be an instant landmark in the area as Gio Ponti's Pirelli tower overlooking Milan's central station was in the late 1950s. The intersecting axes of the station and *broletto* divide the vast area into four rough quadrants, each devoted to a different program requirements—research facilities, university functions, single-family residences, and speculative office development.

LA PIAZZA DI "ÜSKÜDAR" A IJTANBUL

ÜSKÜDAR SQUARE

ISTANBUL, TURKEY
1986

Üsküdar is a suburb of Istanbul located across the Bosporus, on the Asian side of the Turkish capital. Built into a hillside, this bustling port town is a mix of ramshackle structures, sprawling open-air markets, and imposing mosques casually arranged in an semi-circle facing the Golden Horn, Istanbul's harbor. Rossi's competition entry for the redesign of Üsküdar's main square reinforces the existing layout with the insertion of civic-scale structures, bestowing on this typically Turkish town the presence of a twentieth-century international port. Rossi's mix of references is a deliberate attempt to capture the eclectic spirit of Istanbul and its amalgam of Roman and Byzantine architecture.

In this award-winning, but unrealized scheme, Rossi replaces existing ferry stations along the banks of the Bosporus with 300-foot-long glass-topped steel sheds to dramatically mark a place where, in effect, Europe ends and Asia begins. Adjacent are docks for smaller vessels arranged in front of restaurants and bars that, in the other direction, spill over onto a paved central square. Along one edge of the port, are four barrel-vaulted hotels along a waterfront promenade. Behind the hotels are four towers containing offices and apartments. Between the hotel and the shopping center is Rossi's proposal for a museum of the city, contained in stacked brick and stone polygons—a modern day minaret.

LA VILLETTE HOUSING

PARIS, FRANCE
1986

Rossi's low-cost housing in the northeast of Paris, near the Parc de La Villette, is, *de facto*, a comment on the transitory nature of contemporary architectural styles. Located next to one of French president François Mitterand's lavish *grand projets*—the recently completed Cité de la Musique by Christian de Portzamparc—and forming a casual quadrangle with existing apartment buildings whose overwrought geometry pale by comparison to Portzamparc's building, Rossi's structure strikes a note of surprising simplicity. Whereas Portzamparc broke his program—concert hall, music conservatory, and music education institute—into separate pieces each meant to represent a different musical, Rossi gathered the various functional requirements of his—post office, shops,

apartments—into an L-shaped block topped with modified zinc mansards. This arrangement appears a humble version of the *hôtels particuliers* of Paris's master builder, Baron Haussmann.

The 350-foot length of long facade is broken into two pieces to make a cross axis into the communal courtyard. The front end is punctuated by a cylindrical tower clad in French postal blue and yellow aluminum, and the back is a blank brick expanse punctured beneath the cornice by a giant exhaust duct. Apartments ranging in size from one to five rooms are arranged among the second through seventh floors, with commercial space on the ground floor. The exterior is faced in a combination of stucco and Noyant, a local stone identical to that employed by Haussmann.

Early sketch showing postal blue cylindrical tower

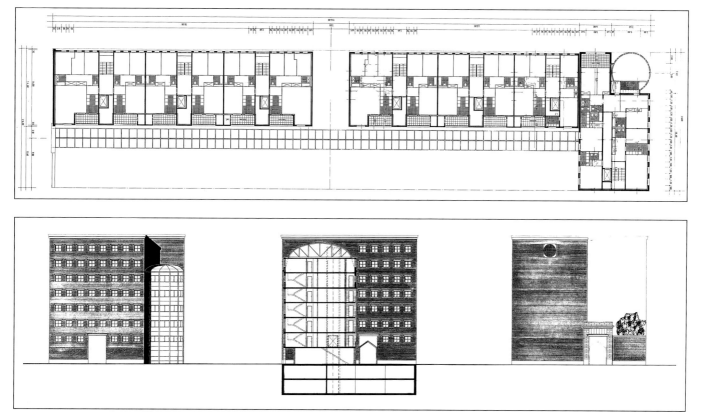

Typical floor plan, cross-section and elevations

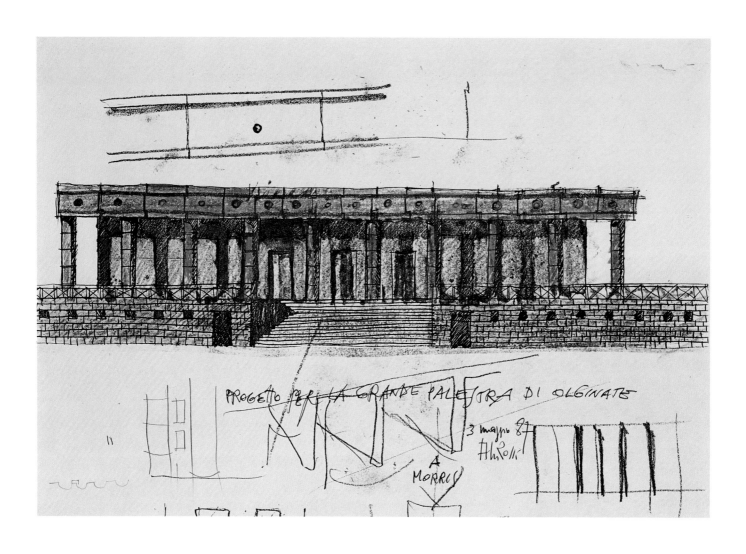

PROGETTO PER LA GRANDE PALESTRA DI OLGINATE

3 maggio 87

A MORRIS

Gymnasium

Olginate, Italy
1987

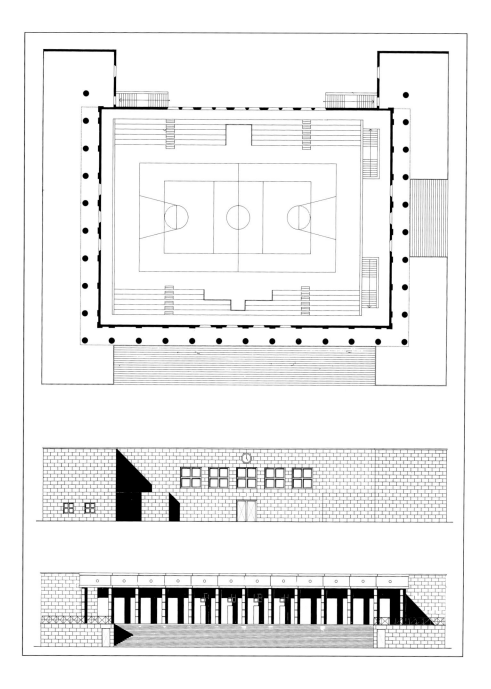

The new gymnasium for Olginate, near Como in northern Italy, is designed for an existing plateau between the village and the lake. The building is set atop a cement base and is framed by a widely spaced peristyle of cement columns whose hammered finish gives them the appearance of granite. A grand stair faces the lake to the north, distinguishing an otherwise blank facade (the idea of a gridded windowless front facade is explored more fully in the design of Hotel Il Palazzo). The public entrance is at the top of a set of steps placed in the center of the west facade, while student access is by way of two modest staircases flanking the back of the building, which faces the rest of the campus. These second-floor entries lead to the top of the spectator bleachers, which step down to the gymnasium floor. Locker rooms and offices line the perimeter, tucked into the base.

HOTEL IL PALAZZO

FUKUOKA, JAPAN
1987

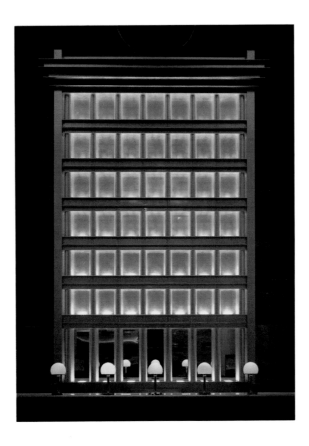

This hotel in Fukuoka, Japan is only part of an ambitious plan to stimulate the redevelopment of the port city's Haruyoshi district by Mitsuhiro Kuzuwa, owner of JASMAC (Japan Store Management Center). In fact, Rossi's master plan for the entire district shows the hotel surrounded by a vast entertainment complex. By the time the initial phase of the project began in 1987, Kuzuwa had amassed a substantial portion of real estate in the district and was already a successful hotelier (although his chain of pay-by-the-hour "love hotels" was clearly *not* to be the model for Rossi's project). Shigeru Uchida played a crucial role. His official title was "creative director," and as such he helped select Rossi and the other designers of the complex's four bars and a discotheque. In addition, he and his Tokyo-based office, Studio 80, designed the hotel interiors. Rossi understood that his role in the internationally-minded developer's plan was to create "a new image for the waterfront." What Rossi found lacking among the jumble of modernist buildings and traditional Japanese *yatai*—demountable bamboo shacks that serve food at small counters—was a semblance of urban order and a monumental focus, which he was to provide.

Aptly named, the seemingly inaccessible Il Palazzo, "The Palace," is set atop a stepped stone base (fulfilling setback requirements) and projects a seven-story windowless face to the canal below. Solid amber-colored travertine columns and chemically aged copper lintels form a gridded superstructure on the facade, creating a bold yet sober presence amid the honky-tonk flamboyance of this port of call. But for all its outward aloofness, Il Palazzo is a surprisingly good neighbor. The slab of guest suites that rises above Barcelona architect Alfredo Arribas's disco and rows of gable-topped pavilions—which contain bars by Ettore Sottsass, Gaetano Pesce, Shiro Kuramata, as well as by Rossi and his partner, Morris Adjmi— form an ordered enclave. The inside of Rossi and Adjmi's bar, *El Dorado*, is dominated by a 20-foot-high gold-leafed model of the hotel's facade.

To explain Il Palazzo's most controversial feature, the absence of windows in the main facade, Rossi recalls E. M. Forster's novel *A Room With a View*, in which a young English lady and her spinster aunt request rooms overlooking the Arno River at a Florence *pensione*. "At the beginning of the novel, the view of Florence is very important," Rossi explains, "but at the end what is really important is the stay at the hotel, the love, the life of the hotel. " Noting that the front rooms of Il Palazzo still have oblique vistas of the canal—a waterway not nearly as picturesque as the Arno—Rossi concludes, "What is even better than an empty room *with* a view, is a life-filled room *without* a view."

101

*Perspective, and site plan showing the area of
future development along the river*

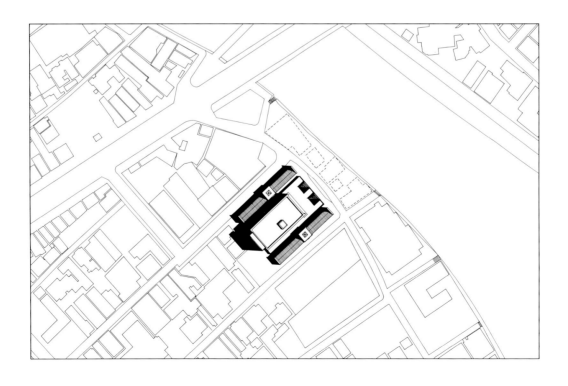

View of the hotel in context

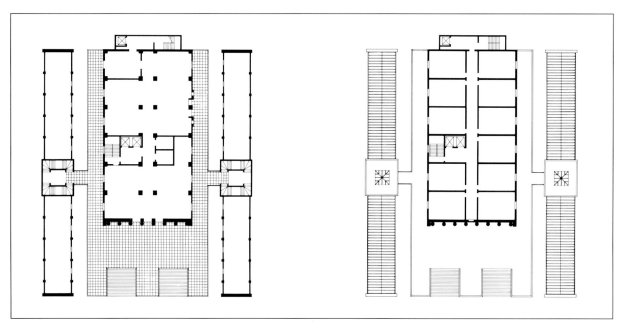

Piazza level and typical floor plans

Early sketch

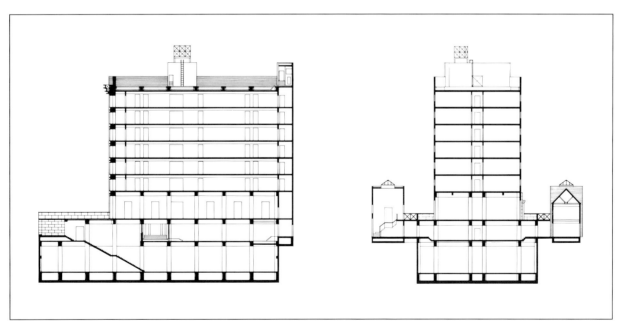

Longitudinal and cross-sections

Details of the building (clockwise from upper left, opposite): view of the stair tower from the west, view along the Vicolo della Luna, view from the main building along the pedestrian bridge to the stair tower, interior view of the stair tower; this page, El Dorado Bar

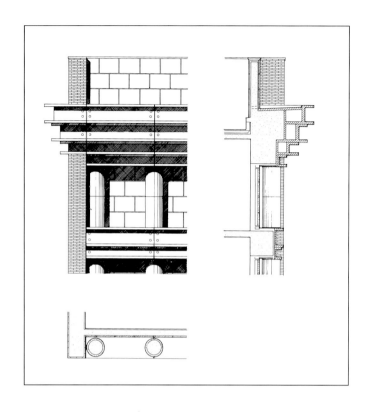

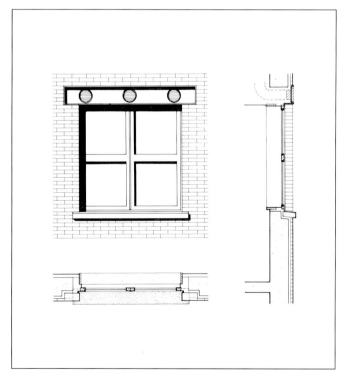

MONUMENTAL ARCH

GALVESTON, TEXAS
1987

In 1987, Rossi was commissioned to design a triumphal arch to span a street in Galveston, Texas's historic Strand district. The arch was to be the centerpiece of the 1988 Mardi Gras celebration. The year before, to help celebrate Texas's 150-year anniversary and reinvigorate flagging "town spirit," the city had reestablished an 1880s tradition of building festival arches along the Mardi Gras parade route, inviting seven high-profile American architects to help mark a mile-long stretch.

For the next pre-Lenten celebration, the organizers decided to adopt a Venetian-inspired theme and, appropriately enough, a Venice-inspired architect. Rossi was selected. Unfortunately, funds were low following the ambitious schemes of the previous year, and Rossi's arch wasn't constructed until money was raised from local boosters in time for Mardi Gras 1990, when the theme was the decidedly un-Italian "Carnaval do Brasil."

The project consists of four 35-foot-high red and white striped lighthouse towers arranged in a 45-foot square along the edge of the street that leads to the port. During Mardi Gras, spectator stands were inserted between the towers for parade watchers. The arch itself is a gridded metal truss, which supports a trio of national and regional flags.

Years before receiving this commission Rossi had visited Galveston while lecturing at the University of Houston; he had been so struck by the Gulf Coast city's charm that he had noted his impressions in his 1978 introduction to the American edition of *The Architecture of the City*. For Rossi, the white clapboard houses, church steeples, and lighthouses of Galveston, similar to the fishing towns of Cape Cod, meld into a tableau of architectural Americana. His design of the festival arch is meant as a "souvenir" of those impressions.

LIGHTHOUSE THEATER

TORONTO, CANADA
1987

The Lighthouse Theater was built for a site-specific arts installation mounted from June through September of 1988 at the R. C. Harris Water Filtration Plant on the banks of Lake Ontario in Toronto. The exhibition was organized by Hennie Wolff and Visual Arts Ontario (VOA) as part of its ongoing "Art in Architecture" program and included the work of eighteen architects and artists. The projects reflected the architects and artists' responses to areas they chose inside and outside of the plant, an operational water purifying facility servicing the Toronto area.

Rossi's architecture seems ideally suited to the massive structures housing turbine engines, pumps, and filter pools. Rather than compete with the existing monumentality, however, his design is an affectionate hybrid of ancient Roman theaters and New England maritime beacons—a European relic washed ashore and made into a navigational guide. Rossi's theater is a semi-circle attached to a rectangle, with wood bleachers facing a backdrop of three partial facades, including an excerpt of his own Hotel Il Palazzo, framed by two clapboard towers. A red and white striped lighthouse rests on an abstracted "pylon" overlooking spectator seating.

Instead of being the venue for performances, the theater became a principal player in a local drama. Nearby residents objected to the structure's presence on a plateau along the water's edge, claiming the open-air seating would encourage loitering. VOA moved the theater away from the lake, to a grass-covered traffic island between two local byways. This lighthouse was landlocked, an ironic turn of events for Rossi's first completed project in North America.

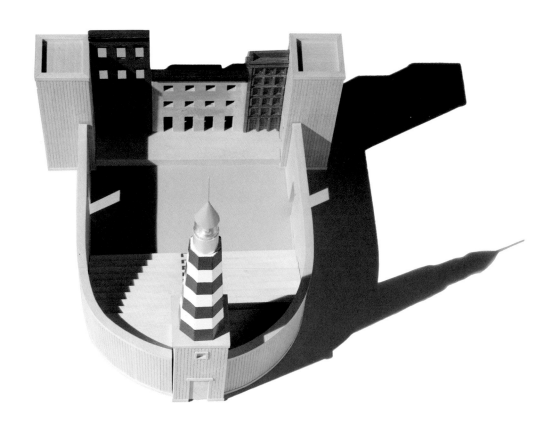

Model view of the final scheme

View of the theater from the south

114

The text within the early sketch reads:

THE
LIGHTHOUSE'S
THEATRE
WITH TWO
SCENES –
A – The Tragedy
B – The Comedy
AR
88

Early sketch

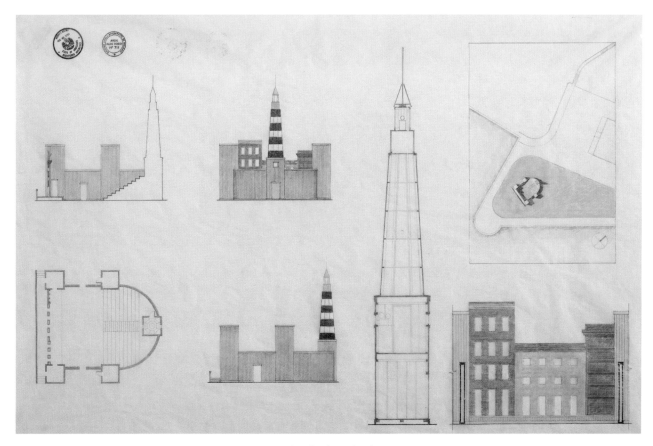

Drawings for the early scheme

DEUTSCHES HISTORISCHES MUSEUM   BERLIN   FR 88

MUSEUM OF GERMAN HISTORY

BERLIN, GERMANY
1988

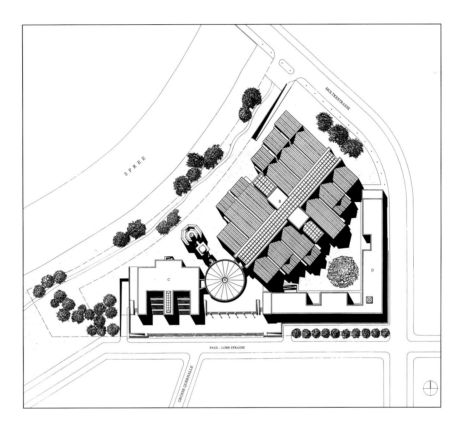

In June 1988, Rossi defeated over 200 German and a dozen other European architects in an invited competition for the design of the Museum of German History in Berlin. No one was more surprised than Rossi himself, who had assumed that he, and his entry, would be judged "politically incorrect."

In a country that has seen an impressive array of new museums either completed or under construction during the past decade, the idea of a museum devoted to the country's long, and, at times tumultuous, history met with great resistance. And certainly the choice of a "foreigner" to give a national monument physical form did not make the project more palatable to the German public. But Rossi is no stranger to Berlin. In fact, he has been a frequent visitor to what is now the center of a unified Germany since the early 1980s, when he was one of an international roster of architects invited to build housing as part of the International Building Exhibition (IBA), an urban program to rebuild areas of the city destroyed by World War II. What is evident from the jury's selection is their desire for an impressive civic presence, one whose abstract forms incorporate an understanding of Germany and its past, and, more importantly, provide an enduring, uplifting message for the future.

The site for the museum is a triangular parcel along the Spree River not far from Berlin's historic center. Rossi and associate Massimo Scheurer's winning entry is oriented in two directions simultaneously. A series of gabled sheds (exhibition space), which resemble the storage hangars of an active dock line the river's edge in a configuration that, for Rossi, establishes them as a contemporary "cathedral."

Facing the city is a group of more formal urban elements, bracketed by a portico that alludes to an earlier Berlin museum builder, Karl Friedrich Schinkel. The elements include a massive cylinder (the museum entrance) rendered in the typical Berlin blend of brick and glass and two carved out brick rectangles—containing meeting rooms, a library, and a theater—with two-story windows pointing downtown to, in Rossi's words, "bring the light of Berlin into the museum's interior and, to a certain extent, brighten the shadows of history with the city's youthfulness."

The scheme has been modified since its initial presentation: the main thoroughfare between the entrance and the exhibition space is now a skylit galleria, and one of the hangar-like pavilions was eliminated as part of a cost-saving reduction in overall program space, a possibility foreseen in some of Rossi's early sketches.

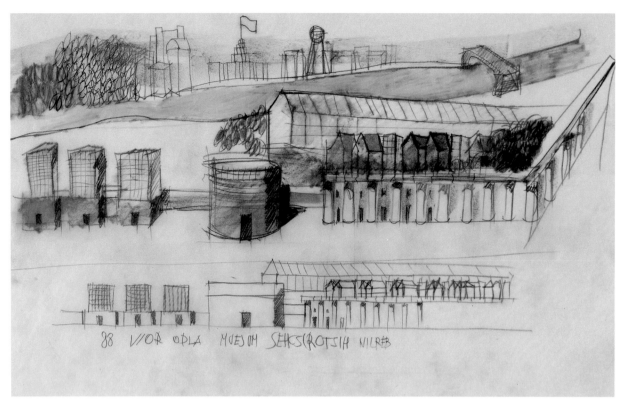

Study sketch for Paul-Lobe Strasse elevation

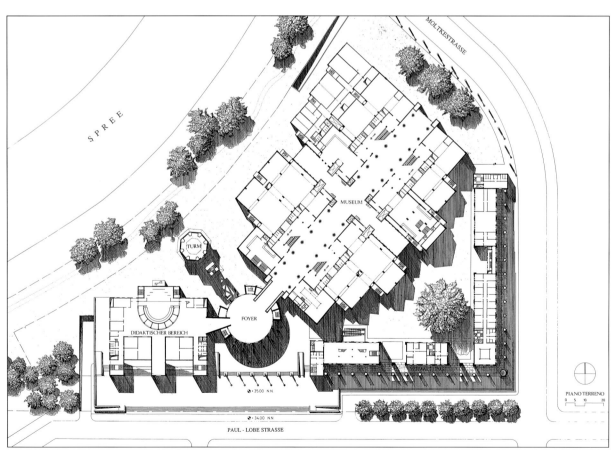

Ground floor plan

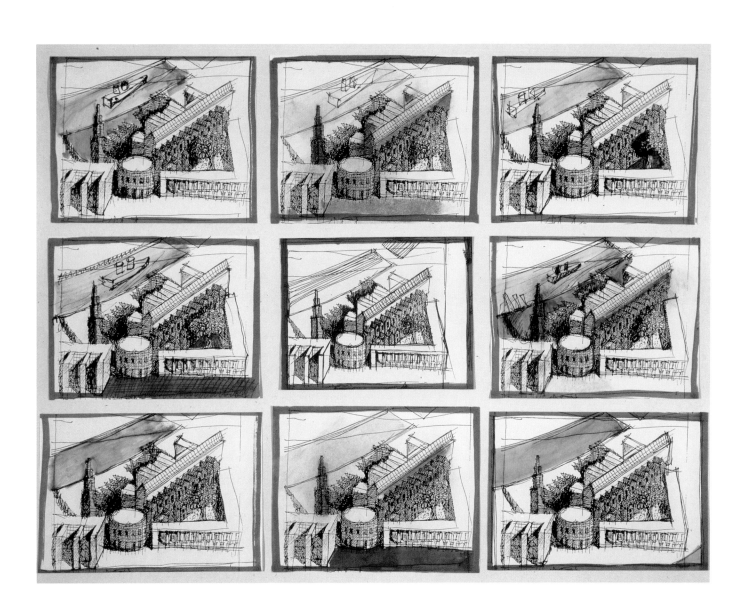

Model view showing elevation along Paul-Lobe Strasse

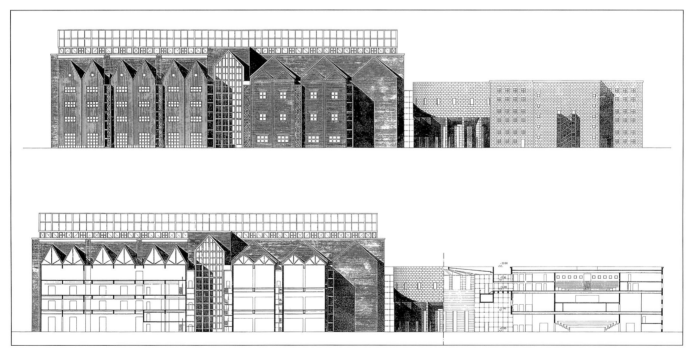

North elevation and longitudinal section

Model view showing elevation along Spree River

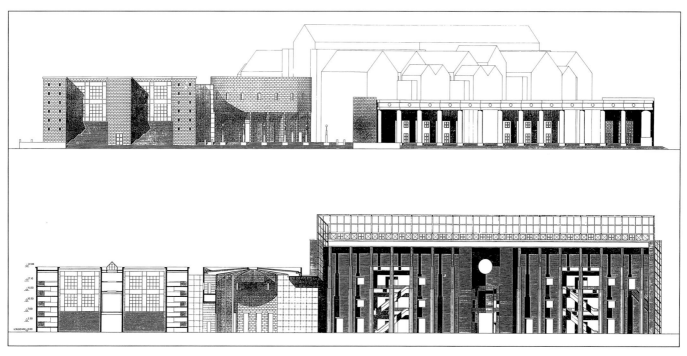

Principal elevation and section through the galleria

hT 39,00

+12,00

6.00 COMMER___le

COMMERCIA

COMMERC

garage

PALAZZO DELLO SPORT

MILAN, ITALY
1988

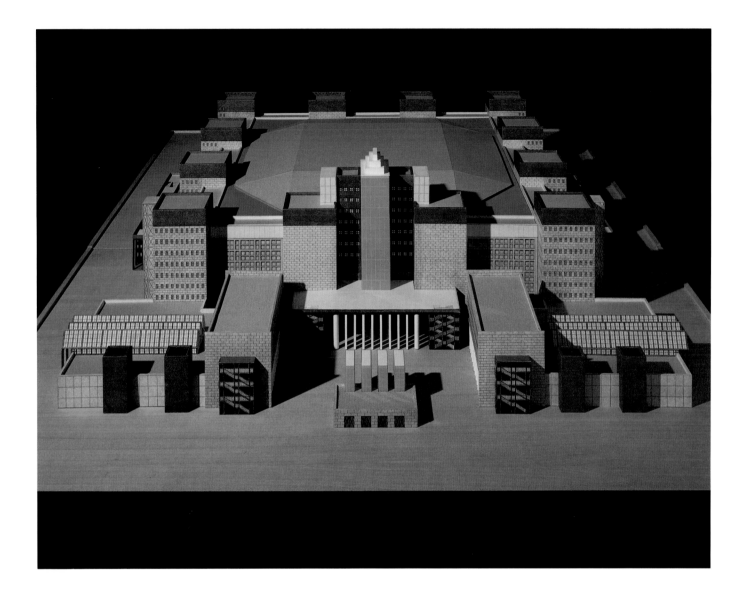

The Palazzo dello Sport is one of a new breed of urban entertainment meccas. Meant to accommodate an array of sporting and musical events in a covered hall, the 255,000-square-foot facility, located on a site adjacent to Milan's new San Siro open-air soccer stadium at the western edge of the city, has state-of-art facilities for both uses, making it the most important arena of the Lombard region. An adjacent shopping center, hotel, and 200,000-square-foot office building further increase the gigantic proportions of the complex.

The center of the complex is the 22,000-seat arena, which can be reconfigured for different sporting events. Twelve masonry towers form the perimeter of the arena and are joined by retail and office space; additional commercial space and a parking garage are located underground. The main entrance to the arena is framed by massive

brick walls topped with copper gable roofs. Rossi himself was daunted by the dimensions of the program and, as his early sketches for the project show, he pondered the relationship of scale and quality in other, more traditional civic monuments. He looked to the Milan cathedral, which he has long admired for its sheer size, noting that observers perceive it as "a mountain of stone, a quarry of itself, and stronger or richer than its stylistic incongruities." Projecting his design against the backdrop of such monuments, Rossi was able to break down the diverse components of Palazzo dello Sport's functional requirements into separate structures clustered around the arena, much in the way "tiny shops and poor dwellings lean on a cathedral." The analogy is particularly appropriate in economic terms, since the arena is intended to serve as a financial enticement to the district.

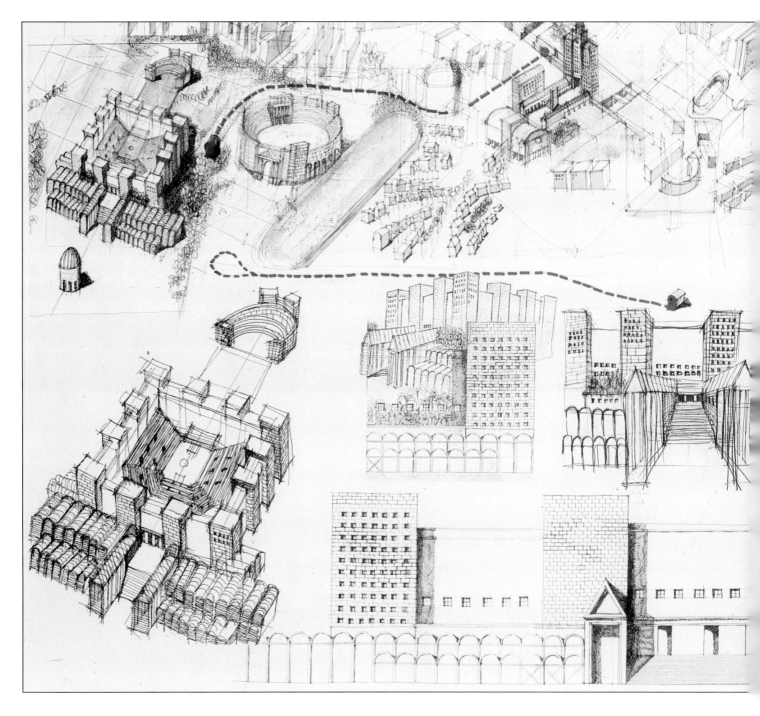

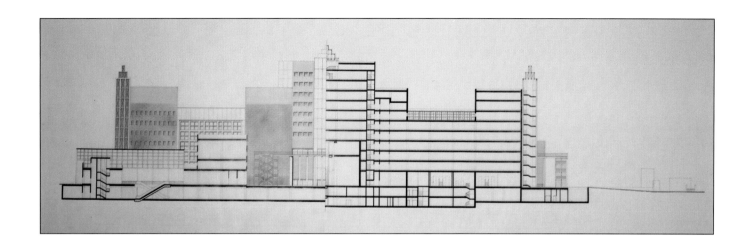

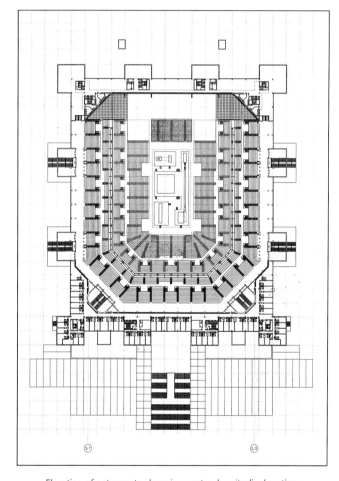

Elevation of entrance to shopping center, longitudinal section, early sketch showing project in context of Milan, and first floor plan

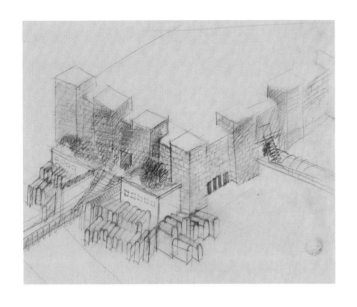
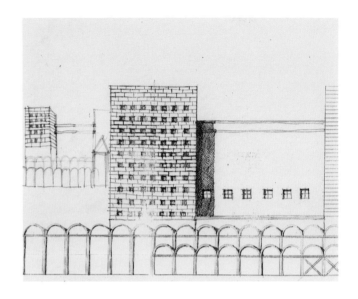

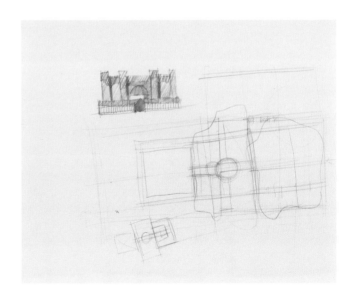

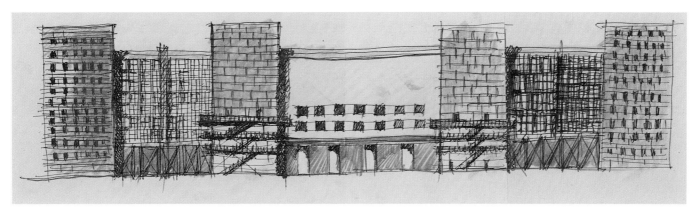

Early sketch of principal elevation

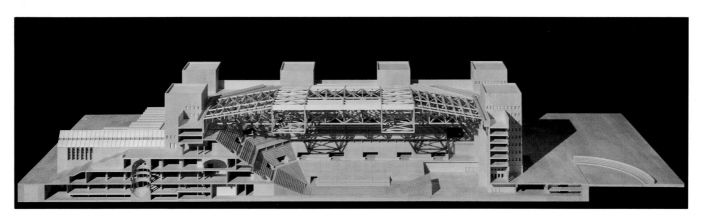

View of the sectional model

DUCA DI MILANO HOTEL

MILAN, ITALY
1988

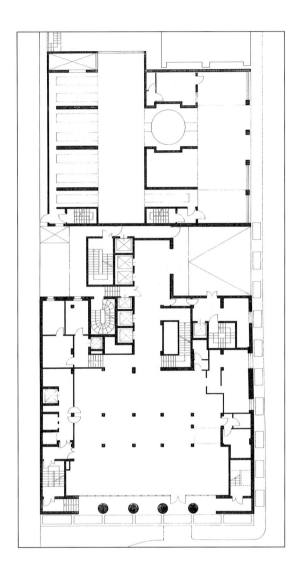

The prestige of the some 40 owned or operated hotels of the venerable Compagnia Italiana di Grandi Alberghi (CIGA) is only enhanced by the publicly-held company's association with its principal shareholder, the Aga Khan, the titular head of the Muslim people, distinguished in architectural circles for his patronage of design. Living up to its high-style reputation, CIGA has begun renovation of its properties throughout Europe, including its four outposts in Milan, of which three—the Duca di Milano, the Principe di Savoia, and the Palace—are on neighboring sites of the city's vast traffic hub, the Piazza della Repubblica.

In 1988, Rossi was commissioned to redesign the newly-acquired Duca's crumbling exterior shell as part of the hotel's overall expansion program, which included an interior scheme by CIGA's in-house designers. Rossi and associate Giovanni Da Pozzo responded to the daunting dimensions of the Piazza della Repubblica with an equally formidable front facade: a two-story entrance portico juts out from the main volume of the eleven-story structure. Four massive marble columns support a row of square windows framed by steel beams that appear to be at once structural lintels and giant decorative horizontal mullions. From the stone base of the hotel reception and restaurant rises the granite-turning-to-brick tower of the guest suites, whose massive expanse is subdivided by six engaged columns. Overlooking a local byway to the north, the Duca presents a restrained brick face to its more glamorous sister, the Principe di Savoia. In the back, along the service road of Via Galilei, are newly-made bricked-up windows—an ironic symbol of modernity.

Detail of entrance

Detail of Via Marco Polo elevation

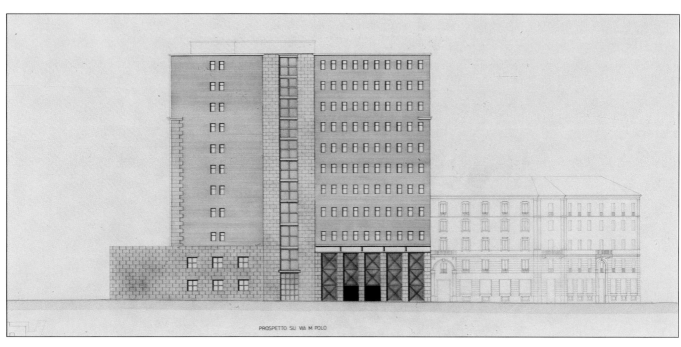

PROSPETTO SU VIA M. POLO

Via Marco Polo elevation

131

THE HAGUE AREA DEVELOPMENT

THE HAGUE, NETHERLANDS
1988

Rossi's scheme for the redevelopment of an area of The Hague, judicial seat of the Netherlands, has been altered since it was unveiled in 1988. The initial proposal, shown here, for a rectangular parcel sandwiched between the bustling harbor of the port city and a residential neighborhood spread along the edge of a narrow lake, combines new construction with renovation of the nineteenth-century slaughter houses.

Designed with Hague-based associate Umberto Barbieri, Rossi's plan shows a gradual decrease in building height and volume from one edge of the site to the other. A 1,500-foot-long wall of apartment buildings with ground-floor commercial space acts as a three-dimensional "sound barrier" and visual screen along a highway, which the city has planned to circle the harbor, while maintaining the scale of commercial high-rises located across the water. On the opposite perimeter of Rossi's site is a row of single-family brick houses—old-fashioned town houses that relate in scale and character to the adjacent residential quarter designed by Dutch architect H. P. Berlage in the early 1900s. In between is the renovated slaughterhouse, with a restored glass-topped galleria serving as an enclosed corridor between various offices and artisan studios. A row of four-story apartment buildings linked by a communal lawn completes this city within a city.

133

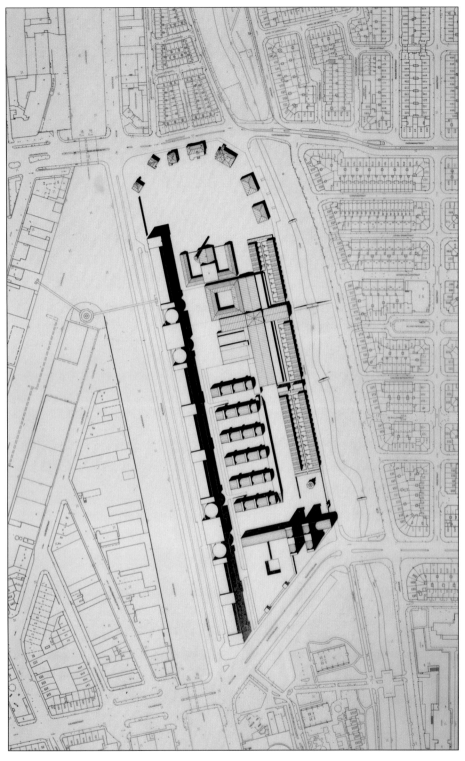

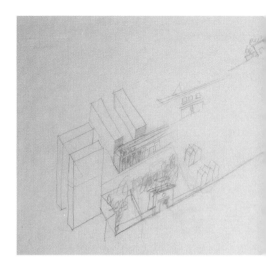

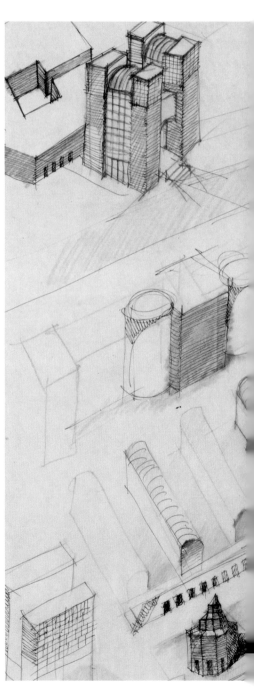

Site plan showing the area of redevelopment, and conceptual sketches

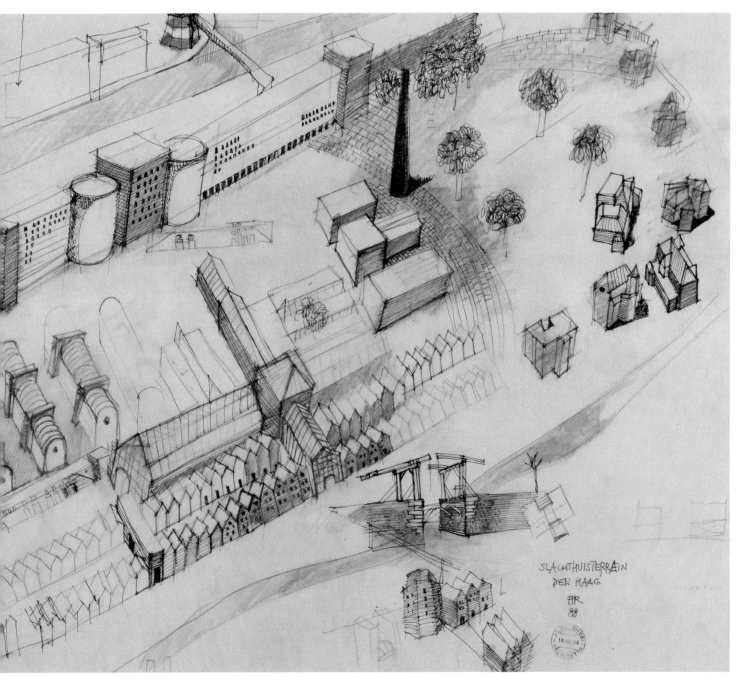

SLACHTHUISTERREIN
DEN HAAG

HR
88

PISORNO AREA DEVELOPMENT

MARINA DI PISA, ITALY
1988

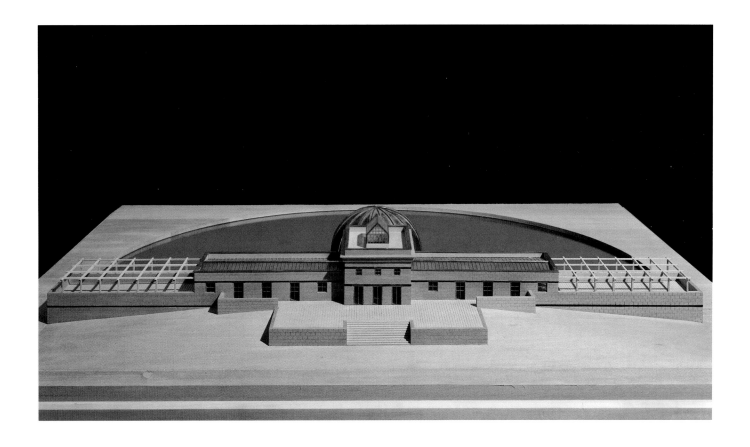

This project for a 70-acre site along Italy's west coast involves demolition, renovation, and new construction. The focus of the project is the former Forzano Film Studio, opened in the mid 1930s by Gioacchino Forzano on a lot near Pisa, in an area known as Pisorno. The growth of the Italian movie industry in general, and of studios that filmed on big constructed sets in particular, caused Forzano to add two more buildings to his original complex of three on an adjacent parcel in the early 1940s.

During World War II, the studio was appropriated first by the German and then by the American Army as storage. Not until 1950 were the buildings returned to their original use. With the rise of neorealism in post-war film, theater-like sets were in less demand, and studios like Forzano's were replaced by location shooting. Forzano went bankrupt in 1958, and his studios were closed.

For the next two decades assorted redevelopment plans were put forth; primarily schemes for subdividing the area into residential neighborhoods or industrial zones; but local residents hoped to maintain the existing scale of the community.

In 1987, a new scheme, backed by the Società Pisorno, advocated a more sensitive scheme. Relying on Tuscany's growing reputation as a resort, it also holds greater promise for financial success: the entire area around the film studios is to be transformed into a hotel and recreation complex, while maintaining the existing ratio of building volume to open land. Toward that end, Rossi's scheme calls for the demolition of 697,000 cubic feet and the construction of 686,000 cubic feet.

The various components of the project are organized around a main axis that connects what will be an expanded golf club to the parking lot. Flanking this path are the double rows of colored stucco "houses" of the Casa Albergo. Interconnected by walkways and covered ramps, the units are broken down into two types: those in the front row have flat roofs while those in the back row, which have sleeping lofts, are topped by barrel vaults.

Between the Casa Albergo and the parking lot is what remains of the 1940s additions to the Forzano Film Studio: the area's historic center, recast as a convention center with an exhibition hall, five auditoriums, a bowling alley, and a restaurant. The three original studios are consolidated into the 150-room Hotel Tirrenia with a central courtyard. New facades of alternating bands of white and black marble allude to the summer colonies of the 1930s as portrayed in the movies.

All of the buildings are respectful of the site in both their sources of inspiration and scale: architecture, according to Rossi, that is deliberately "minute with respect to nature."

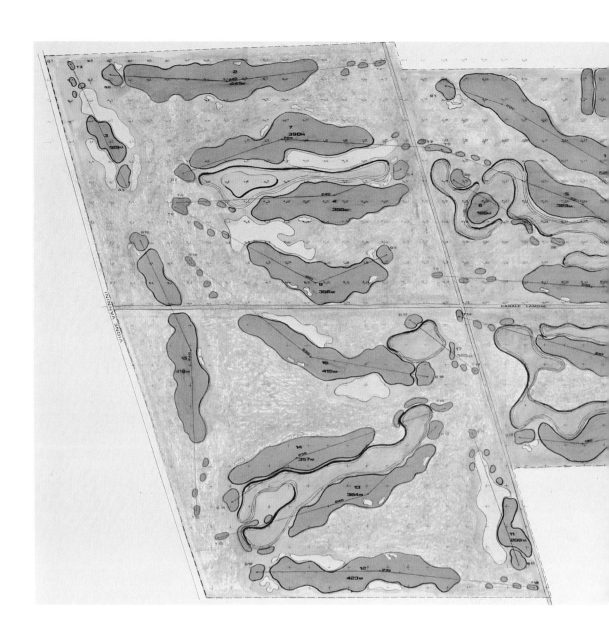

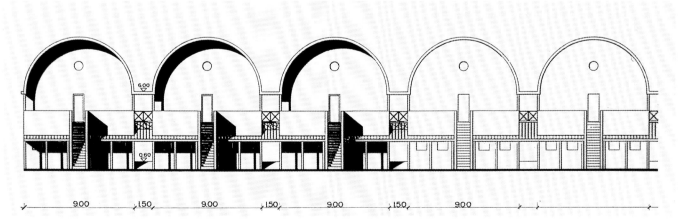

Row house elevations of the Casa Albergo

138

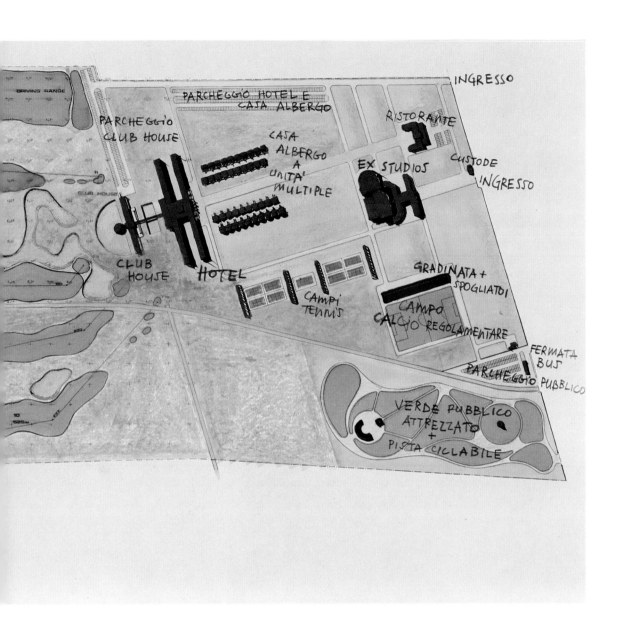

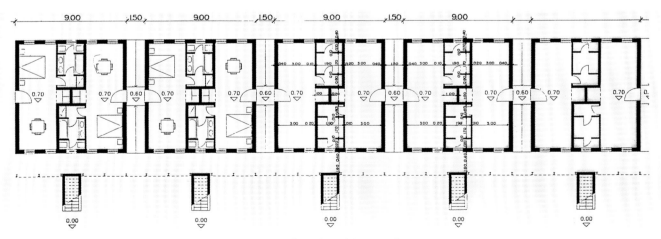

Ground floor plans of the Casa Albergo

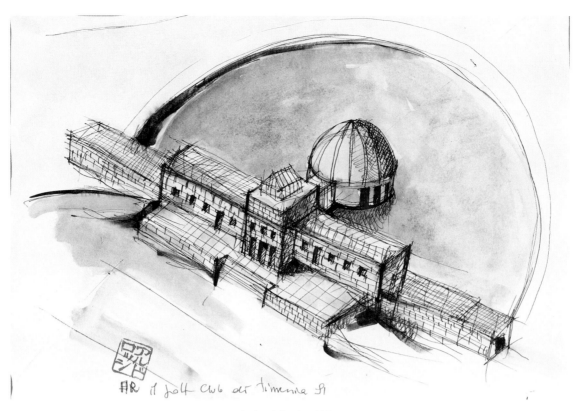

Study sketch for the clubhouse

Study sketch for the Hotel Tirrenia

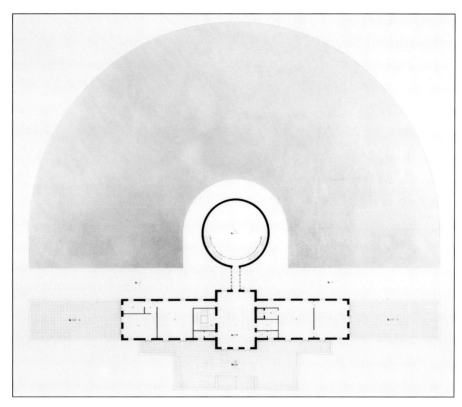

First floor plan of the clubhouse

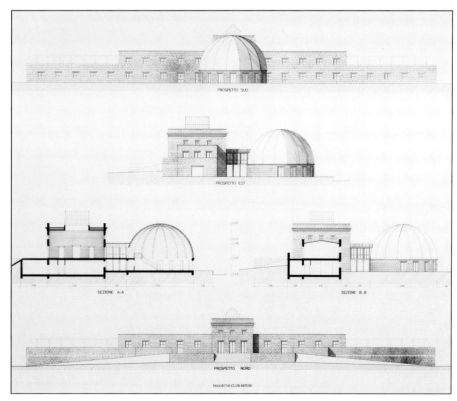

Elevations and cross-sections of the clubhouse

CENTER FOR CONTEMPORARY ART

VASSIVIÈRE, FRANCE
1988

The French Ministry of Culture joined with the powers-that-be of the region of Limousin in central France, and a local business consortium to finance a new museum of contemporary art on the remote island of Vassivière. In a lake between the towns of Limoges and Clermont-Ferrand, the 173-acre island is known for its lush forests and rolling countryside. On a hilltop site overlooking the water is the newly-completed modern art museum, designed by Rossi with French architect Xavier Fabre, a former student of his at the Zurich Polytechnic. The facility is made up of two parts: a brick lookout tower that resembles a lighthouse and a long, gable-topped gallery. The tower is meant to reinforce the verticality of surrounding trees, while the gallery, which is connected to it, mimics the horizontality of the plains. Inside are exhibition spaces, artists' studios, and a library.

Side elevation and tower

Detail of entrance

Interior view through the corridor to the gallery

Interior view of gallery

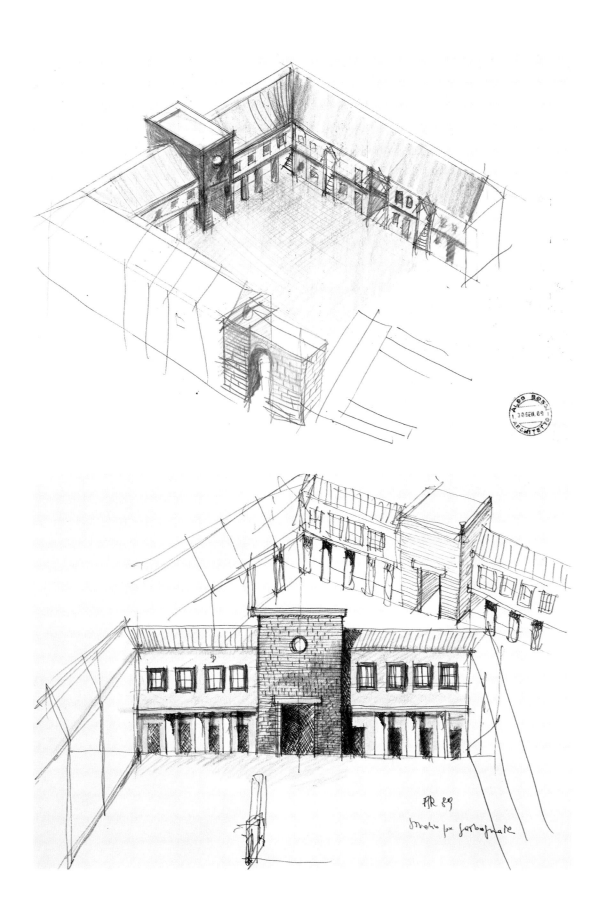

AR 89
studio per forbofinale

CORTE DEL CHIODO

GARBAGNATE, ITALY
1988

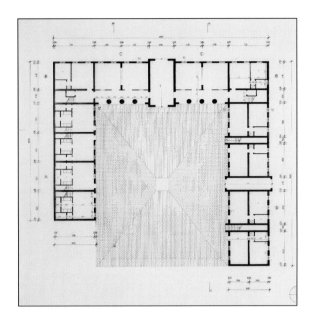

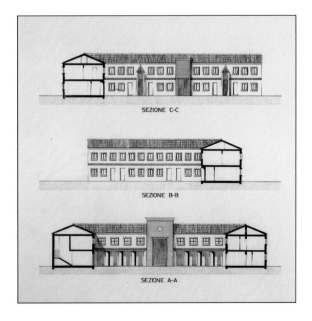

Rossi's proposal for low-cost housing in the Milan suburb of Garbagnate, located some 60 miles to the northeast of the city, is part of a reevaluation of town planning in the region. In general, the program calls for renovation and new construction in downtown districts that, in Rossi's words, "have been destroyed and damaged by a sudden and abnormal growth." His scheme focuses on Corte del Chiodo and draws on the courtyard configuration typical of apartment complexes in Lombardy. The two-story U-shaped structure, clad in traditional plaster, opens toward adjacent apartment buildings to the south. A brick tower punctuated by a clock marks the main entrance. Communal meeting rooms are located on the ground-floor of the north wing and permit access to the terra-cotta-paved courtyard from a covered portico; one- and two-bedroom units are located above and in adjacent wings.

AMERICAN HOUSE / PENNILVANIA

WHITE

HAMBURGER'S HAUS.
HAMBURGER'S HAUS
PENNSILVANYA
DOMESTIC ARCHITECTURE

NY
88

POCONO PINES HOUSE

MOUNT POCONO, PENNSYLVANIA
1988

Many architects begin their careers by designing houses; often their first clients are their parents. Not Rossi. After completing a villa in Versilia, Italy—a series of interlocking cubes sheathed in white plaster that incorporates references to the stripped-down forms of Adolf Loos—in 1960, and a Ticino vacation compound—of which only the guest cottage was completed—Rossi did not build another single-family house for nearly three decades, though, during that period, he consistently built *housing* (mostly low-cost).

In 1988 a young American developer asked Rossi to build three houses ranging in size from 2,000 to 2,700 square feet on one-acre lots spread among neighboring developments in eastern Pennsylvania. Inspiration for these speculative houses came not from the work of Loos, but, more appropriately, from American residential vernacular. The gabled roofs, dormers, prominent brick chimneys, and painted clapboard siding of the houses are meant to be a blend of suburban and farmhouse imagery.

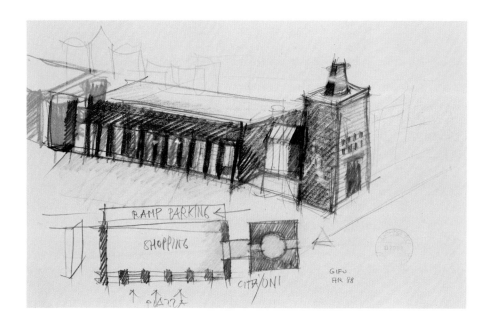

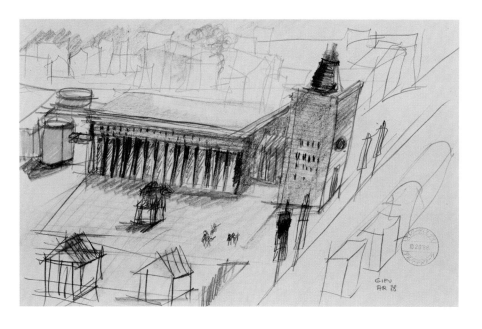

CENTRO CITTÀ COMMERCIAL AREA

GIFU, JAPAN
1988

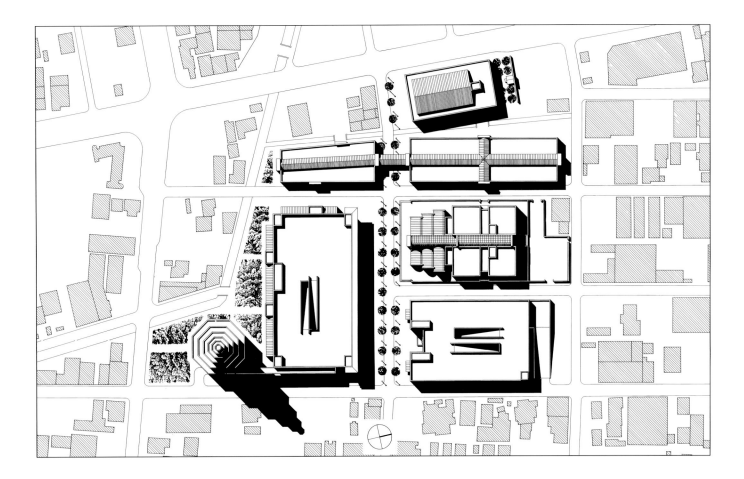

After starting work on Hotel Il Palazzo in Fukuoka, Rossi was offered other commissions in Japan with Shigeru Uchida and his firm, Studio 80, acting as interior space planners. In 1988, Rossi was asked to design a commercial complex for retail conglomerate UNY in the Japanese city of Gifu. UNY, one of Japan's largest "General Merchandising Stores" (GMS), is based in Nagoya and operates retail stores around the country. In recent years, competition among the GMS's has become fierce and companies have devised increasingly elaborate methods of distinguishing themselves to potential customers. Such publicity-generating "marketing techniques" have included GMS-sponsored baseball teams, company museums, and the commission of high-profile architects.

This project rests on the site of a former metal factory located in the economically-depressed southern section of Gifu. As is typical in UNY developments, which are largely based on the company's analysis of American and European models, a portion of the complex is devoted to selling UNY clothing and other goods, while local merchants and outposts of international manufacturers are incorporated to give regional character and a worldly flair.

Because land in Japan is so expensive, providing sufficient parking to satisfy zoning requirements is a particular problem, often resolved in the manner seen here; it costs less to structurally reinforce buildings to support parking on the roof than to furnish sprawling ground-floor lots. Since the storage of cars was of such importance, Rossi made the parking ramps to UNY's rooftop lot into a tower and a marker of the entire complex. The six individual buildings of the complex are spread across several existing city streets. The streets in between the various buildings are not UNY's property and are to be kept intact. Rossi proposes repaving them, forming an outdoor courtyard between three four-story structures: the UNY outlet, the food market, and entertainment building with its traditional Japanese garden in its back yard. The communal courtyard is dominated by a triangular bronze fountain inset into the blank, brick, south facade of the food market. A two-story "fashion court" spans the main thoroughfare of the complex (the pedestrian bridge is an optional component of the design); the building's corrugated metal sides and red metal roof house high-price merchandise. Near the fashion court is a four-story health club.

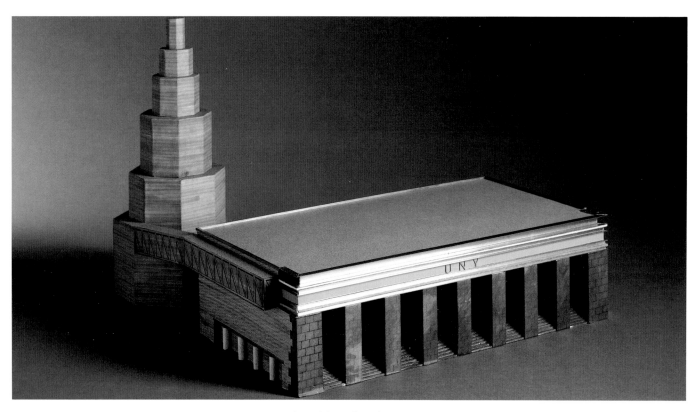

Early model view from the piazza

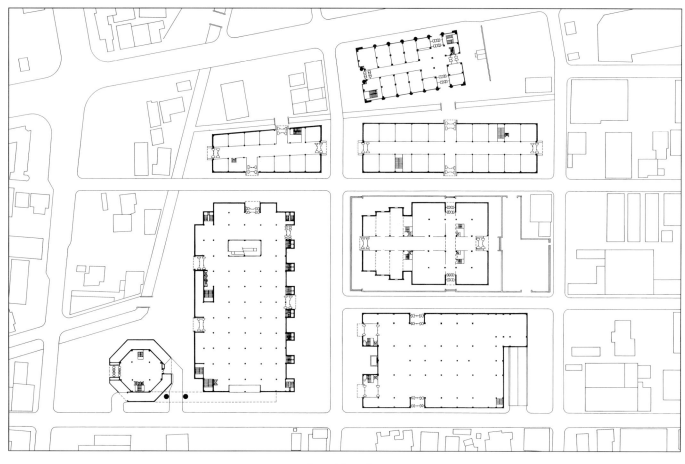

Ground floor plan

Early model view from the southwest

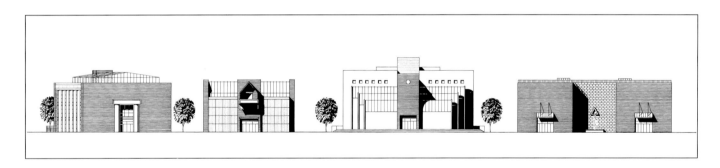

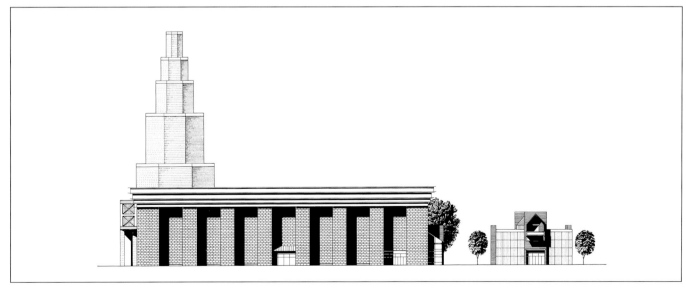

South and north elevations

Via Croce Rossa Monument

Milan, Italy
1988

Despite Rossi's international prominence, he had built few projects in his home town by the end of the 1980s. Since the completion in 1973 of the Gallaratese housing block, located in the outskirts of Milan, Rossi's projects for the Lombard capital have existed largely on the drawing board. In 1988, however, Metropolitana Milanese, the city's public transportation agency, gave him a prime, though modest-sized, site at the intersection of Via Manzoni and Via Montenapoleone, two of the city's most fashionable streets. The program involved the design of a monument to help transform the entrance to the new Croce Rossa subway station into a public piazza.

At first glance the project looks remarkably similar to Rossi's entry to the 1962 competition for the Monument to the Resistance—a giant hollow cube covered with commemorative inscriptions and the names of resistance fighters who died in battle. Although the resistance monument was never built, it was clearly on Rossi's mind when he designed the Croce Rossa monument—a cube without a top and a front face that holds a staircase to the sky. Placed at the back of the rectangular plaza, the monument is flanked by rows of mulberry trees indigenous to the Lombard region, bronze street

lamps, and granite-block benches. A drain bisects the granite paving of the plaza and water flows from a triangular fountain at the back of the monument. The staircase and the surrounding walls are covered in a rare pinkish-grey Candoglio marble identical to the stone of the Milan cathedral.

When completed in 1990, the monument was not universally well received; it was criticized alternately for being inappropriate and useless. Because the project was effectively government-sponsored, some of the criticism may have been purely political. (Italy has a long history of politics in the architectural arena.) Also, the dedication, which took place not long after Rossi received the profession's most prestigious award, the Pritzker Prize, was an ideal opportunity for some critics to disparage Rossi, architecture's acknowledged hero. No stranger to controversy, Rossi remained steadfast against demands for the monument's removal. "They can't destroy it," Rossi said of the solid construction. But the controversy quieted as the Milanese began using the plaza as the architect had intended— basking in the sun or eating a *panino* on the steps—proof that this monument to a different kind of resistance has been successfully absorbed into Milan city life.

View of the monument from Via dei Giardini

Model view from Via Manzoni

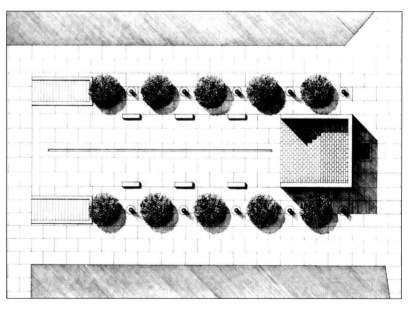

Site plan

GFT Comune di Settimo Torinese

Turin, Italy
1988

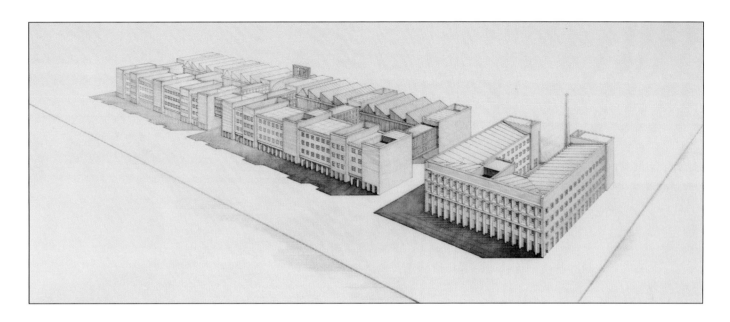

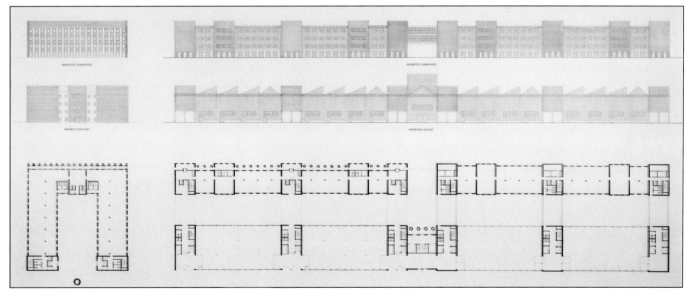

This project, Rossi's second for the apparel consortium Gruppo Finanziario Tessile (GFT), is planned for the eastern edge of the northern Italian city of Turin, in an area known as Settimo Torinese. After completing GFT's new headquarters, Casa Aurora, on a prominent site in downtown Turin, Rossi was asked to do a scheme that would provide for the gradual relocation of the company's manufacturing facilities from the city's historic center to its less zoning-restrictive, and less expensive, fringe. Rossi's inclusion of an independent office block, to be used initially as sales offices, also anticipates the projected reunion of factory and corporate headquarters.

The office building is a "U" that opens toward a brick smokestack. Joining two four-story wings, is the central streetfront facade dominated by rows of stacked stone columns. Adjacent is the factory, which consists of two strikingly distinct parallel wings joined by covered pedestrian bridges. Along the street, are the more formal masonry structures of the fabric-cutting workshops and behind are the brightly-colored, interconnected metal sheds of the textile weaving studios. Although the gabled sheds are a surprising departure from Rossi's well-established repertoire, they are bracketed by brick towers at all corners, recalling the familiar massive blank brick surfaces of Casa Aurora.

YATAI

NAGOYA, JAPAN
1989

In 1989 a world design exposition was held commemorating the 100th anniversary of Nagoya. As part of the exposition, the Nagoya-based UNY Group, a retail conglomerate, sponsored its own pavilion and invited an international group of architects to design twelve individual installations. The architects were asked to incorporate their interpretations of a *yatai*—a traditional Japanese stall that can be folded up and reassembled at another location—into the chosen theme of "festival."

Movable architecture was not new to Rossi, who had designed a floating theater for the 1979 Venice Biennale. For the World Design Exposition, Rossi again examined architecture in motion, this time in a more whimsical manner. His contribution to the exhibition was a display of European festival masks, and in his imagined scenario the most famous Italian storybook character, the puppet Pinocchio, serves as festival impresario. In this three-dimensional fairy tale, Pinocchio is seated at the wheel of a shiny red tractor hitched to four

pavilions. The pavilions are childlike versions of Rossi's own architecture—"the old and shaky constructions that may not last too much longer and that only exist in the artificial world of the theater"—mounted on clunky, wooden wheels. Inside the pavilions are masks and western costumes. But there is a serious side to this fanciful tale, as Rossi explains in the written brief that accompanies the project: "This is Pinocchio's *yatai*. Pinocchio is not really a puppet. His destiny or the motivation of his life in the end is to become a boy and then a man. Therefore, Pinocchio is a difficult person, easy but also neurotic, in between two worlds."

To help Pinocchio realize his dream of leaving his artificial world behind and becoming a real boy, Rossi has given him a high-tech tractor for his journey into manhood. Says Rossi: "Pinocchio accepts all of his responsibilities and in order to defend himself against harm drives a tractor to confront all the adversaries of the journey… Pinocchio has faith in technology and a better world."

MONUMENTO URBANO
ZAANDAM

ALDO ROSSI
1989

This stack of brick polygons stradling two gabled sheds does not make its use immediately apparent: it is a sculpture museum for Zaandam, a city in the western Netherlands. It is Rossi's first completed project in the country where he has maintained an adjunct studio with associate Umberto Barbieri since collaborating in the 1988 competition to redesign a section of The Hague.

ART GALLERY

FUKUOKA, JAPAN
1989

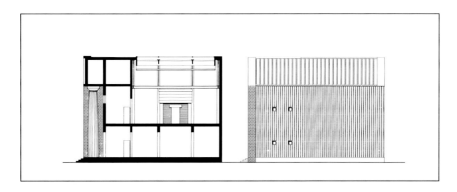

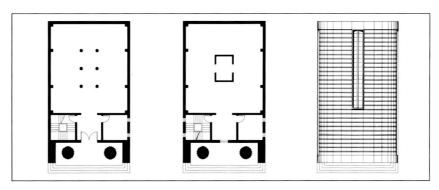

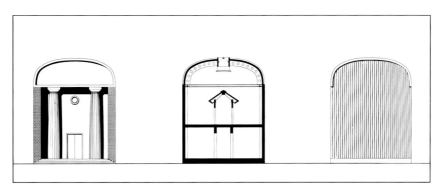

After hiring Rossi to design Hotel Il Palazzo, JASMAC (Japan Store Management Center) and its owner Mitsuhiro Kuzuwa commissioned an art gallery on a nearby site in Fukuoka. Like many large Japanese corporations, JASMAC is making a concerted effort to elevate its public profile by employing a variety of prominent European architects, using their celebrity status as both a corporate esthetic imprimatur and marketing tool.

The building itself is meant to send a message: the art gallery, for a collection yet to be assembled, is further proof of the client's commitment to the arts. Another notable feature of the project is that the facility is to stand for only three years, until JASMAC is able to acquire an adjacent property and build a full-fledged museum.

Whether intentional or not, Rossi's design is an appropriately ironic comment on architectural permanence, or, in this case, the lack of it. In dramatic contrast to the seemingly flimsy corrugated metal siding that sheathes the 50-foot by 30-foot structure, the entrance is dominated by two 26-foot-tall fluted plaster Doric columns, classically correct in form, though not in material. Behind this grand portico is the stucco facade framed by two brick fin walls. Inside are two floors of open display space, with a stairwell and private office tucked into the front corners. The second story is dominated by a demountable wood pavilion intended for special exhibitions, making the gallery into a sanctuary for a traditional Japanese construction.

RESTAURANT AND BEER HALL

SAPPORO, JAPAN
1989

This restaurant and beer hall is the third Rossi project for JASMAC (Japan Store Management Center). The site for the project is in Sapporo, the largest city of Japan's northern-most island of Hokkaido, once covered by dairy farms and now the last frontier of Japanese urban development.

The original plan for the building was to make a communal beer hall for four of the major Japanese beer manufacturers, with JASMAC acting as facility developer and operator. The idea met with resistance from the beer manufacturers, who opted to maintain separate premises.

Rossi's design accommodates a multitude of drinking and dining experiences. The scheme incorporates four separately accessed double-height bars with suspended L-shaped mezzanines. The bars are expressed on two exterior facades by stacked bays of matte aluminum columns and lintels subdividing red-painted metal window frames; the columns decrease in size as they rise toward a steeply gabled roof, which prevents the heavy snow build-up common to the region. (The other two facades butt against adjacent buildings and are left blank.) Entrance to the building is at a diagonally cut corner between two brick fin walls, which support a white marble clock tower protruding above the building's cornice. Small windows in the tower overlook an ancient shrine across the street. The fourth floor is a single-story communal kitchen, distinguished on the exterior by grids of glass block.

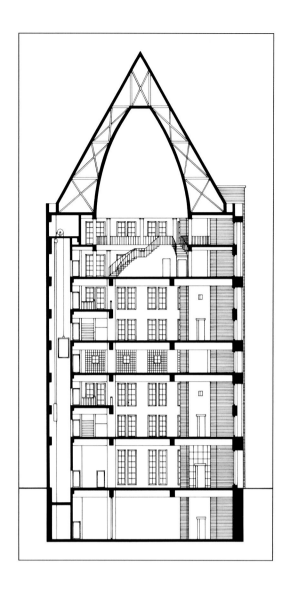

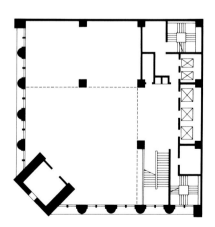 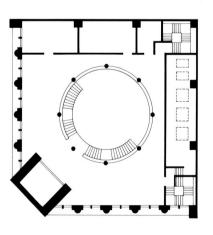 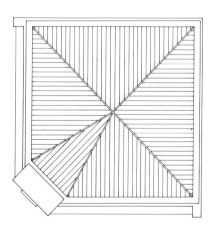

Cross-section, ground, mezzanine, and roof plans

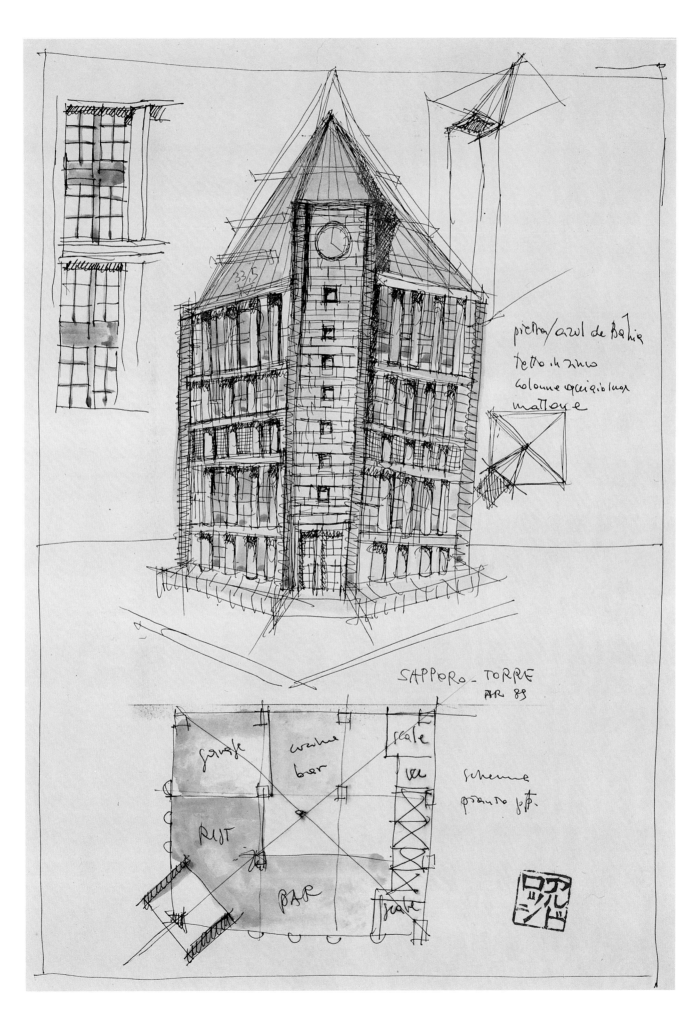

pietra/azul de Bahia
tetto di zinco
colonne ceraig bluse
mattone

SAPPORO - TORRE
AR 89

schema
pianto pt.

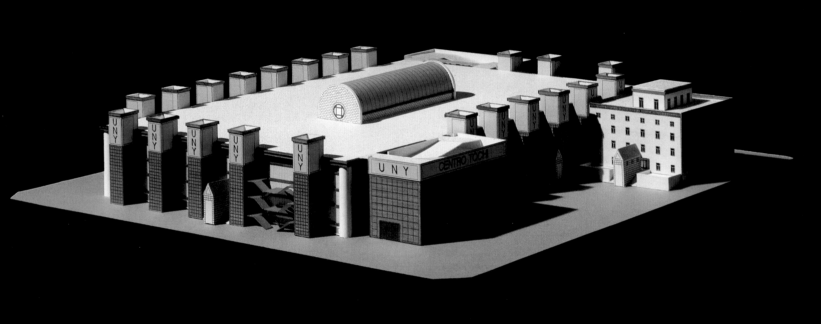

UNY SHOPPING CENTER

NAGOYA, JAPAN
1989

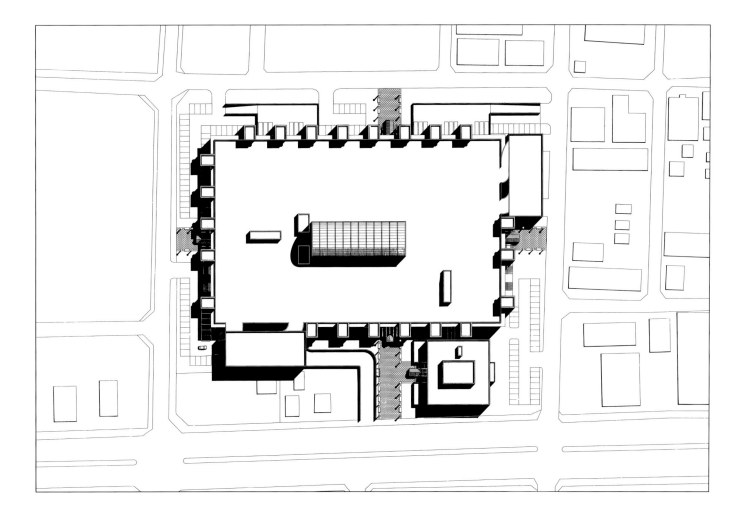

After designing a shopping center for UNY in Gifu, Japan in 1988, Rossi was asked the next year to do another project for the retail conglomerate's home base in Nagoya. Before World War II, Nagoya was the center of military hardware manufacturing. During the war, the city was heavily bombed by the Americans; most of its infrastructure was destroyed. Since then, the local economy has been rebuilt as a service industry.

Like Gifu, the site for this project is in a financially-depressed section of town, called Tochi. What distinguishes the shopping center in Tochi from the one in Gifu is that it is not broken into several components dispersed over separately owned or leased parcels, but rather is consolidated into one enormous structure measuring 450 feet by 285 feet, not including an adjacent restaurant.

Rossi was asked to give exterior form to a partially predetermined physical layout. His initial scheme, based on Roman town-planning principles, divided the complex into four distinct quadrants, each arranged around an interior courtyard. The plan, which provided for future growth along the *cardo* and *decumanus*, was revised to satisfy new interior requirements. This revision, also shown here, is dominated by a single, central courtyard. The courtyard has a barrel vault with a coffered ceiling protruding from the flat roof of the structure. The first, second, and third floors of the complex are given over to four principal zones: UNY, food purveyors, "health/culture" facilities, and the fashion quarter. The basement, fourth floor, and roof are designated for parking.

Twenty-two metal-grid towers, each containing fire stairs, surround the metal-paneled exterior. The towers are not evenly spaced around the perimeter of the building due to internal circulation requirements. Rossi inserted additional fire stairs in between towers on the south side, making an accordion-like connection that focuses attention away from the unsymmetrical arrangement of the towers. Indian sandstone paving defines courtyards in front of the four entrances to the shopping center. Attached to the center is a four-story restaurant in what looks like a giant Italianate villa, complete with such domestic touches as a rooftop balustrade.

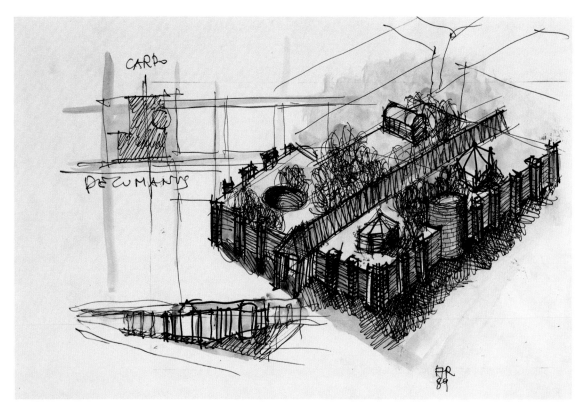

Sketch of early scheme

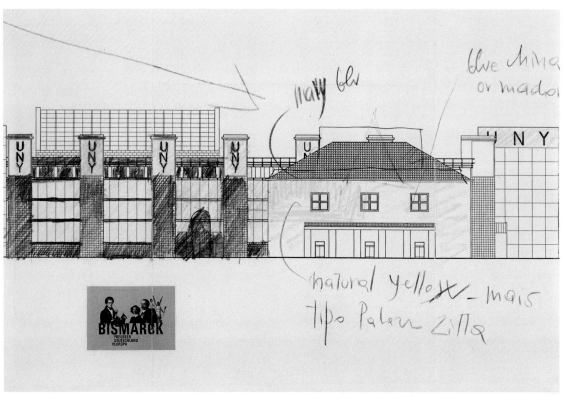

Study drawing

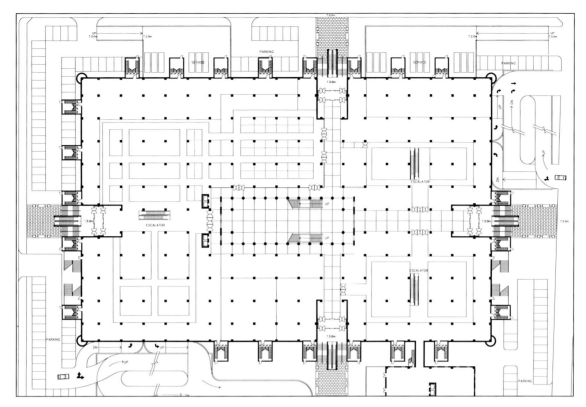

Ground floor plan

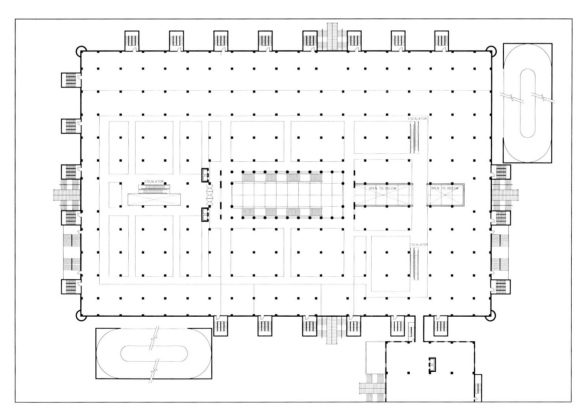

Third floor plan

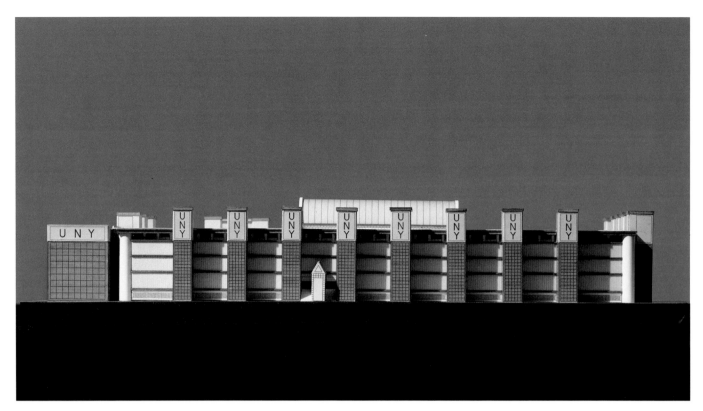

Model view from the east

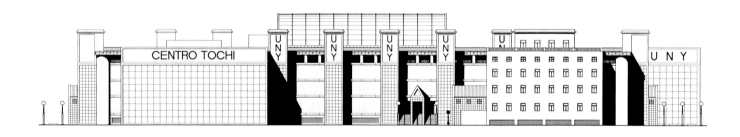

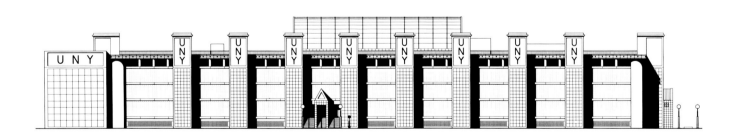

West and east elevations

Model view from the south

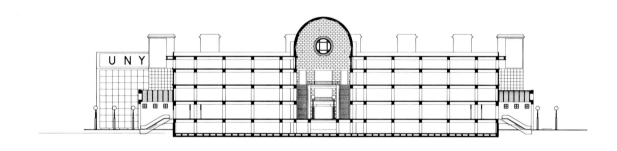

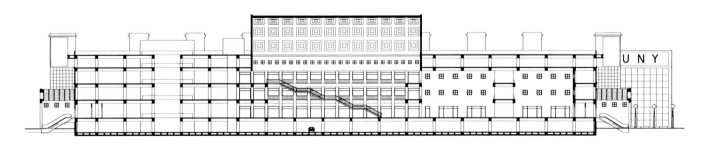

Cross-section and longitudinal section

AMBIENTE SHOWROOM

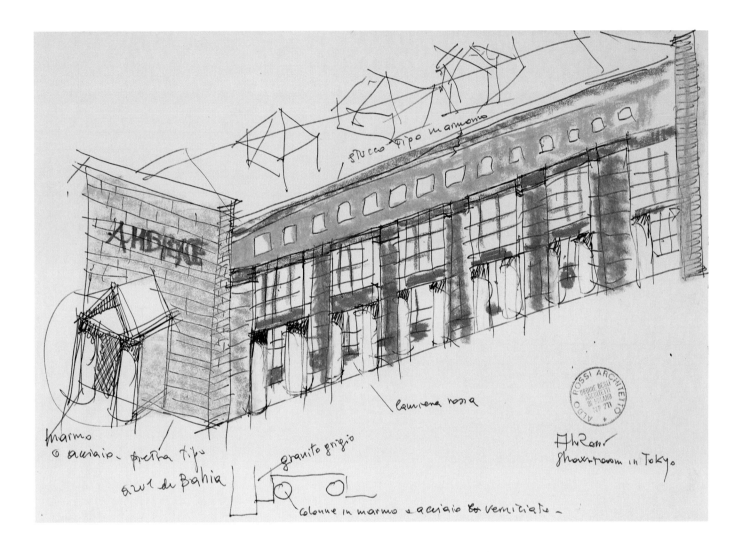

Ambiente is a Japanese importer and distributor of European-made designer furniture. One of the manufacturers that Ambiente represents is the Italian company Molteni, producer of several Rossi designs, including the Milano and Parigi chairs and the Carteggio cabinet. In 1989 Ambiente asked Rossi to design the company's new showroom in an area of Tokyo populated by architectural offices and fashion studios.

Rossi's design conforms with the residential scale of the neighborhood by maintaining the standard building height of 30 feet. The three-story structure's front facade of blue Brazilian stone is punctuated by three red-painted metal square windows and topped with gold-colored brass parapet coping. White Carrara columns and a pediment mark the entrance.

On one side of the building, five bays of columns and lintels form a grid over a white stucco surface. (The other long side abuts an adjacent building.) In the back of the building a fire-stair tower is framed in stainless steel panels. Skylights serve as light wells for the interior.

studio per il Cimitero di Rozza

CEMETERY

ROZZANO, ITALY
1990

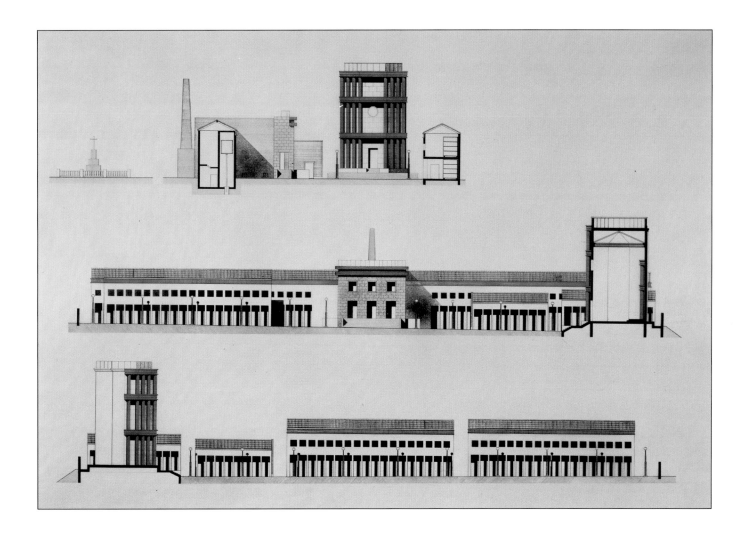

It is perhaps Rossi's unusual fate that, albeit unwittingly, he built his professional reputation on the design of a burial place. His winning competition entry for the San Cataldo Cemetery in Modena in 1971 catapulted him to international prominence for his frank assessment of the program as a "city for the dead," an achievement that some attributed to mere morbid fascination.

Two decades later, Rossi's work at Modena still continues, as does his ability to integrate a city for the dead with the city of the living. "As cities grow, the cemeteries grow," is Rossi's wry assessment of the status of cemeteries. Referring to models both Anglo-Saxon/Germanic (where cemeteries are made into benign park-like settings) and central European (where cemeteries are civic monuments), Rossi argues that through history cemeteries have become a repository not only of human life, but also of monumental architectural form. The grand avenues and well-tended tombs of these final resting places are a backdrop for the worship of the dead, a practice that, in Rossi's opinion, prolongs worldly ties and makes cemeteries "not necessarily...sad or melancholy places."

Rossi's second commission for a cemetery, in the northern Italian town of Rozzano, reuses many of the elements of Modena, but in a more outwardly representational arrangement. He left an existing brick wall to define the perimeter of the enclosed compound with the graveyard on one side and a group of buildings on the other. The street that leads into the compound ends opposite a chapel. Marking the edges of the street are the long linear slabs of the columbarium—gable-topped structures lined with recesses for cinerary urns. In the center of this informal piazza is the crematorium, which is dominated by a smokestack. In front of the building is a row of benches surrounded by trees and streetlamps— poignant reminders of the "city of the living."

Roof and ground floor plans

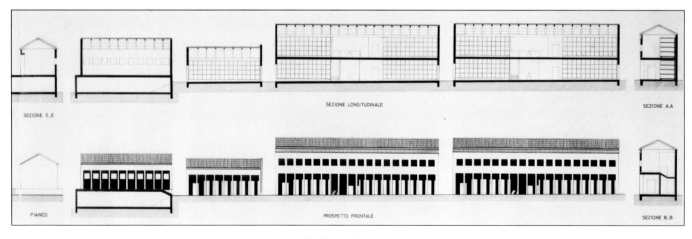

Elevations and sections

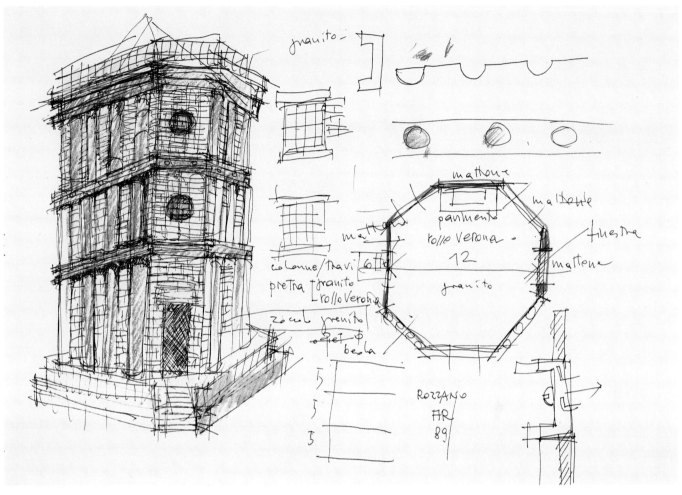

Early sketch for the chapel

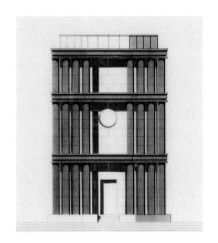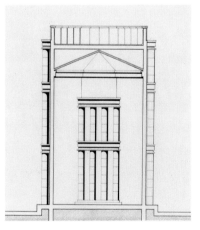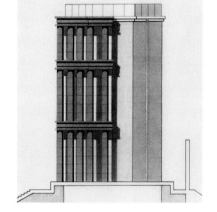

Elevations and section

LIBRARY

SEREGNO, ITALY
1990

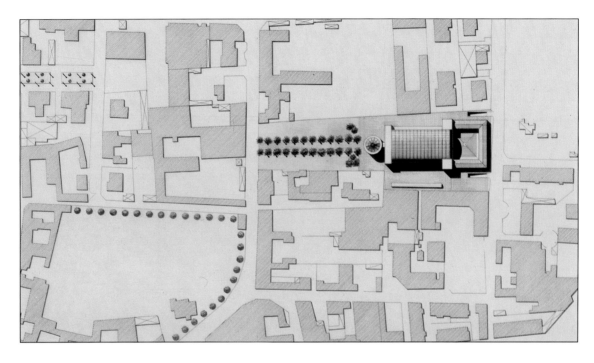

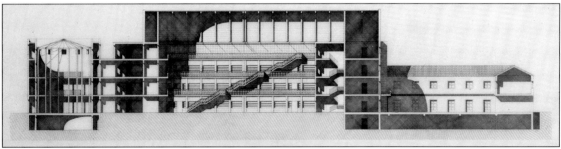

In 1990 Rossi won a competition to design a branch library for the Italian town of Seregno. The centerpiece of Rossi's proposal—a long hall topped with a barrel vault—was influenced in both form and content by Etienne-Louis Boullée's circa-1780 design of the Bibliothèque Nationale in Paris. After his first proposal for a royal library had been rejected as too expensive, Boullée presented the regime of Louis XVI with an unusual, less-costly alternative: he planned to vault an existing Parisian courtyard measuring 300 feet by 90 feet, making, in his words, "a vast Basilica lit from above, which would house not only our literary heritage, but also what we have reason to expect in times to come."

Though never built, Boullée's grand vision lives on in Rossi's more modest scheme for Seregno, which consists of three main parts: a cylindrical entrance, a Boullée-inspired hall (reading room), and a hollow square (children's stacks and audio-visual facilities). Capped by a steel and glass crown, the brick cylinder is coated with tinted stucco. The reinforced concrete structure of the reading room uses a nine-foot module for window openings; wood beams support the vault of the copper roof. Stone clads the rectangular hall and flanking stair towers, which separate the children's book stacks of the courtyard building from the stacks of the main hall. The narrow courtyard building permits natural light to fill the interior from both sides.

MIXED-USE COMPLEX

TURIN, ITALY
1990

The giant blank portal of Rossi's Casa Aurora (1984) faces due south, marking the juncture of two of Turin's principal thoroughfares, Corso Giulio Cesare to the east and Corso Emilia to the west. In an attempt to diversify the company's financial investments beyond retail manufacturing, Casa Aurora's owners, Gruppo Finanzario Tessile (GFT) in association with Dora Immobiliare, devised a plan of speculative commercial and residential development for the block surrounding Casa Aurora and commissioned Rossi to give it physical form.

The first phase of the project slated for construction is an office building along Corso Vercelli, parallel to Corso Giulio Cesare. The second phase, known as Dora Immobiliare Giulio Cesare, incorporates existing manufacturing sheds along Corso Giulio Cesare; it fulfills zoning requirements temporarily suspended during the design of Casa Aurora by maintaining a streetfront wall and a set back of thirty feet. The first three floors of the building are designated for retail space, with the remaining floors accommodating offices. Between the office building and the mixed-use building is a schematic design of an apartment building that also has ground-floor shops, and abuts an existing building located on the only parcel of the block not owned by the two companies. The entire complex is unified not only by shared architectural elements like brick towers, painted steel cornices, and repetitive rows of square windows, but also by a newly-landscaped interior courtyard, whose access is restricted to block residents and employees.

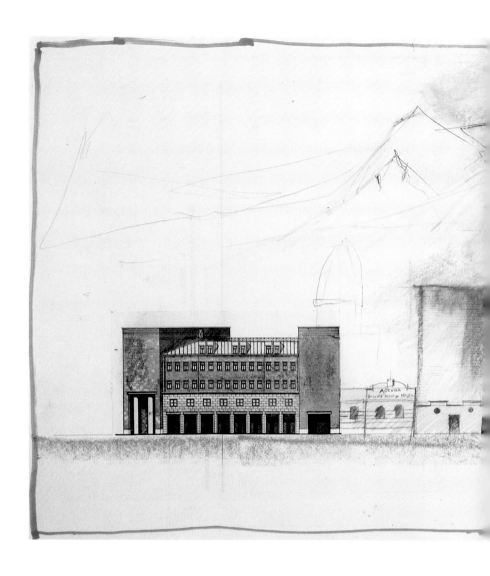

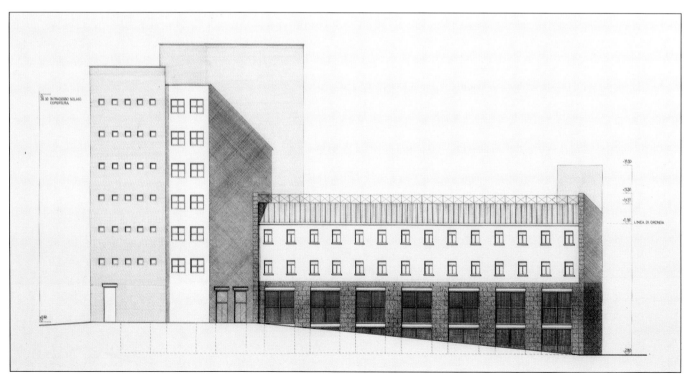

North elevation

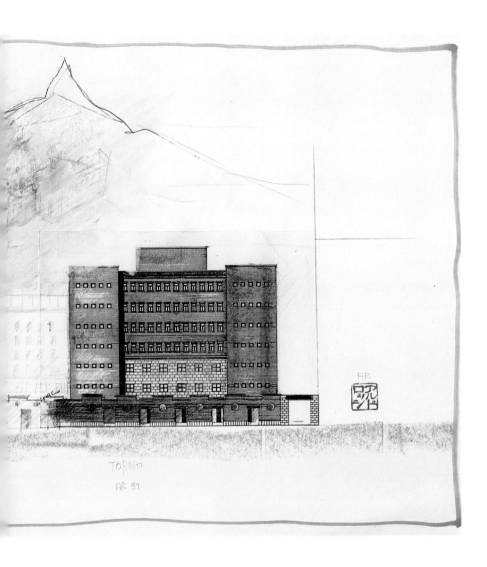

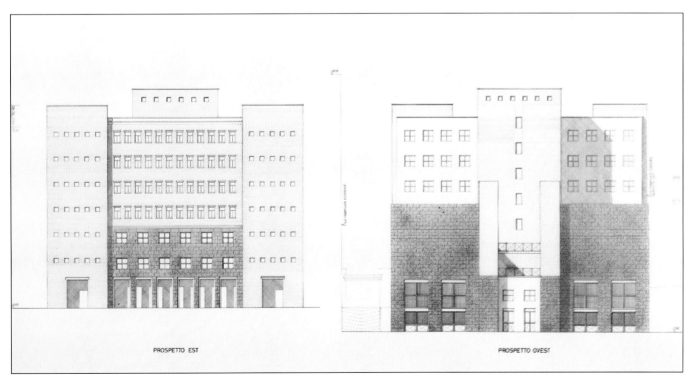

East and west elevations

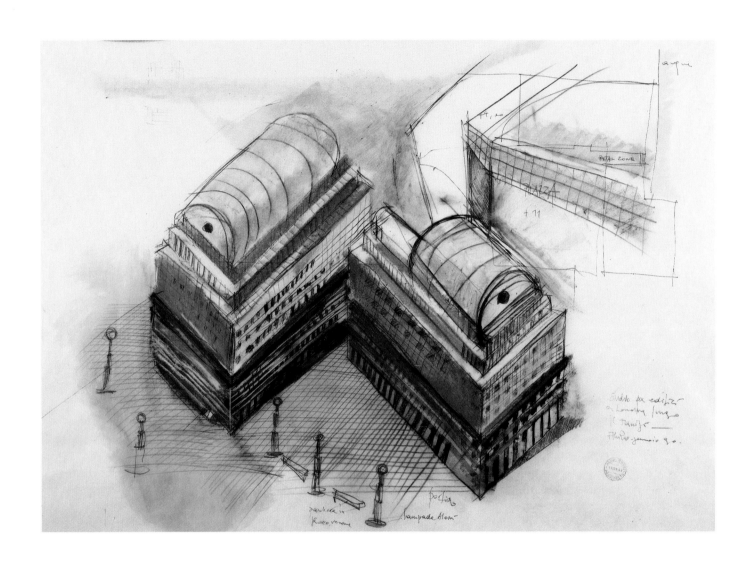

CANARY WHARF OFFICE COMPLEX

LONDON, ENGLAND
1990

In the 1980s the vast docks spread along the Thames River to the southeast of London entered a new phase in their long history. Changes in shipping methods over the preceding twenty years had gradually made the network of wharfs and warehouses obsolete. By the early 1980s commercial activity along the Thames had halted, leaving the port facilities abandoned and some 55,000 workers unemployed. This fate was shared by ports all over Britain—a condition that the British government sporadically began planning to correct in the 1970s. In London's case, the future of its dock lands remained uncertain throughout the seventies as battling political factions offered opposing proposals for renewal. While the Labour Party advocated a plan for public housing, the Conservatives backed a mixed-used complex that would transform the riverbanks into a city center all its own, complete with office buildings, shops, hotels, and housing. Private developers had their own schemes. The combined ineffectuality of a convoluted public planning process and the growing power of private interest groups led to a turning point in 1979 instigated by a Conservative administration, the creation of what became known as an "Enterprise Zone."

Although the exact origin of the Enterprise Zone (EZ) remains a subject of debate, what seems clear is that it is a textbook solution to remedy the "urban blight" of older metropolises. The basic premise of the EZ is to foster new industry in impoverished districts; special considerations would be granted to local entrepreneurs, who, the argument goes, would develop businesses with regional flair. In April 1982, London established an EZ that suspended land tax on new developments and, in effect, eliminated many of the obstacles to obtaining the necessary building permissions. Included in the EZ is

Canary Wharf, Toronto-based developer Olympia and York's proposal for some 10 million square feet (the figure is in constant flux) of office space spread across a 71-acre parcel of land. Not surprisingly, the establishment of the London EZ drew immediate criticism, primarily for contradicting its essential purpose, which was to cultivate local industry and free-market growth and not to provide financial incentives for foreign investment.

It is against this high-stakes financial backdrop that architects from around the world were commissioned to design what will be a new city of 50,000 white-collar workers. For an architect like Rossi, steeped in the history of his native landscape, it is a welcome opportunity to build where the presence of the past is negligible—and to contribute to what he calls "the most advanced experiment for creating the city."

Currently under construction, Rossi's project consists of two buildings that form the corner of a public square on one side and line the river's edge on the other. Rossi envisions his main building to be like a basilica, with an enormous artificially aged copper barrel-vaulted roof. A portico connects both buildings to the plaza. Along the water, the cast-iron colonnade and metal panel facade of the second building recall the industrial sheds of the old dock lands. The basilica building will be clad with pink and red stone. In his preliminary visits to the site, Rossi became fascinated by how differently stone is perceived in different climates. His overriding image for the new financial center is guided by what he calls "The Stones of London" (his play on Englishman John Ruskin's 1851 book, *The Stones of Venice*), and the "austere air that they [will] assume in the sky, in the mist of London."

Early sketch

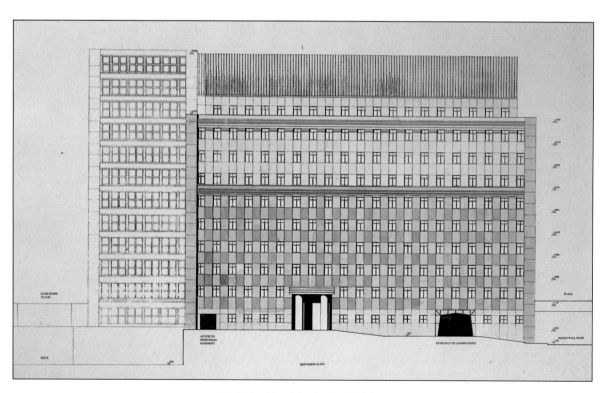

North elevation of the 'basilica' building

190

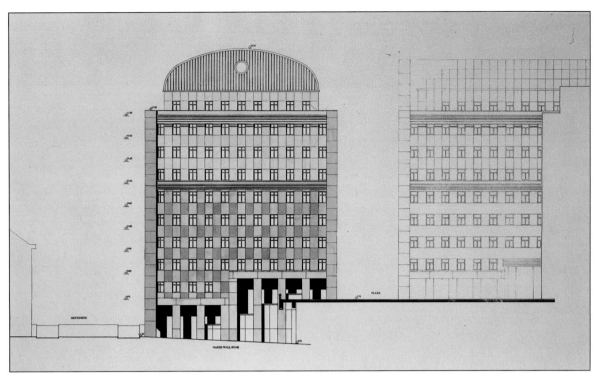

West elevation of the 'basilica' building

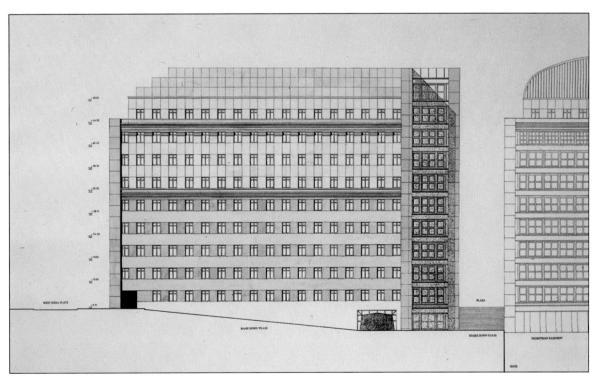

East elevation

MAASTRICHT ALDO ROSSI 91
MAGGIO NY

VERLUST DER MITTE

BONNEFANTEN MUSEUM

MAASTRICHT, NETHERLANDS
1990

Rossi's design of the new Bonnefanten Museum in Maastricht, the southernmost city of the Netherlands located close to the Belgian border, rests on a fifty-four-acre parcel along the River Maas in what is known as the "Ceramique" district. Situated between the historic heart of the city and the twentieth-century municipal seat, the museum is the symbolic center of an extensive ten-year building program that includes 1,600 single-family houses; 210,000 square feet of offices; a 60,000-square-foot hotel; 60,000 square feet of sundry "cultural activities"; 15,000 square feet of retail and restaurant space; and 13,000 square feet of underground parking. Construction of the museum is scheduled to be completed by the end of 1993.

Directly adjacent to Rossi's site are the Weibenga Halls, built by architect Jan Gerko Weibenga in 1912 for ceramic production— hence the name of the complex and the district. The Provincial Government of Limburg's plan is to retain the halls as "an industrial-archeological monument," refurbishing them for exhibition use, and to give the actual museum, until now housed in a converted department store in downtown Maastricht, the physical presence appropriate to what museum officials are promising will be a modern art collection of "international stature."

Rossi's proposal shows a four-story E-shaped structure, punctuated at its central tine by a double chimney-like stair tower attached to the cupola-topped museum café. The three parallel wings are joined by an entrance lobby along the eastern edge of the site. The lobby leads to a grand stair that connects the various galleries, Rossi's response to museum director Alexander van Grevenstein's request that the architect provide "a place where the visitor has to pause a moment…an impressive spatial gesture, which serves to remind people where they are."

Above, study sketch; at right, ground floor plan and studies in plan, section, and elevation

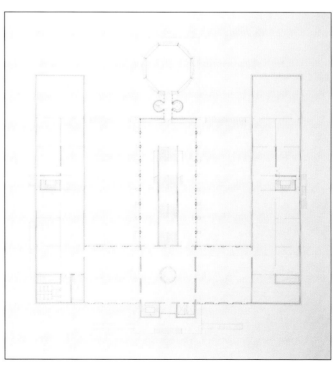

194

195

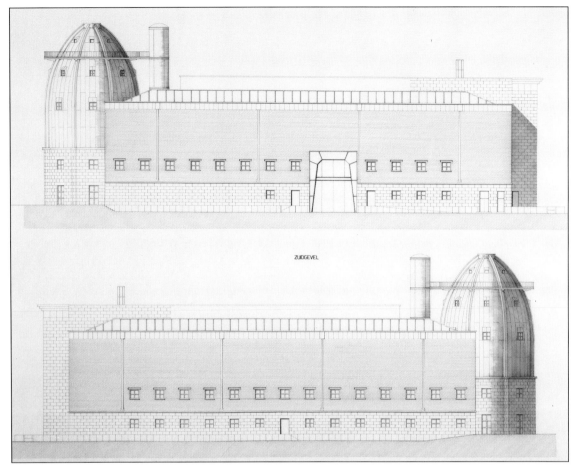

South and north elevations

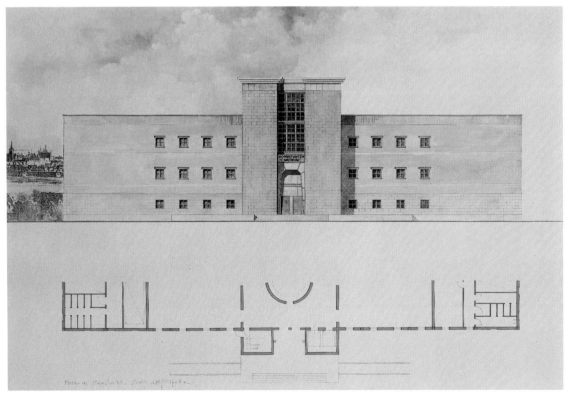

East elevation and plan detail

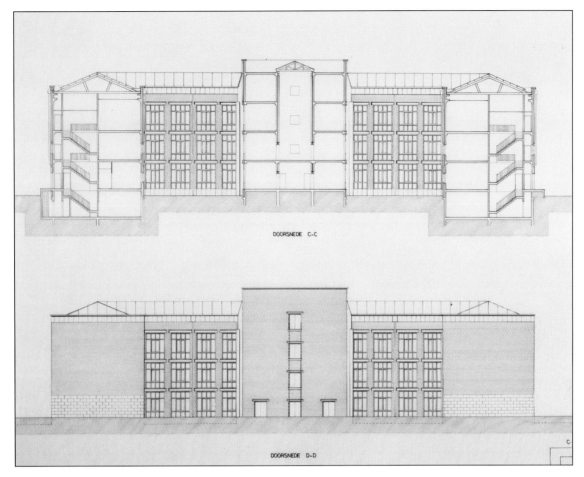

DOORSNEDE C-C

DOORSNEDE D-D

Cross-sections

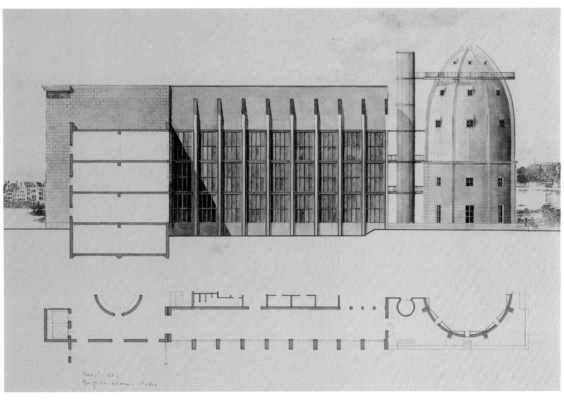

Longitudinal section and plan detail

197

SAN CARLO ALLA BARONA CHURCH

MILAN, ITALY
1990

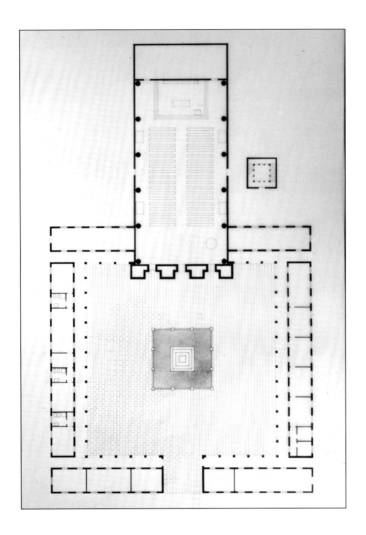

In the design for the church of San Carlo alla Barona in a Milan suburb, Rossi contemplated the relationship between a community and its place of worship. Rossi sought to reconcile his role as an architect with his beliefs as a Catholic—a task he considers particularly difficult in an era dominated by secular concerns. To Rossi's mind, current religious practice has lost the immediacy of ancient times, when the religiously observant "had a more natural rapport with the Church itself and the order of the Church was the order of architecture."

Rossi's scheme supplies a monumental focus to a peripheral section of the city where any semblance of urban order has dissolved; it provides the architectural equivalent of religious guidance. The project is in effect the liturgical sequence in three dimensions and consists of three main components: church, bell tower, and cloister. Appropriately, Rossi uses the parochial functions of the cloister to give civic presence to the complex: load bearing walls of the cloister form a square frame around a semi-public courtyard. The plaster piers of the portico are framed in terra-cotta tile to enhance the appearance of depth.

The church is connected to the cloister with a frontispiece of four, giant, engaged columns, whose massive granite base and more modest brick shafts form niches for statues of the Patron Saints of Milan. Inside the church, the only decoration is the exposed structure of the gabled shed: round steel columns, a steel truss roof, and industrial-size windows. A bell tower of brick-faced reinforced concrete coated in plaster overlooks the complex from behind the cloister. In the center of the enclosed courtyard is a protected sagrato—consecrated ground—paved in stone and dominated by a wooden cross.

Rossi proposes modest materials throughout so as not to detract from the "foundations" of Catholicism, thereby, "illuminating the severity of the work and of the sacred, a severity that is alive."

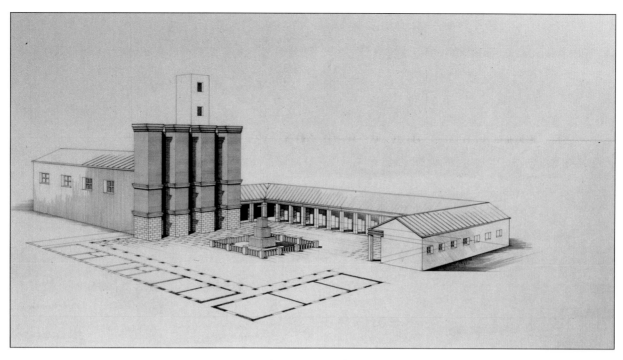

Cut-away perspective

Elevation study

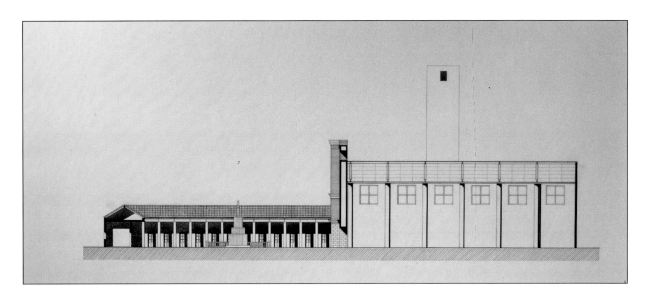

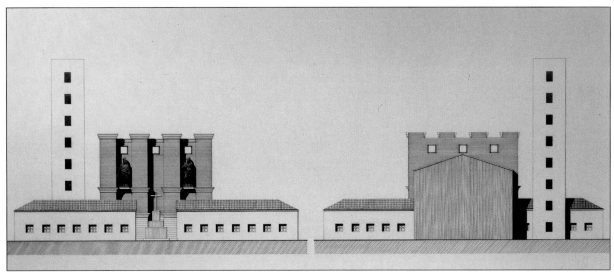

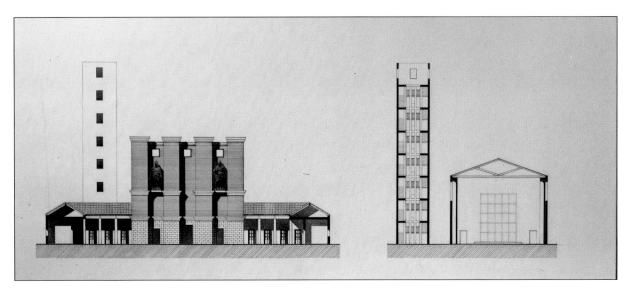

Longitudinal section, front and back elevations, and cross-sections

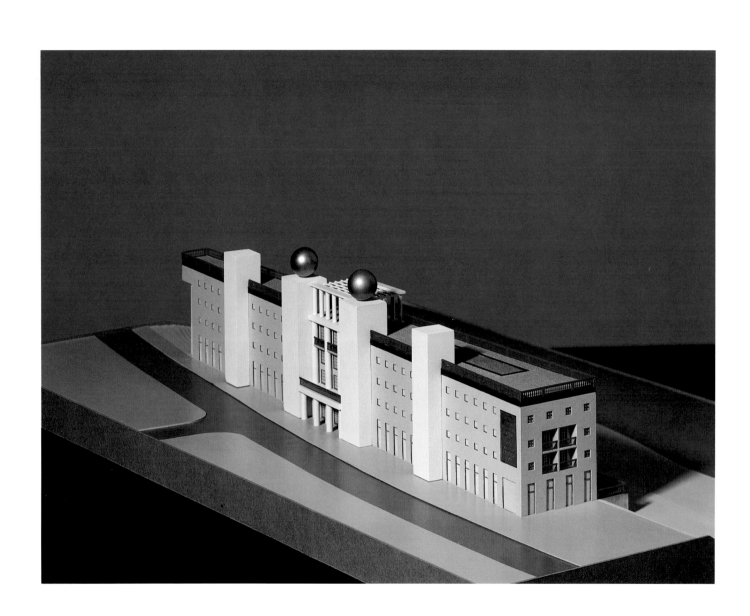

Hotel Ocean

Chikura, Japan
1990

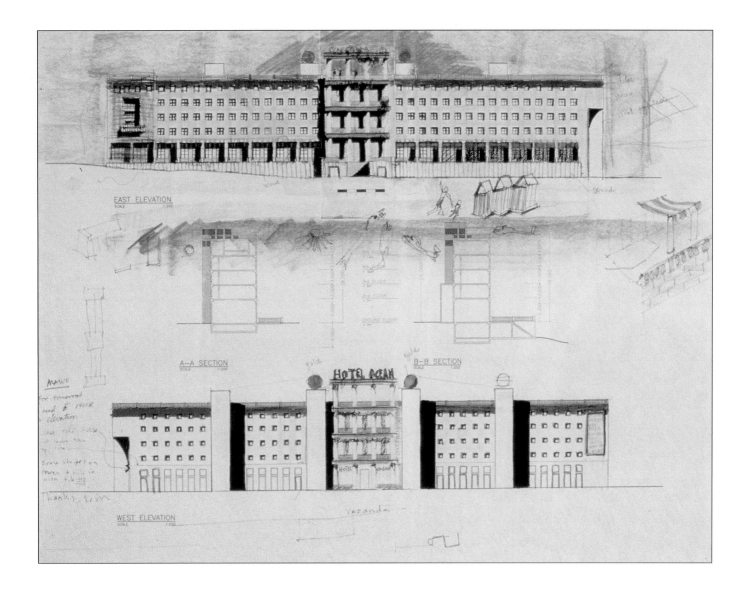

In 1990 Japan set out on a decade-long building spree of new airports, highways, magnetic-levitation railway systems, housing, and waterfront development, which, when completed at the outset of the new millennium, will represent a capital outlay of some 3.2 trillion dollars. About 9 billion dollars of the overall amount is earmarked for a bridge over Tokyo Bay to connect Tokyo with the Chiba prefecture. Although construction of the bridge has yet to begin, plans are being made to take advantage of the shortened route from Tokyo and the neighboring city of Yokohama to the seaside towns along Chiba's eastern coast.

One such project is the Hotel Ocean, a proposal for Chikura, a fishing town on the southernmost edge of Chiba. The site for the hotel is a wedge-shape property along the Pacific Ocean. It was not possible to disguise the long, narrow shape of the site, and Rossi's design, with its repetitive rows of windows and seemingly endless rooftop balustrade, revels in its sheer length. Its 315-foot-long yellow stucco facade comes to a forcible end in a ten-foot diameter column that contains a fire stair.

Only forty feet wide, the boat-shaped hotel has thirty rooms with large suites located above the main entrance. Framing the entrance is a giant wood trellis flanked by protruding stair-towers, topped with spheres finished in gold leaf. All of the guest rooms overlook the ocean, while the hallways and stair towers face a road in the back. Set into the back facade is a bronze panel engraved with the hotel's name and the proclamation "Who Ever Enters This Hotel Will Be Forever Lucky."

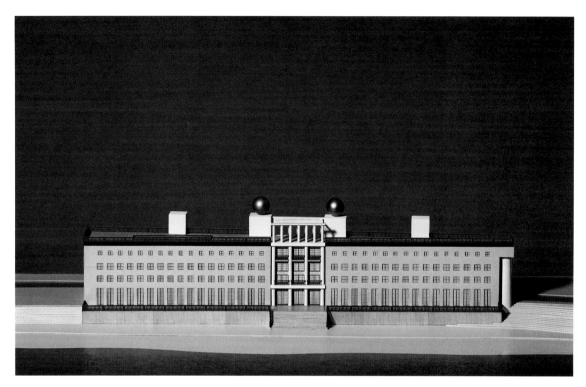

Model view from the beach

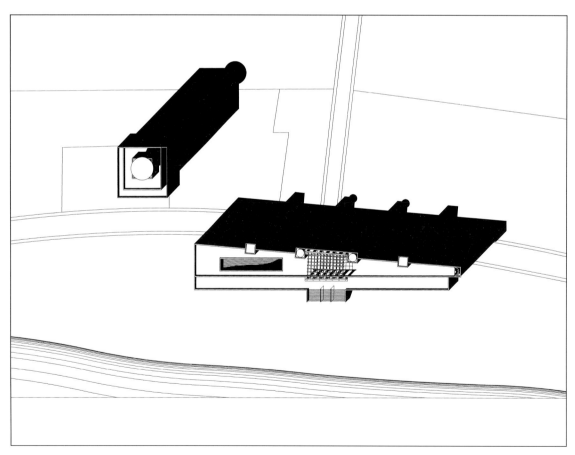

Site plan

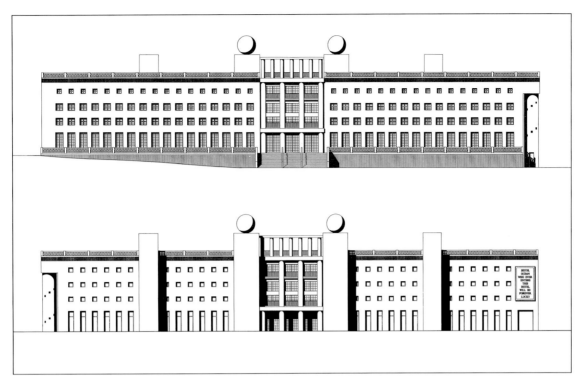

Beach front and street elevations

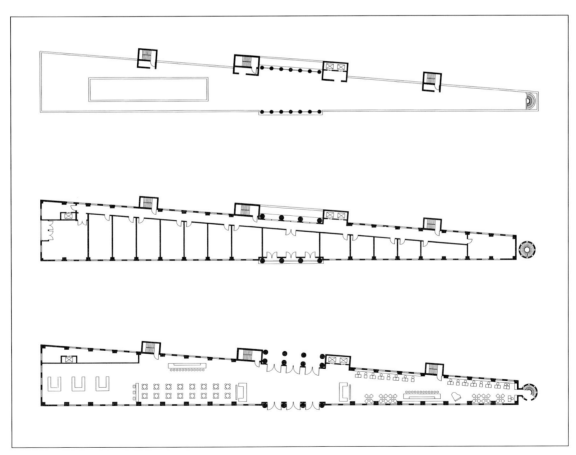

Ground, typical, and roof plans

ASABA DESIGN STUDIO

TOKYO, JAPAN
1990

This studio for graphic designer Katsumi Asaba was influenced by Asaba's adherence to *feng shui,* an ancient Chinese practice that dictates the placement of rooms and buildings in accordance with certain environmental and mystical phenomena to ensure "harmony" with nature and good luck. According to the principles of *feng shui,* Rossi's design of a 30-foot square structure that virtually fills a cramped Tokyo site had to be appended with two protruding entrances at the front and side corners, which would allow spirits to enter and exit.

Rossi's three-story structure is based on his interpretation of the traditional Japanese residential architecture of the surrounding neighborhood. Between two brick fin walls is the stucco front facade and its two rows of painted aluminum-framed windows with sliding wood shutters, a Westernized version of Japanese screens. The front pavilion is covered in bronze panels and the side pavilion is sheathed in a more modest stucco; both have roofs of blue ceramic tile, similar to the huts built by Japanese farmers in the 1960s.

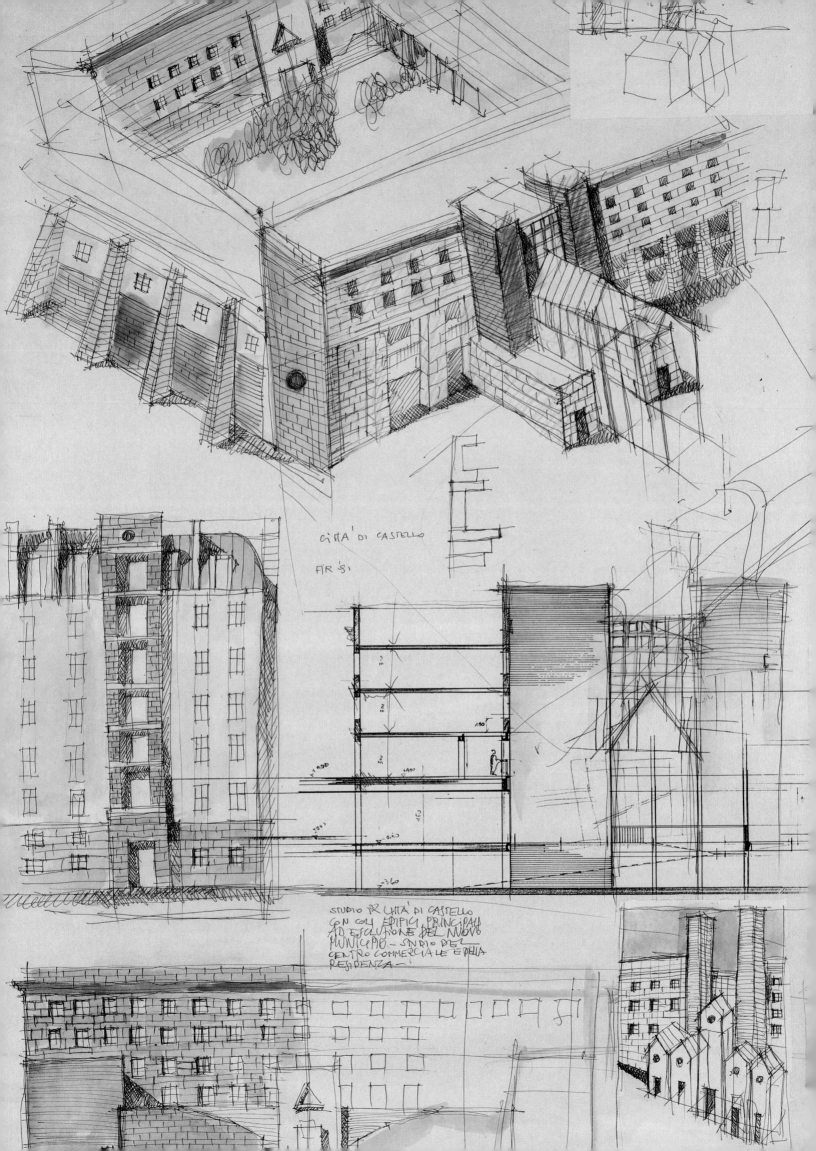

CITTÀ DI CASTELLO

FIR'SI

STUDIO PR CITTÀ DI CASTELLO
CON GLI EDIFICI PRINCIPALI
AD ESCLUSIONE DEL NUOVO
MUNICIPIO - STUDIO DEL
CENTRO COMMERCIALE E DELLA
RESIDENZA -

LORENTEGGIO PUBLIC HOUSING

MILAN, ITALY
1990

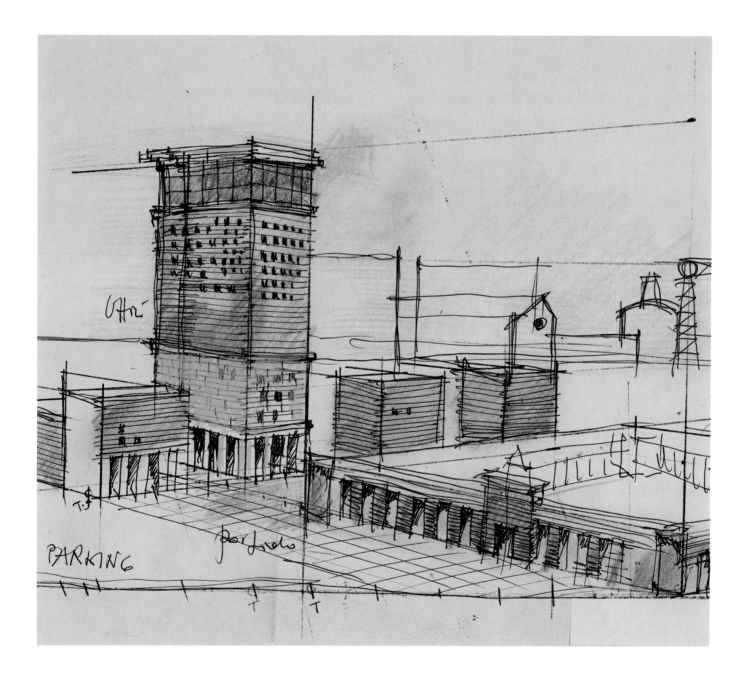

This mixed-used project is for a site to the southwest of central Milan located at the intersection of Via Lorenteggio and Via Bisceglie. A series of barrel-vaulted sheds totaling 58,000 square feet accommodates the commercial component of the program. The residential component is contained in three ten-story structures and one fourteen-story structure totaling 152,000 square feet; this easily satisfies local zoning requirements which stipulate that the residential part of a mixed-use project must exceed fifty percent of the overall volume.

Four towers of the apartment complex run along the southern perimeter of the site, arranged in a 300-foot-long row perpendicular to Via Bisceglie. Facades of yellow plaster and granite are topped by zinc roofs, in the manner of a traditional Milanese *palazzo*. The sheds of the commercial building are surrounded by two-story porticos, which serve as a transition between parking and indoor shops. Entrances from Via Lorenteggio and Via Bisceglie are indicated by brick towers banded in blue and white ceramic tiles, reminiscent of Rossi's earlier design of the Centro Torri shopping center in Parma.

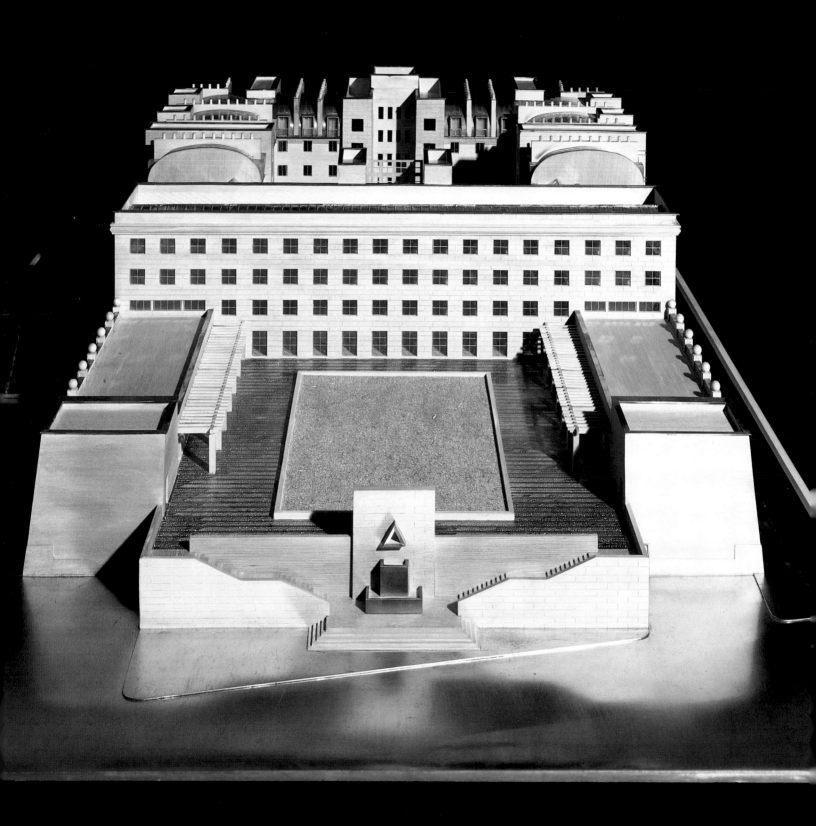

RESIDENTIAL COMPLEX

CITTÀ DI CASTELLO, ITALY
1990

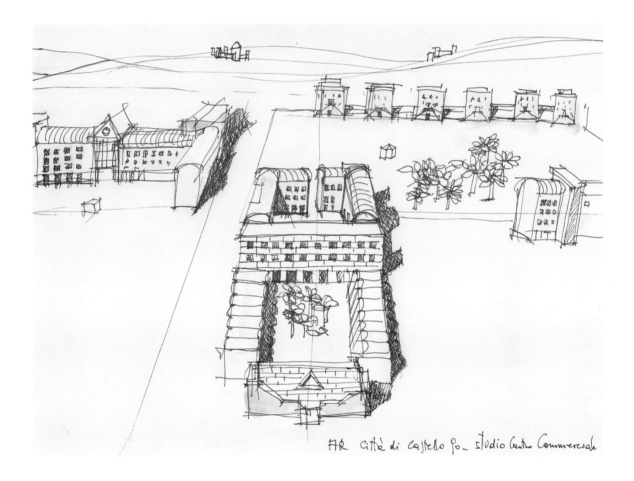

FR Città di Castello Po- studio Centro Commerciale

Città di Castello is located between Florence and Rome, the virtual heart (and soul) of Italy. "The image of central Italy is the image of Italy. In other words, if an image of Italy exists, this is it," says Rossi of this "Castle City."

If Città di Castello is Italy incarnate and Rossi's work is the three-dimensional distillation of that image, then this scheme for a mixed-use development is the convergence of inspiration and interpretation, a real-life enactment of *The Architecture of the City*. Outside the walls of the old city, on the site of derelict industrial buildings, the project is envisioned by the architect as an urban-scale "cul de sac." Rossi's proposal is made up of three main components: a town hall adjacent to a new train station, apartments grouped around a public garden, and a "commercial center" with shops, offices, a market, and more apartments.

The town hall has a two-story colonnade that forms a "C" around a paved piazza; parking is underground. Brick towers mark the corners, and the wings are a mustard-colored plaster. A gabled portico connects the piazza with the long copper-topped sheds of

the bus stop and with the train station beyond, where pavilions containing ticket booths and waiting rooms are clustered around a long brick wall.

To the south, apartment complexes bracket a public park on two sides. The first "apartment building" consists of six three-story square structures—a row of Italian villas in stucco with terra-cotta balustrades. The second "apartment building" comprises three separate three-story volumes set atop a common base of grey stone, which contains parking.

To the west of the park along a new road is the commercial complex, organized around two courtyards that are separated by the rectangular volume of an office building. Barrel-vaulted buildings have shops tucked in the ground-floor colonnade and five floors of apartments above. An iron and glass frontispiece joins this complex to the office building, the raised courtyard, and the brick stalls of the market. This raised courtyard overlooks historic Città di Castello and is connected to the street thirteen feet below by staircases flanking a triangular fountain.

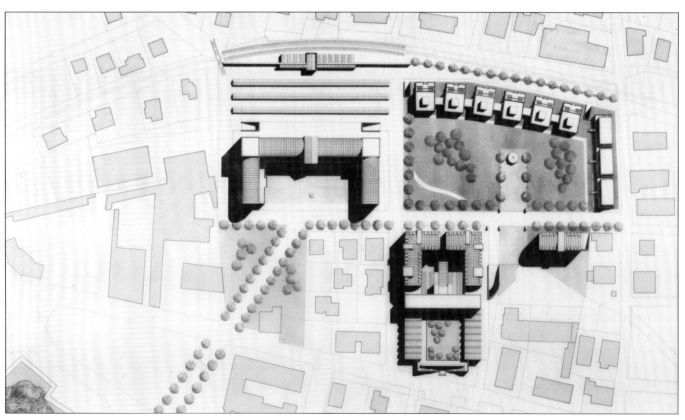

Site plan

FIR 90 studio px Città di Castello. Il nuovo Municipio e altri edifici.

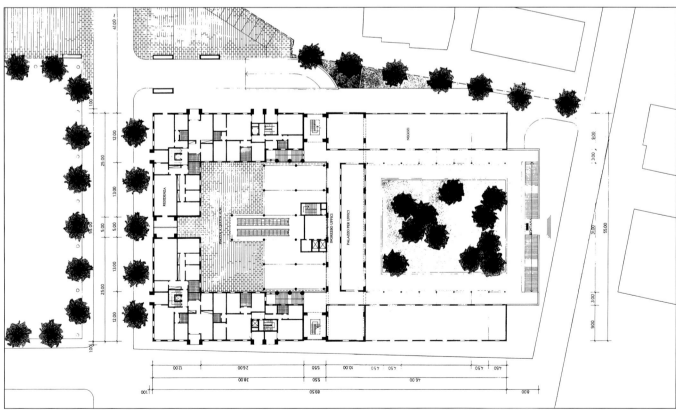

Typical floor plan

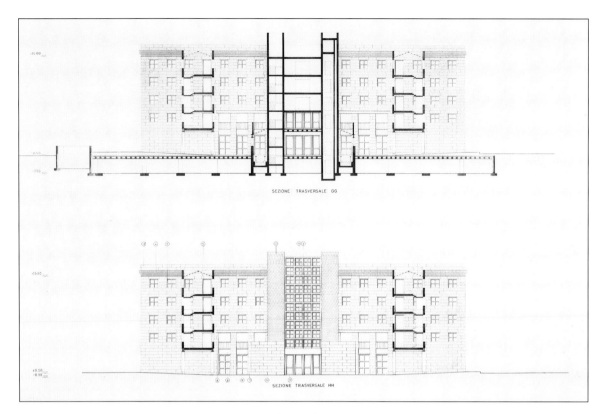

SEZIONE TRASVERSALE GG

SEZIONE TRASVERSALE HH

Cross-sections

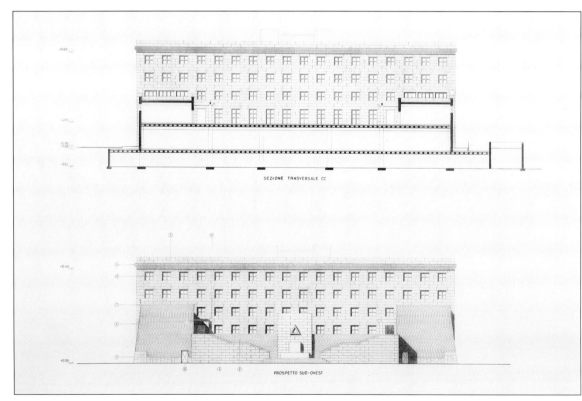

SEZIONE TRASVERSALE CC

PROSPETTO SUD-OVEST

Cross-section and southwest elevation

214

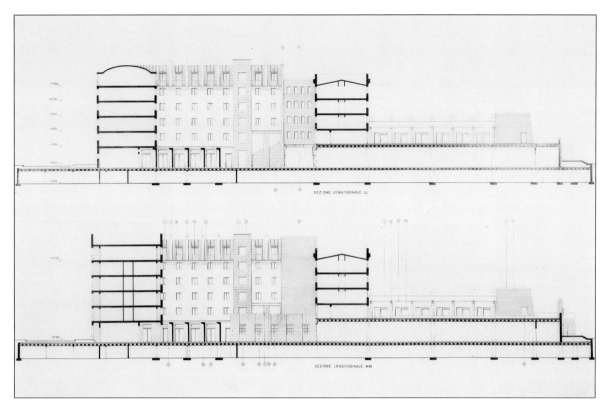

Longitudinal sections

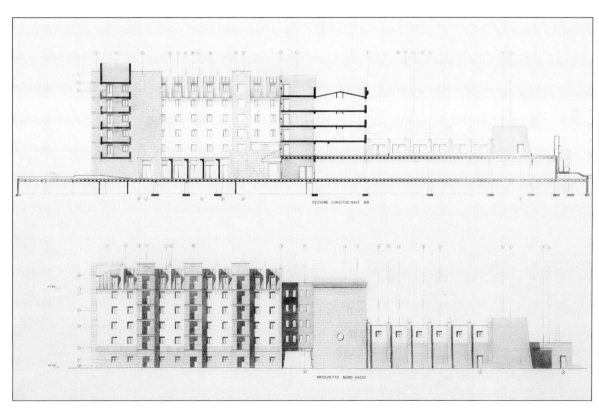

Longitudinal section and northwest elevation

FRONTE LAGO

VILLA ALESSI

LAKE MAGGIORE, ITALY
1991

Rossi's relationship with the Alessi family and their tabletop company officially began in the early 1980s with his participation in the "Tea and Coffee Piazza"—eleven architect-designed sterling silver tea and coffee services, produced in a limited edition, meant to bring a new level of celebrity to the former supplier of metal parts. Since then, Rossi has designed more mass-marketable objects made of stainless steel for the Italian manufacturer; his La Cupola espresso maker, Il Conico tea kettle, and Il Momento wrist watch are icons for the home and body.

Rossi's work for the design-minded Alessis has not been confined, however, to tabletop products: he did a scheme for a studio and lookout tower for the lake district estate of Alberto Alessi in 1986 before the general manager's nephew, Stefano Alessi, commissioned this house overlooking nearby Lake Maggiore. Rossi's design retains a garden wall around the property which was partially destroyed during World War II. The four-story structure contained within is an amalgam of residential- and civic-scale elements: sandwiched between two flat brick facades with quoined edges is a steel barrel-vault punctured by dormers. In the back, balustrades outline three stacked balconies, making the structure appear a hybrid of a plantation manor and an urban town house.

Rossi himself is aware of the unusual effect and says of the project: "It is particularly interesting to me, because for the first time it's possible for me to be inspired [by] (and in some way to imitate) the romantic style, which combines local characteristics with Classical or historical elements."

217

BIENNALE
VENEXIA
ARCHITETTURA

QUINTA MOSTRA
INTERNAZIONALE
DI ARCHITETTURA

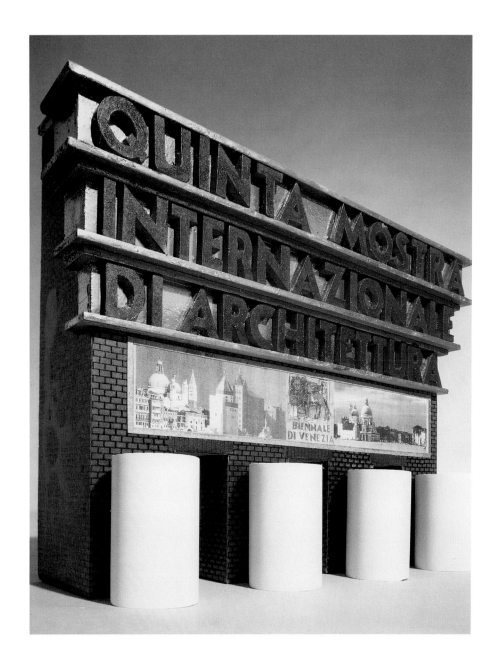

Contrary to its name, the Venice Biennale does not occur with regularity. The island city has hosted an official series of architectural events and exhibitions since 1979, most recently in the public gardens facing the canal of San Marco—the traditional site of the more established art Biennale. Rossi was one of many international architects asked to contribute to the exhibition in 1991. (In 1979 he designed a temporary theater and in 1985 he designed a portal.) Rossi's 1991 portal is, like his other Biennale creations, an excerpt of his architecture: a metal skeleton sheathed in a brick veneer is topped with giant cornices that announce the show. Three massive metal columns flank doorways; and above a giant mural depicts the Venetian waterfront with Rossi's floating theater of 1979.

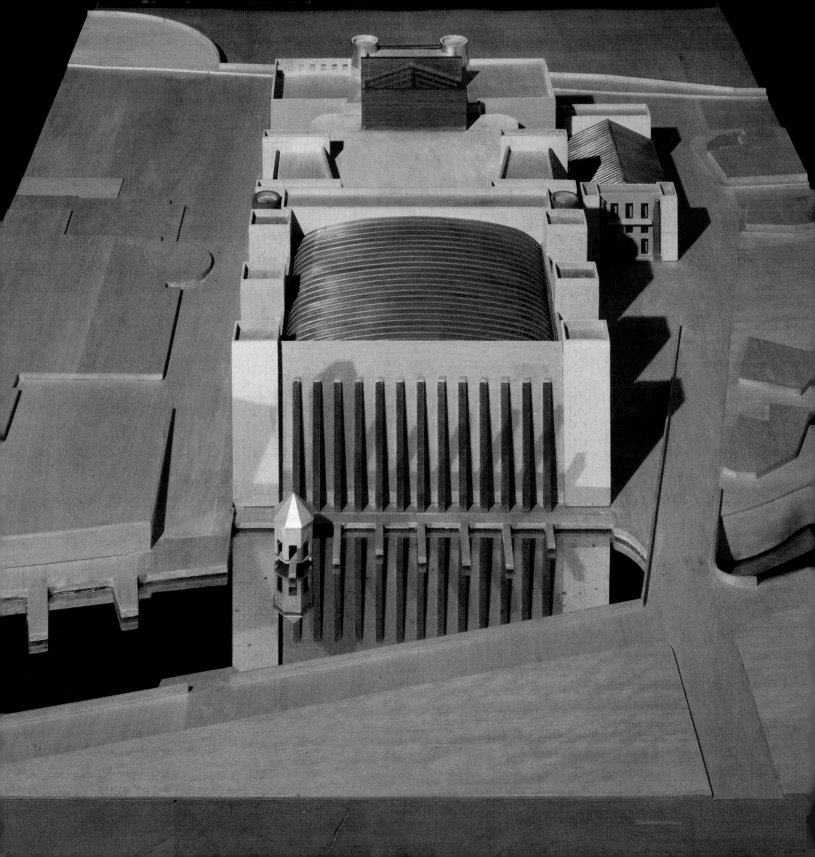

PALAZZO DEL CINEMA

VENICE, ITALY
1991

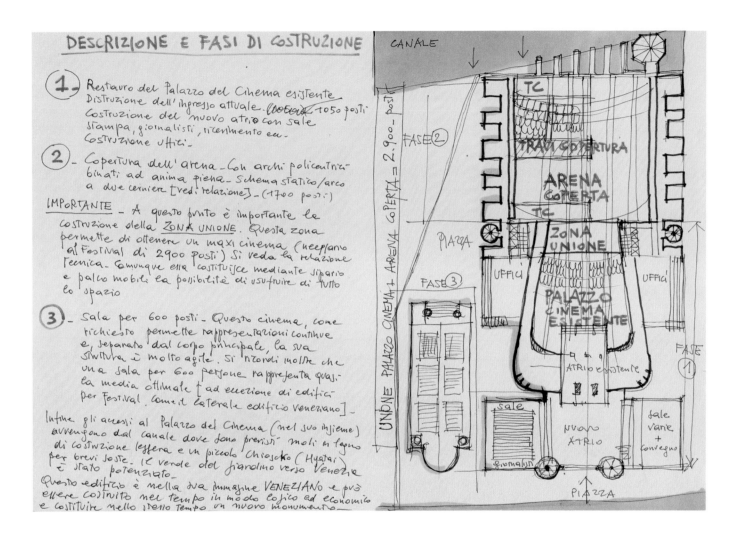

The Lido, part of the island city of Venice, is a summer refuge for high-rollers and fast-laners with its ritzy casinos and top-dollar hotels. Come September, however, when most of the tourists have gone home, another high-style group flocks to the city's south side for the Venice Film Festival. Though the names have changed, each year the cast stays the same—actors, directors, critics, and other assorted movie lovers have been attending premieres for over 60 years in what is now the outmoded Palazzo del Cinema.

Rossi, along with associates Giovanni Da Pozzo and Massimo Scheurer, in a recent entry to an invited international competition, proposed an expansion of the existing "Movie Palace" comprising three parts to be built in stages over several years. The first phase of the project calls for the renovation of engineer Luigi Quagliata's 1937 structure (which was partially remodeled by Quagliata in 1952, and, in plan, resembles the bottom half of a violin), to transform it into a state-of-the-art 1,200-seat theater. The second phase converts an outdoor arena in the back into a 1,700-seat theater by covering it with a metal-framed barrel vault; the arena is lined on the exterior by a series of piers along the canal for water arrivals. (When necessary, walls can be slid open to combine both theaters into a giant playhouse.) The third phase of the project addresses public-related facilities: a hall for press conferences, offices, and a grand foyer for receptions are contained in a new masonry frontispiece framed by chimney-like stair towers. Adjacent is an independent 600-seat screening room with a curved bay facing a piazza.

Over the years, Rossi has done several designs for Venice, where he has taught since the early 1970s. Save for his Biennale commissions—the floating theater and portals, none of his major Venetian projects have been realized, having fallen prey to lengthy political squabbles. With this scheme, Rossi, a film student-turned architect, hopes to cast one of his own buildings in a central role in a city that has been such a focus of his career, and fully participate in what he describes as "the world of love, adventure, terror; in that world of the cinema that always surprises us."

Early sketch

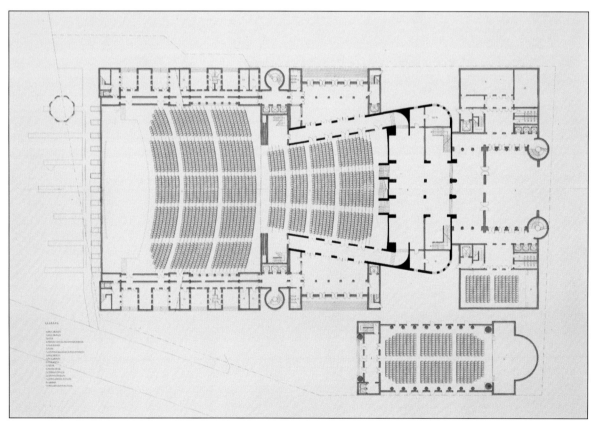

Ground floor plan

222

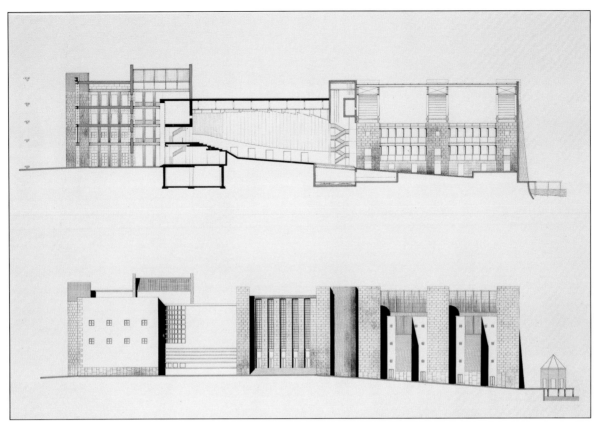

Longitudinal section and elevation from piazza

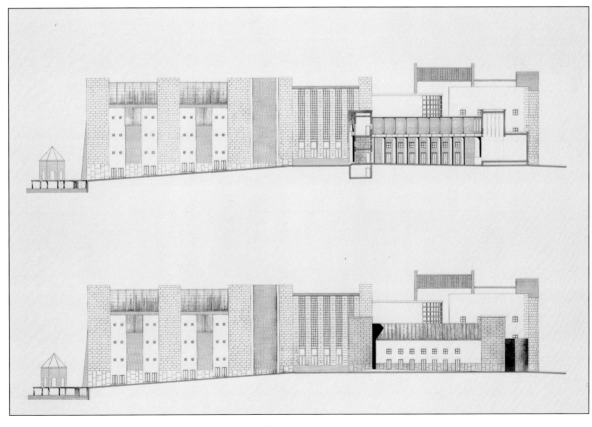

Longitudinal section and elevation

PALAZZO CONGRESSI

MILAN, ITALY
1991

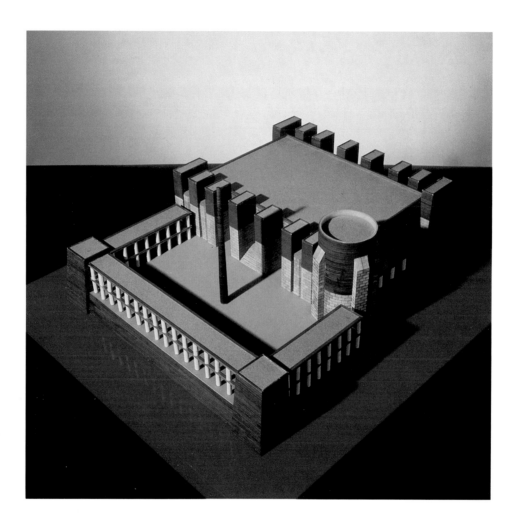

In 1982 Rossi did a preliminary proposal for Milan's new tribunal hall—the spires and grand public spaces of his Palazzo Congressi are a compendium of the city's monuments. His second proposal for a civic assembly, shown here, accommodates a similar program, but now is only part of a larger plan to redevelop a 57-acre parcel of Milan's south side with a convention center, hotels, apartments, television studios, and a renovated fairground for fashion and furniture exhibitions, making this sector of the Lombard capital a "high-performance machine" in the service of culture.

There is an underlying irony that in order to bring the services of the city into the twenty-first century, Rossi looks to the past, namely the now outmoded *arengàrio*, or magistral hall. Though its internal amenities are in need of updating, the overall image of the *arengàrio* is as potent today as it was when constructed in the thirteenth century. As with his design of the Carlo Felice Theater in Genoa where he integrated new construction with a partial recreation of architect Carlo Barabino's 1828 design, Rossi manages to strike a precarious balance between ancient forms and modern technology, giving new meaning to both.

The scheme, developed with associates Massimo Scheurer and Luca Trazzi, consists of two rectangular blocks: one a grassy courtyard framed by a two-story pergola, the other the enclosed volume of the giant assembly hall and its support functions. Rising above the subterranean parking garage, which is beneath the outdoor courtyard, is a brick smokestack that marks the spot where factories of car manufacturer Alfa Romeo once stood—an industrial monument that Rossi admires for its "formal beauty and for its song of the worker's history." A cylindrical tower braced by medieval buttresses acts as a hinge between the entrance courtyard and the congressional palace, containing inside a bar, a restaurant, and meeting rooms. The massive volume of the steel-trussed main hall is flanked by stair towers that resemble the sentry towers of an ancient castle—an ensemble that achieves Rossi's goal to create a"work of our time, and a work that is without time."

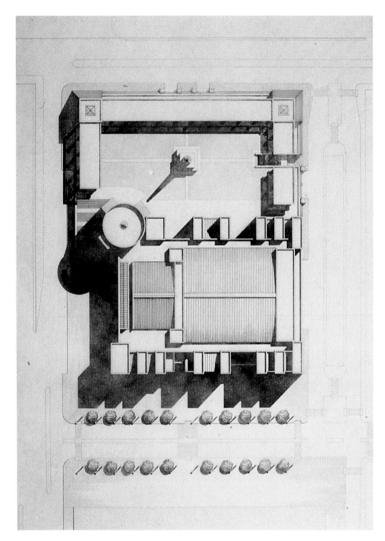

Site plan and third floor plan

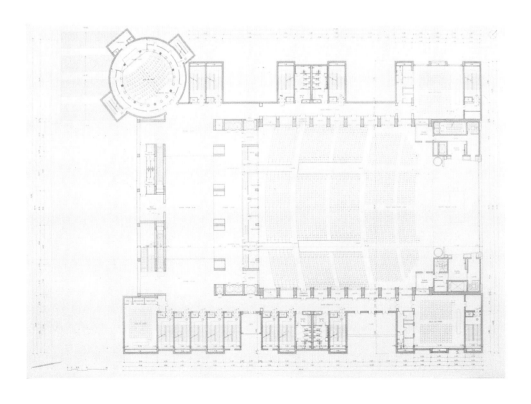

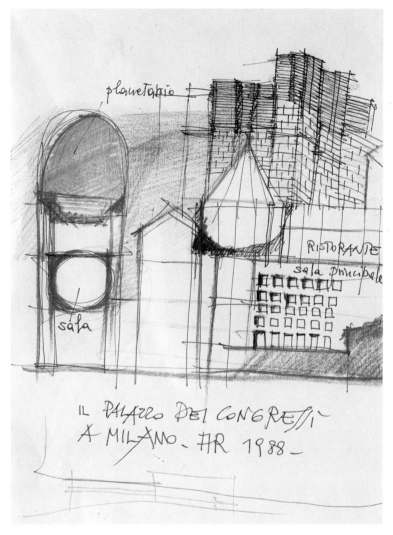

Studies for section and entry elevation

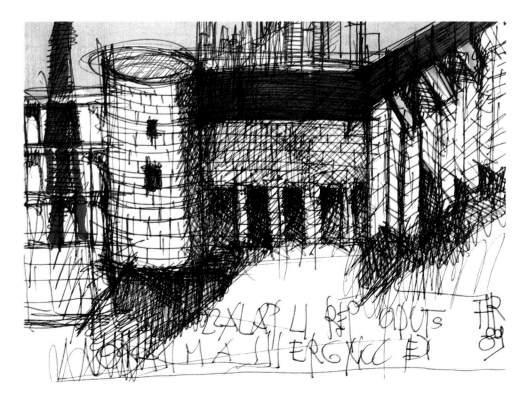

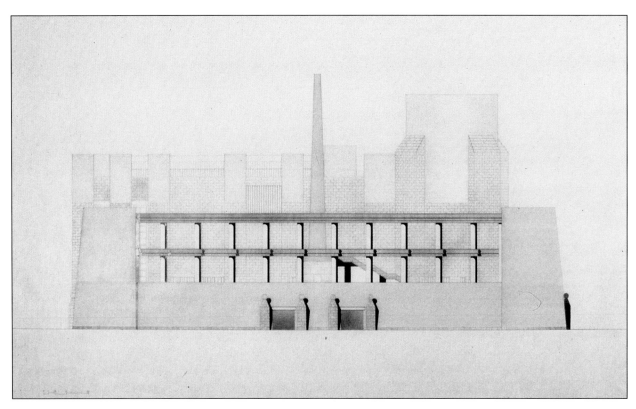

North elevation

East elevation

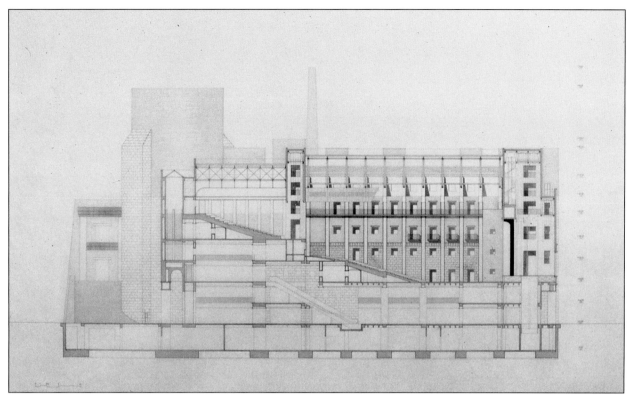

Cross-section through the assembly hall

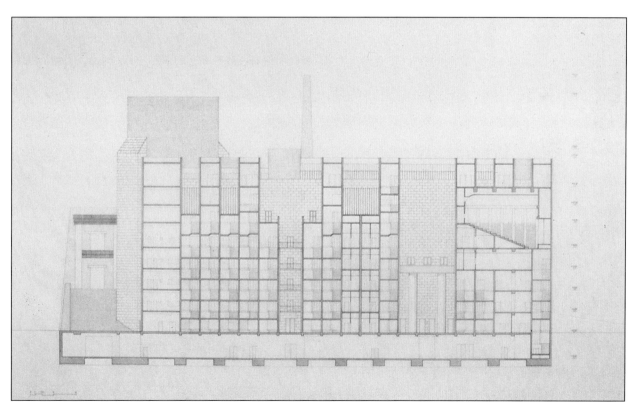

Cross-section through the stair towers

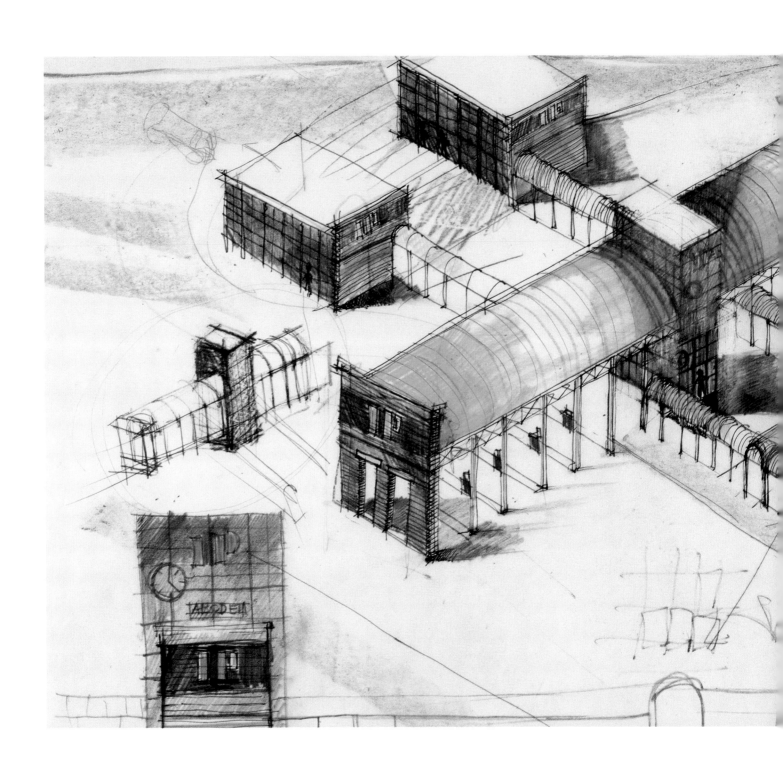

IP GAS STATION

PROTOTYPE
1991

At first glance, it would seem an unlikely commission for an architect with a reputation as a high-brow academic: to design a prototype gas station for a national petroleum company. Nevertheless with this scheme, Rossi, who has built his practice as a civic-monument maker, proposes what may be in fact the late twentieth-century landmark *par excellence*: the prototypical gas station that repeats itself along the Italian autostrada. In Rossi's preliminary sketches, the filling station is given monumental presence by its enormous metal barrel-vault roof which is bracketed by brick walls. Enclosed barrel-vaulted corridors connect the station to a road-side restaurant, creating a series of courtyards and arcades, as if it were a grand compound.

231

UBS OFFICE COMPLEX

LUGANO, SWITZERLAND
1991

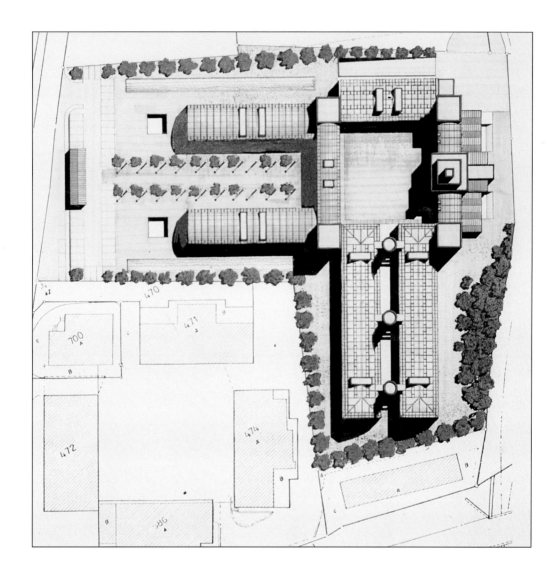

Rossi's entry to an invited competition for the new headquarters of the Union Bank of Switzerland (UBS) envisions a small working village rather than one multi-use megastructure. The project is based on Rossi's reading of the historic urban role of banking facilities. In the last century, he notes, "the bank and the stock exchange were the principal buildings of the bourgeois city." For Rossi, financial institutions today have the power to provide "urban dignity." The site for this new urban-scale development is in the town of Manno, near the alpine resort of Lugano, comfortably nestled in the Swiss canton of Ticino. Rossi's proposal consists of a square courtyard bounded by buildings with ground-floor porticos on all sides. To the west is an avenue lined with trees and office buildings leading to the main complex. Rossi suggests that these buildings can be leased to independent tenants or given over to the banking school. Along the

western perimeter is a barrel-vaulted office building with the official entrance and security check in the center. The main offices for UBS are housed in two long pavilions with clerestories and gabled roofs that echo the mountain peaks in the background. Between them are an alley, permitting natural light and air to enter from both sides, and three brick chimneys that contain bridge-like connections between both buildings. Opposite is a local post office contained in a lower gabled structure. On the eastern edge is the barrel-vaulted structure of the company cafeteria; the building is punctuated by a stepped brick tower—an industrialized campanile with a giant clock facing the courtyard. Inside the tower is a spherical conference room. Four brick towers contain elevators for handicap use and connect to underground parking, marking the corners of the communal courtyard with Swiss precision.

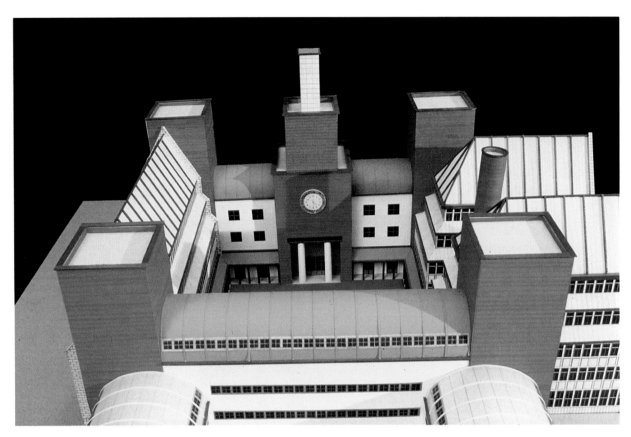

Model view showing tower and courtyard
Elevation, longitudinal and cross-sections

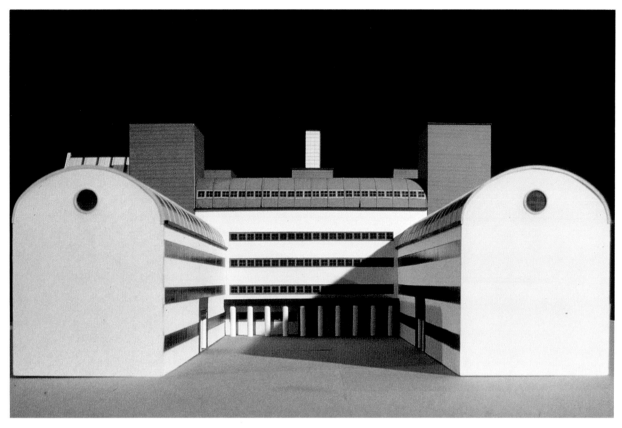

Model view showing entry forecourt
Ground floor plan

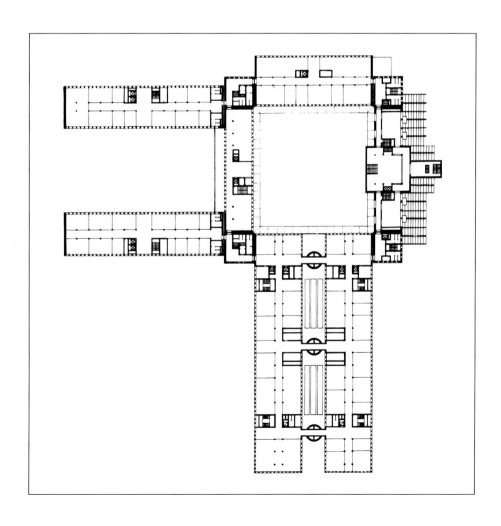

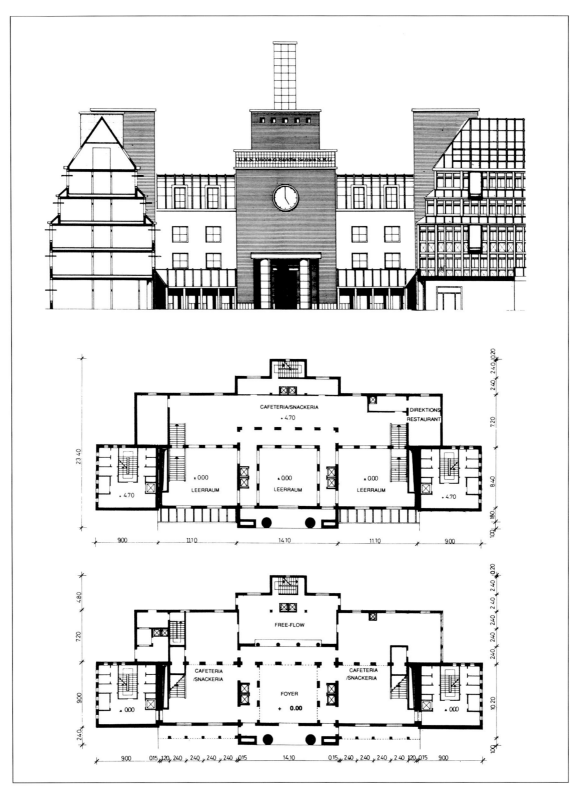

Detail of longitudinal section and plans

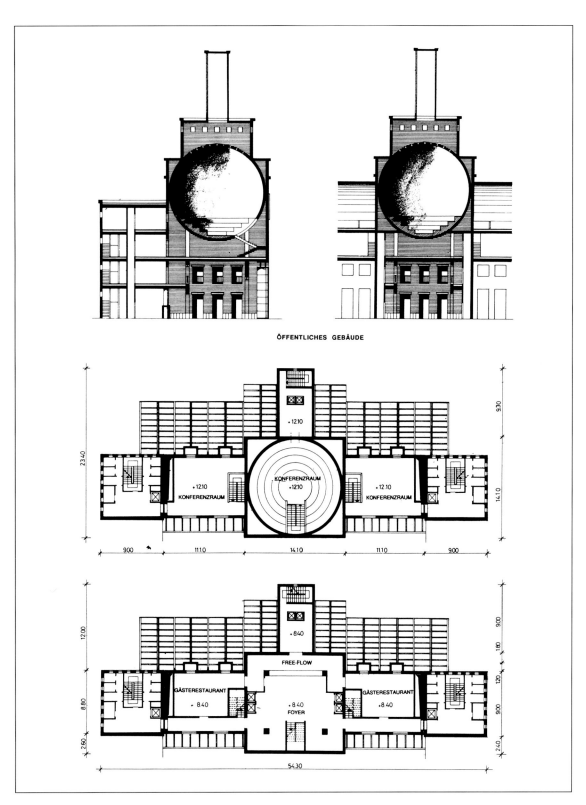

ÖFFENTLICHES GEBÄUDE

Tower sections and plan details

DISNEY OFFICE COMPLEX

ORLANDO, FLORIDA
1991

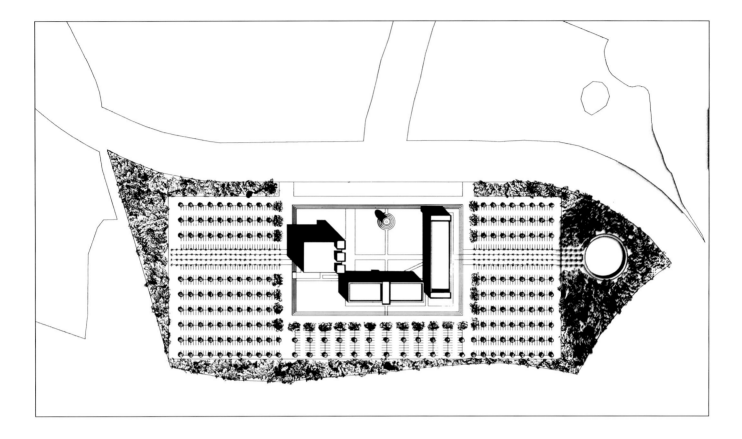

Rossi's design of an office complex in Florida with the Disney Development Company (DDC) as the principal tenant is his first project for the motion-picture/theme-park consortium. Designing for a site outside the confines of DisneyWorld, Rossi was able to escape the dilemma facing the many world-class architects currently working on projects at Disney's home base of Burbank, California and its resort properties in Orlando and France: the provision of a captivating "theme," or three-dimensional story line, as if the building were a character in one of Disney's animated films. Portrayed in the popular press as an ivory-tower academic turned loner-architect, Rossi hardly seems a likely choice for a company whose corporate mandate demands upbeat, "entertaining" architecture. But for an office complex in what is slated to be a several-thousand acre "utopian" new suburb of Orlando, named Celebration, Disney, appears to be getting serious.

The scheme comprises three office buildings with a combined square footage of 370,000 in addition to a 1,800-square-foot "folly." Rossi looked for historical reference to the main square of Pisa, the Campo Santo, and the deceptively casual arrangement of its four principal structures: the cathedral, the cupola-topped baptistery, the belfry (the famous Leaning Tower of Pisa), and the linear block of the cemetery, which serves as a backdrop for the sculptural assemblage.

Phase one of the project, scheduled for construction in 1992, consists of a ten-floor curtain-wall structure with a frontispiece of three giant engaged masonry columns (the DDC headquarters), an adjacent six-floor block whose long front facade is broken up by six vertical volumes and a central entry tower, and a folly. Phase two includes a four-floor block opposite the DDC headquarters, which replaces the folly, and the relocation of the folly opposite the middle building. As in the Tuscan city, Rossi's various sized and shaped volumes are unified by a grass-covered piazza and common exterior materials such as red limestone cladding and artificially-aged copper mullions, spandrels, and cornices.

Early sketch with folly

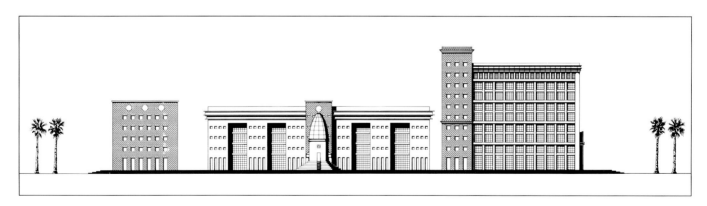

North elevation

Piazza study

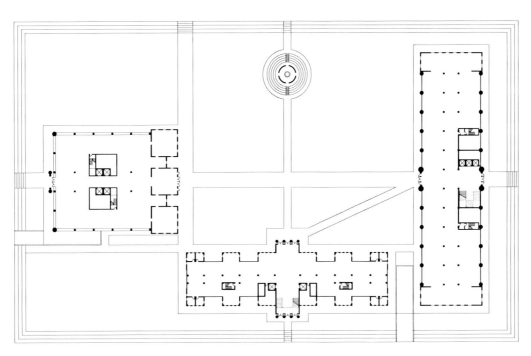

Ground floor plan

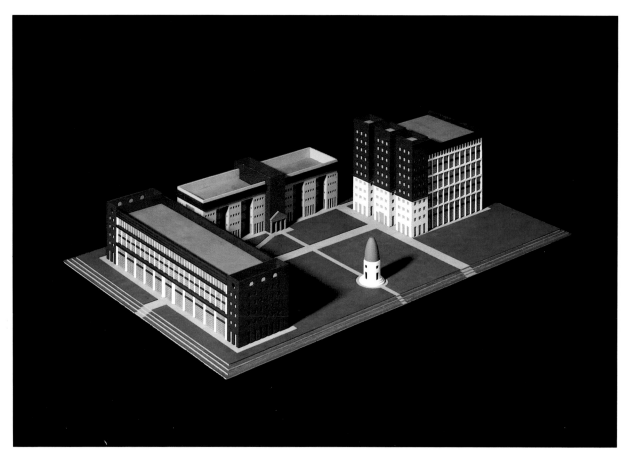

Model view of the final scheme

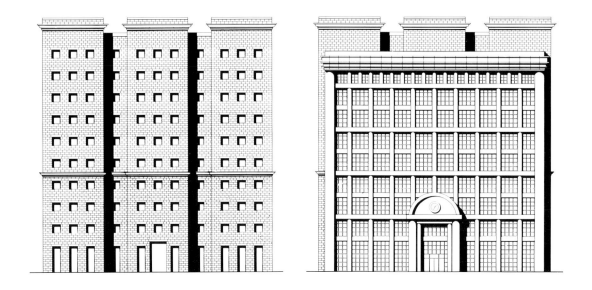

East and west elevations of building A

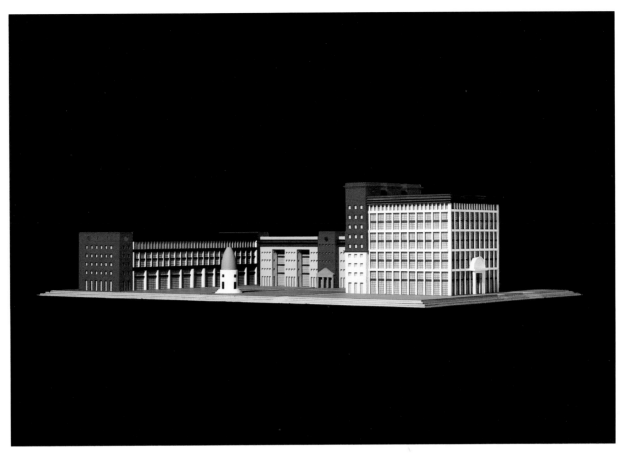

Model view from the northwest

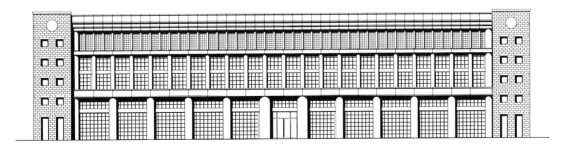

North elevation of building B
East elevation of building C

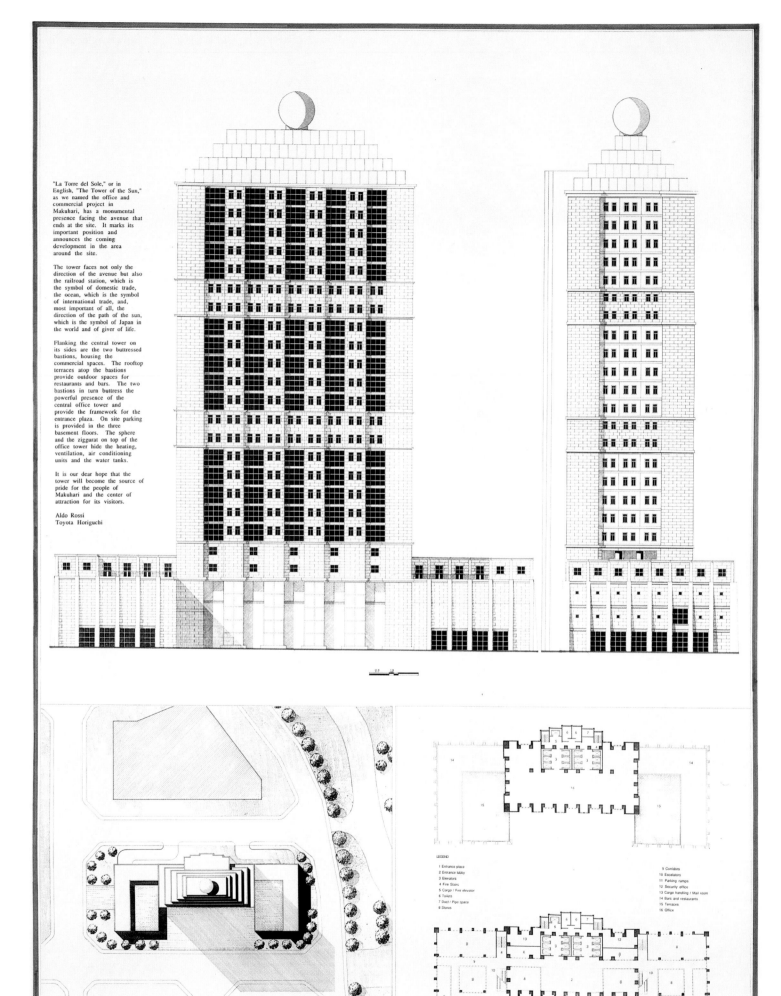

"La Torre del Sole," or in English, "The Tower of the Sun," as we named the office and commercial project in Makuhari, has a monumental presence facing the avenue that ends at the site. It marks its important position and announces the coming development in the area around the site.

The tower faces not only the direction of the avenue but also the railroad station, which is the symbol of domestic trade, the ocean, which is the symbol of international trade, and, most important of all, the direction of the path of the sun, which is the symbol of Japan in the world and of giver of life.

Flanking the central tower on its sides are the two buttressed bastions, housing the commercial spaces. The rooftop terraces atop the bastions provide outdoor spaces for restaurants and bars. The two bastions in turn buttress the powerful presence of the central office tower and provide the framework for the entrance plaza. On site parking is provided in the three basement floors. The sphere and the ziggurat on top of the office tower hide the heating, ventilation, air conditioning units and the water tanks.

It is our dear hope that the tower will become the source of pride for the people of Makuhari and the center of attraction for its visitors.

Aldo Rossi
Toyota Horiguchi

LEGEND

1 Entrance plaza
2 Entrance lobby
3 Elevators
4 Fire Stairs
5 Cargo / Fire elevator
6 Toilets
7 Duct / Pipe space
8 Stores

9 Corridors
10 Escalators
11 Parking ramps
12 Security office
13 Cargo handling / Mail room
14 Bars and restaurants
15 Terraces
16 Office

La Torre del Sole

Makuhari, Japan
1991

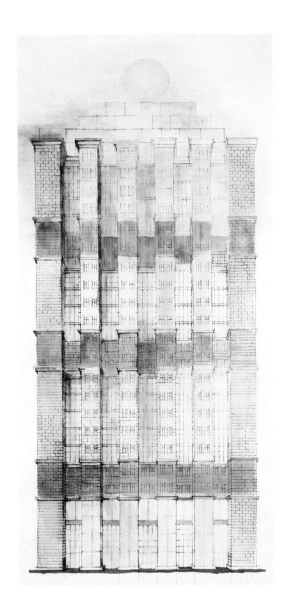

Planned for a site in Makuhari, a city in Japan's Chiba prefect, "La Torre del Sole" or "The Tower of the Sun," is a 24-story structure with shops occupying its four-story base and offices filling the remaining floors. In plan, the complex resembles a squat "U" that opens to the southwest onto a local thoroughfare. With the railroad station in the distance, the tower faces "the symbol of domestic trade, [and beyond] the ocean, which is the symbol of international trade, and most important of all, the direction of the path of the sun."

Designed with associates Giovanni Da Pozzo and Toyota Horiguchi, the scheme calls for the parallel side arms to appear as "bastions" to the central volume of the tower. Toward that end, they are rendered in brick and granite and are further supported by brick buttresses. The exterior of the tower is a combination of red Indian sandstone, granite, Portland limestone, steel, and glass. It rises to a ziggurat topped by a gold-painted sphere— monumental camouflage for rooftop heating, ventilation systems, and water tanks.

NATIONAL MUSEUM OF SCOTLAND

EDINBURGH, SCOTLAND
1991

Rossi and associate Christopher Stead's competition entry for the National Museum of Scotland in Edinburgh takes advantage of its site. The scheme uses a natural change in grade to offset the south-facing entry from the principal facade of the adjacent Royal Museum by Robert Adam. Claiming that "a public building should not be so greedy as to occupy the whole of its site," the architects perpetuated what they call the civic tradition of *noblesse oblige* by setting their structure back from the street behind a covered loggia. Galleries, reading rooms, and offices are arranged around a six-floor spiral gallery topped by a skylight.

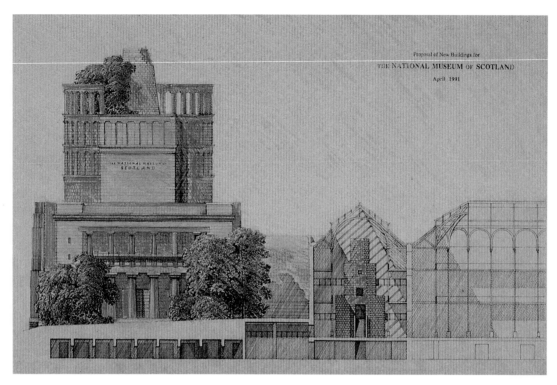

Longitudinal section looking north

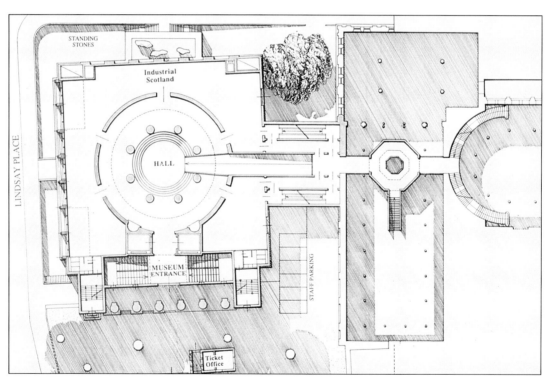

Third floor plan

Longitudinal section looking south

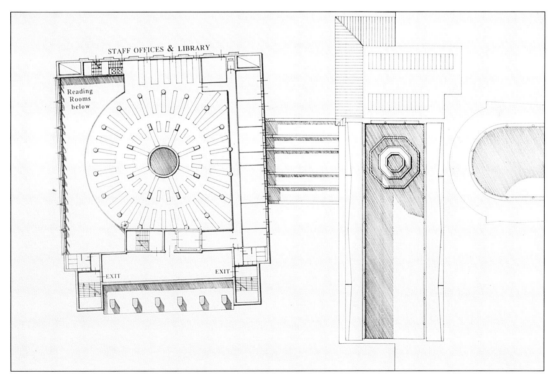

Seventh floor plan

CITY CENTER

KUALA LUMPUR, MALAYSIA
1991

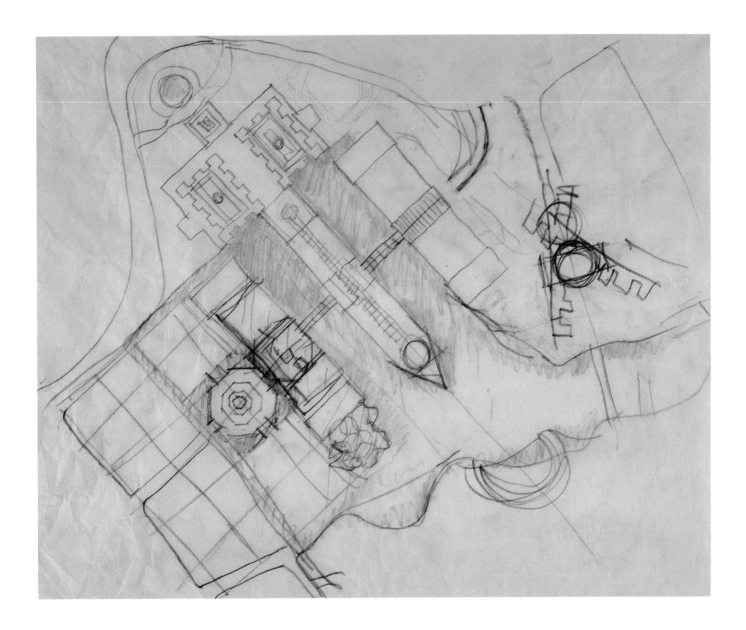

In the spring of 1991, Rossi was invited to compete for the design of a vast complex of offices, stores, and residences in Kuala Lumpur. The client, a private sector-governmental consortium, requested a proposal for the first phase of the project, a fourteen-acre parcel with a body of water in the middle. The program called for three office towers of between sixty and eighty stories; the inclusion of a twin-tower convention hotel was optional.

Rossi's scheme, dubbed "Il Castello" or "The Citadel," configures the required floor area into four, not three, towers so that the headquarters of the national oil company (contained in two 52-story structures) will preside over the adjacent speculative offices buildings (two 43-story structures) and outlines a master plan for the hotel/convention center to the southwest. Set atop a base of shops and restaurants, the angled brick and steel sides of the oil company's twin towers rise to a narrower ziggurat-like top. The towers are joined by what appear to be giant steel trusses, but what are actually pedestrian bridges with porthole windows. Jutting out into the water below is a pier of restaurants, with the *Dogana*—Rossi's reference to the Venetian customs house—at the tip of the pier. Rossi's idea is that the pier will eventually become a principal stop on the city's growing rapid-transit system. Completely orthogonal, the adjacent buildings repeat the pattern of alternating bands of brick, glass, and steel.

Perspective and early sketch showing 'La Dogana'

NORTH ELEVATION 1:500

North elevation and longitudinal section

SECTION X-X 1:500

253

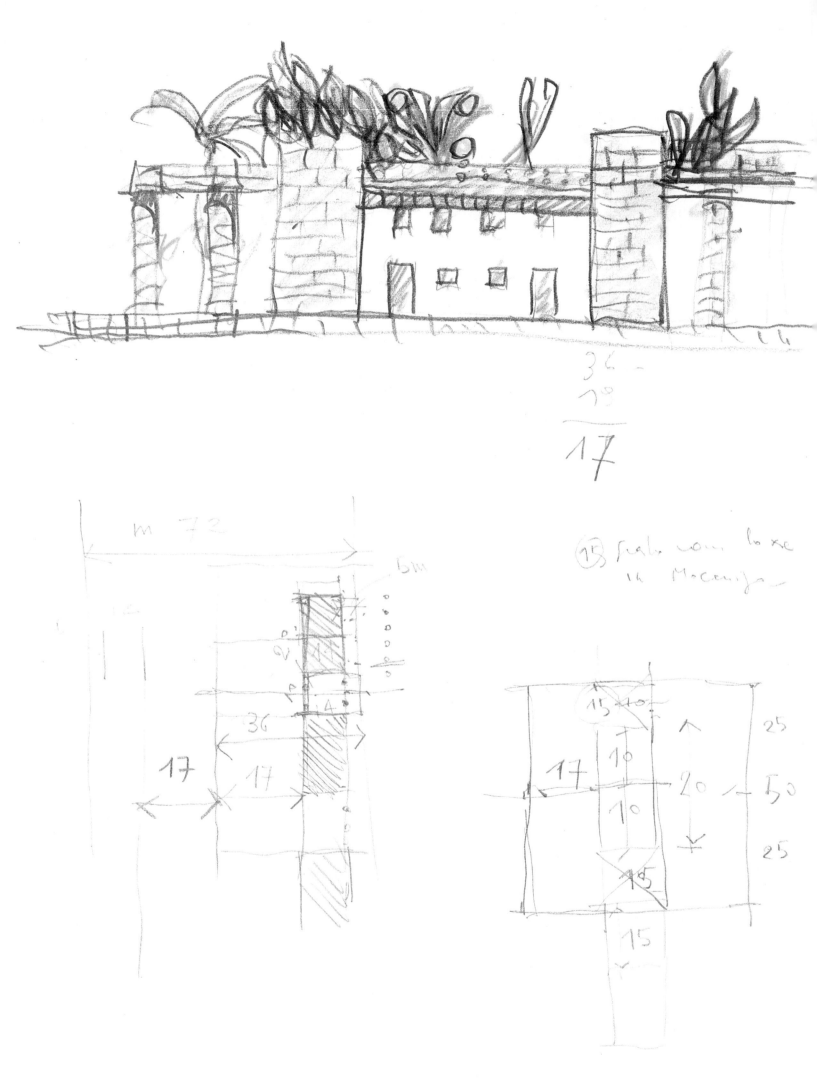

$$\frac{36 - 79}{17}$$

m 72

bm

(15) fub con boxe in Mocenifo

36
17   17

17

15 10   25

17   10
        20 → 50

     10
              25

15

15

HOUSING COMPLEX

BARI, ITALY
1991

The "heel" of the boot of Italy—the province of Apulia—faces the Adriatic Sea and Yugoslavia beyond. Its capital, the port city of Bari, is an agricultural and industrial center that has been growing rapidly in recent years. A planned part of that expansion is a new self-contained district comprising housing, a school, and a commercial complex. The scheme combines aspects of the old town clustered on a promontory with the gridded streets of the new downtown spread out along the waterfront.

Rossi's program consists of 80 two-family homes and the enclosure wall around the entire district, which is located in upper Bari. The design incorporates references to the city's past as a Greek colony with elements of structures indigenous to southern Italy.

The entrance gate has three structures arranged in a casual "U": in the center is a 50-foot-high cone of local white stone that is truncated at the top to admit light into the white-washed interior. The cone is meant to recall ancient Hellenic burial chambers and old Sardinian fort towers. Flanking the gate and clad in a porous rock are two low-slung gate-houses that contain offices and locker-rooms for the guards. Immediately inside the compound is a paved circular piazza dominated by four rectangular towers in brick banded with ceramic tile, versions of Rossi's towers at Centro Torri in Parma. The two-family houses, with their plaster facades and olive-wood window frames, are stripped-down versions of Mediterranean villas. "Simple, severe, and powerful shapes that blend with the earth and indeed seem to have sprung directly from the earth, typical of Apulia and the Mediterranean. In this harsh, sun-washed landscape, architecture is generated by materials: tufa, the white stone of Trani, soil, [and] olive groves," says Rossi of the project.

VILLA A RABILZZO

Site plan

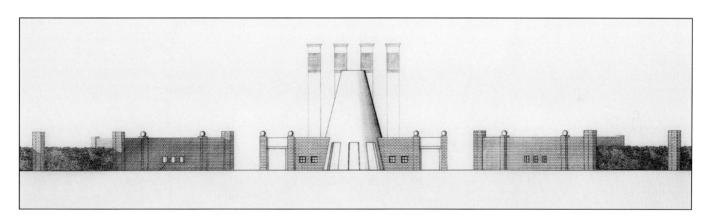

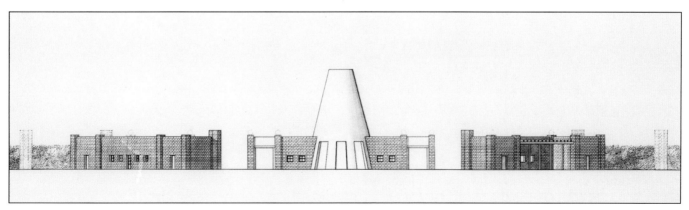

Front and back elevations

LINATE AIRPORT

MILAN, ITALY
1991

Linate Airport is on the eastern edges of Milan. Unlike its newer and more up-to-date sister facility, Malpensa, which is some 70 miles to the northwest of the city, it accommodates domestic and inter-European routes. "Airports are structures that are constantly growing, not only spatially but also technologically and in terms of conception and use of the space employed," observes Rossi. To him, airports provide the initial and potentially overriding image of the city they service—not only do they act as modern-day urban gateways, these self-contained complexes are also cities in their own right. For Rossi, fast-pace developments in areas as diverse as transportation, construction techniques, and security procedures ensure that any airport intended to be futuristic will quickly become obsolete—in both use and appearance—as new technologies

manifest themselves in unexpected ways. (His reference to Paris's Charles de Gaulle airport and its intergalactic imagery, now clearly a product of a 1970s Star Trek fascination, brings his point home.) Rossi's proposal for the renovation and expansion of Linate directly confronts the stated need of a civic "door." Facing the runways and disembarkation areas—what is typically the "back" of the terminal— is his new facade: two columns twelve feet in diameter support a giant steel truss and frame an immense expanse of glass. The glass wall is a grid of Rossi's signature green steel-framed square windows. Set back from this transparent portal into the airport—a preview of the city beyond—are gridded side wings of brick and glass. The project incorporates five new gates that connect to expanded arrival, departure, and baggage-claim areas.

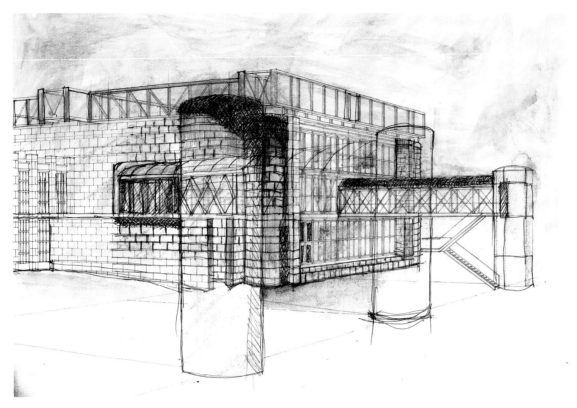

Early sketch showing massive columns

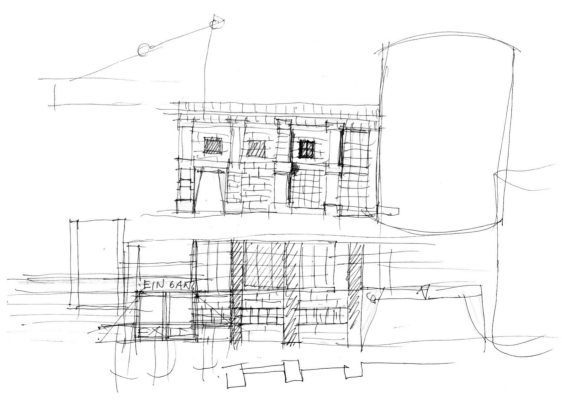

Early study for facade

Model view of principal elevation
Elevation with plan detail and sections

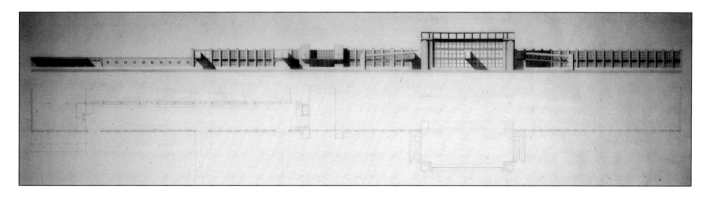

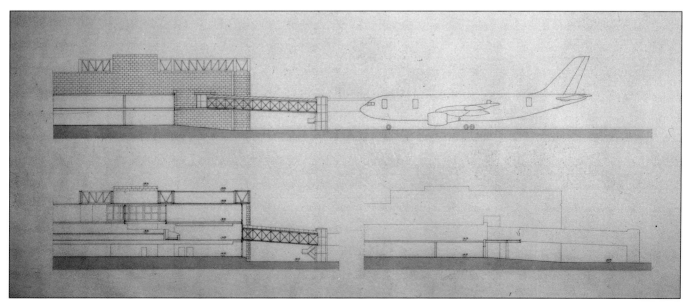

ORTNEC LI
ELXQUTLVC
O CITS AIOE 5
XNORB LEN
PAR 9

studio per studenti
in nuova tipo nuovo

ART ACADEMY

BRONX, NEW YORK
1991

Artist-teacher Tim Rollins and his Kids of Survival (K.O.S) from the Art & Knowledge Workshop, an after-school program for teenagers, are starting an alternative high school of the arts in an area of New York City infamous for its derelict, largely abandoned building stock and overcrowded, under-supervised educational facilities. According to the Academy's mission statement, the proposed South Bronx Academy of Art for artistically-talented students (once classified as "learning disabled" by the public school system) is "intended to serve as a monument to the possibilities of [the area's] youth." In client Rollins, Rossi seems to have found a soul mate—someone who not only maintains that "creativity and education are inseparable," but also echoes Rossi's faith in the power of architecture. It is their shared belief that Rossi's building (certain to be an instant landmark among the mostly charred wreckage of the South Bronx) will instigate the physical "redemption" of the neighborhood.

This "urban rescue operation," as Rossi calls it, is planned for a vacant 2.7-acre parcel, formerly the site of an orphanage and reform school for girls, adjacent to the Corpus Christi Monastery and across the street from the Spofford Juvenile House of Detention. Rossi's master plan retains an existing concrete wall around the perimeter of the property, modified by the addition of two gates—one for the school and one for local residents. The scheme shows one-third of the site occupied by the Academy with some 30,000 square feet of new construction, and the remaining two-thirds transformed into a community park and baseball field.

The preliminary design for the Academy's facility depicts a circular entry portal flanked by administrative offices that lead to a giant cube, which Rollins calls *la sala*, or "great hall." The ground floor of this space contains an informal exhibition area and classrooms; upstairs is a spherical double-height auditorium. The exterior of the cube is treated as a giant four-sided canvas, to be covered with murals by K.O.S., Rossi, or both. Extending from both sides of the "great hall" is a series of interconnected square pavilions to be used as individual studios. Behind the cube is a tower, positioned on axis with the entrance, that also marks the center of a garden path. Shown in Rossi's early sketches as a lighthouse, the lookout tower appears, appropriately enough, as a beacon in the wasteland of the South Bronx.

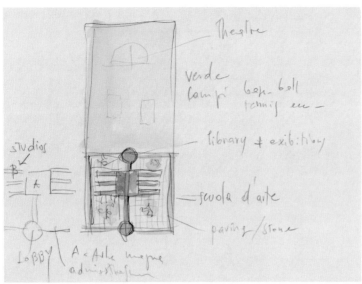

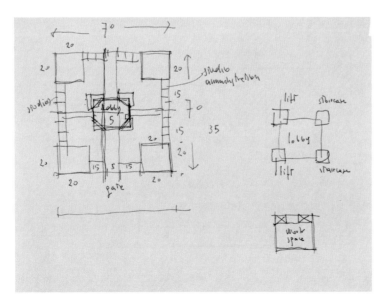

Preliminary sketches

PART THREE

Il Celeste della Madonna
Invisible Distances

IL CELESTE DELLA MADONNA

KAREN STEIN

Aldo Rossi and Pinocchio are an unlikely pair, but they have a lot in common. Both are distinctly Italian; both are from a modest background; both have achieved mythical stature. And Pinocchio is often on Rossi's mind when he designs: "When I draw a piece of furniture, I always remember the strange piece of wood which might have become a piece of furniture, but was then destined to be a puppet and in the end became Pinocchio. Of course, this was a wood of genius, but who is to say that such things don't happen?" In fact, the storybook character could be a Rossi creation: his cylindrical body, gangly columnar legs and arms, spherical head, and cone-shaped nose are Rossi's architecture anthropomorphized. But Rossi sees Pinocchio as a fully-formed character, with the dreams and aspirations of a person: "The motivation of his life is to become a boy and then a man. Therefore, Pinocchio is a difficult person, easy, but also neurotic."

Rossi considers Pinocchio to be "in between two worlds." The same could be said about the architect himself. It is perhaps the similar incongruity of Rossi's firm handshake and scuffling feet—a paradoxical combination of directness and boyish impatience—that helps explain why his work inspires such a range of emotions. The monumental scale of his buildings is the ideal backdrop for our most heroic fantasies, while their blank surfaces seem coated

le caffè dell inretto
FTR. Po | fa alla mattina lei doren
bevi un buon caffè.

with a more uncertain expectation. Since he came into international prominence in the late 1970s, Rossi has remained an enigma, even to his admirers, possibly because his inaccessibility (and the perceived aloofness of his work) has led observers to seek less "difficult" architects. His interest in architectural purity and rationalism was often confused with abstract dogmatism, even though there was ample evidence to prove the contrary. His writings, most notably *The Architecture of the City*, first published in 1966, and *A Scientific Autobiography*, which appeared in 1981, are richly tangled webs of historical analysis and personal observations—a compelling mix of scholarly research and free association.

Rossi's architecture and drawing are the same. His work appears deceptively simple: it consists of a storehouse of geometric volumes—cubes, cones, spheres, pyramids—which Rossi arranges according to program requirements, always guided by traditional building types. In each successive project, he refines his compositions, thriving on the slight permutations from one design to the next; and as time

goes on, it seems that his own work is increasingly his most significant source of inspiration. By constantly reworking the same shapes into a new order with what some consider myopic consistency, Rossi has created an identifiable, even idiosyncratic style that has connections to historical tradition, but escapes simple classifications. He is a loner in the profession, pursuing his speciality as assiduously now, in the height of his popularity, as before he came to the public's attention. In truth, Rossi has made his obstinacy part of his art (and an art out of obstinacy). Although there have been watersheds in his career—his 1971 winning entry to the San Cataldo Cemetery competition, for example—there have been no dramatic turnabouts, no abrupt changes of artistic direction. Unlike other famous artists of our age, Rossi has never had the need to reinvent himself.

Rossi's design for the Venice Biennale of 1979, the Teatro del Mondo, is perhaps the most notable symbol of the architect's professional accomplishment. Built on a barge, the floating theater was pulled into the island city's lagoon by a tug boat. After the Biennale, the theater traveled the coast of Yugoslavia, calling on ports that were former Venetian colonies. The Teatro del Mondo conveyed the mixed messages of a temporary structure inspired by the architecture of the ancients: its audience was impressed by its monumentality, charmed by its old-fashioned decorum, touched by its fragility. As its medieval tower bobbed in and out of view, the theater was at once a startling addition to the city's skyline and comfortably at home—new yet familiar. It is this sleight of hand that characterizes Rossi's work.

When Rossi designs a building, he thinks first of its emotional impact. He goes through a process of identification so complete that he imbues his projects with human qualities, often referring to a particular buildings of his as "sad" or "happy" or, more than likely, "melancholy." He relies on his own intuition, often times as uncanny about places as about people; inevitably, his first impression of a project carries him through.

Rossi is, above all, a storyteller. He tells his stories in words but mostly with drawings and paintings, as well as with buildings. His are hopeful tales of architecture as the beloved protagonist inciting positive change in a community: a new civic structure, for example, is not just a source of pride for local residents, but a beacon of functional clarity and monumental presence that will somehow inspire similar attributes—honesty, valor, dignity—in its users.

Rossi does not just build the backdrop for daily life, he supplies a script. One imagines a visitor crossing the long galleria of the San Cataldo Cemetery in Modena hearing her own footsteps echoing off the concrete paving. Is it not, as Rossi planned, inevitable that she is unnerved by the eerie stillness of the dead whose ashes are stored in vaults above her head, yet relieved at the life-affirming sound of her own steps? Yet his work has been called cold and impersonal because to some it harbors a resentment of its inhabitants for destroying the purity he has so painstakingly created.

Rossi is unique not only for the architecture he produces, but also for the way he produces it. His formal training in architecture was at the Milan Polytechnic where he entered in 1949 as a film student with no particular architectural ambitions, but his ongoing education comes from his powers of observation and his travels around the world. Like original thinkers in other fields, he is part book-taught, part self-taught. Years ago, an Italian magazine asked Rossi for his views on architectural training, presumably hoping to discover the architect's "secret." His answer was characteristically in the form of an analogy: "You can teach someone English, but you can't

teach someone to be Shakespeare," he explained, making a distinction between the basic tools of training and the gift of inspiration.

In what is more than a quaint turn of phrase by someone who heads a professional practice spanning three continents, Rossi refers to architecture as "my trade" or "my craft." In fact, Rossi's Milan office resembles an old-world *atelier*, with all work overseen by the *maestro*. He has a habit of integrating former students into an extended professional family—a close-knit group of surrogate sons and the occasional daughter—and their "headquarters" is what appears to be a rambling apartment in a Milanese *palazzo*. In this "apartment," however, all the rooms are painted shades of blue, ranging from baby blue—a particular hue called *Celeste della Madonna* or "Heavenly Light of the Madonna" that has become Rossi's signature—to azure. Here, surrounded by his paintings, drawings, and curios collected on his travels, Rossi still works much in the way he did when he started his firm, Studio di Architettura, in the early 1960s, as if assuming what he considers the elements of a corporate infras-

tructure—a public-relations consultant or a marketing expert—might somehow adversely affect his work. Whether intentional or not, Rossi's resistance to standard office protocol has become his trusted sieve: those clients (and even colleagues) who make it through have the necessary mettle for his work.

If Rossi the man resists change, Rossi the architect measures it. Using the same shapes over and over, without the decoration that can be attributed to a particular era or style, the passage of time is marked off in their continuous recombination. In their repetition they establish their own tradition. Rossi muses on the similarity of his projects and his urge to remake them. In a well-known passage in one of his notebooks, which were later published as *A Scientific Autobiography*, he writes: "In my projects, repetition, collage, the displacement of an element from one design to another, always places me before another potential project which I would like to do, but is also a memory of some other thing." Yet his interest in self-reference is tempered by his submission to happenstance—the specifics of time and place, the skill of the contractor, the angle of the sun—all those seemingly mundane things that breathe fresh life into each project.

In his constancy Rossi himself has become a measure of the passage of time, swings in his popularity measuring shifts in the architectural profession over the last thirty years. Labeled alternately a fascist or a communist in the 1960s for his avowed sympathy for Stalinist architecture and dismissed from his teaching post at the Milan Polytechnic in 1971 for his support of the student movement, the "radical" Rossi is now admired for his uncompromising common sense. In the past decade Rossi has gone from cult figure to official hero (winning the Pritzker, the self-styled Nobel of architecture, in 1990 made it official), with the disconcerting effect of routinizing his wanderlust into a peripatetic lifestyle that requires him to travel from job site to job site. Like many in-demand architects of his generation, the success of his practice can be measured virtually in the miles he logs on the airplane.

The current phase of Rossi's career began in 1981, when he was invited to participate with other distinguished European and American architects in the International Building Exhibition (IBA) in Berlin to design an apartment building for an area of the city destroyed during World War II. With the Friedrichstadt complex—his first major commission outside the borders of Italy—Rossi, the once-touted "regionalist," went truly international. The IBA marked a turning point in Rossi's work: his frame of reference was suddenly larger than the landscape of his native Lombardy, and his buildings became a deft synthesis of native and global.

At Friedrichstadt, the basic configuration of the building is Rossi's reading of the traditional apartment house type—a structure with a double-loaded corridor that is pushed up along the lot lines to make a continuous streetfront and maximize the "backyard." Blended into the distinctly Germanic rendition of the type—the ruddy brick Rossi attributes to the typical Berliner *Haus*, the steel and glass of Mies van der Rohe, and the glossy ceramic tile of the area—are souvenirs from Italy in the form of corner columns, giant versions of a column on the fifteenth-century Venetian palazzo by Antonio Filarete.

While Rossi's new experience of building in Germany required him to assimilate different cultural traditions and building techniques, it also confirmed the urban theories of *The Architecture of the City*, and gave him renewed confidence. As Rossi's international stature has grown, so has the number of commissions outside of Italy. He has had to reconcile the demands of projects scattered around the world with his hands-on way of working. "I want to find the right way to realize good architecture," he offers in explanation of his decision in 1986 to open a satellite office in New York City with former Institute of Architecture and Urban Studies student Morris Adjmi. The New York office supervises projects in the United States and Japan without altering the structure of the Milan office.

The rush of new commissions in the early 1980s can be partly explained by the passage of time, which allowed observers to grow accustomed to Rossi's work and shed popular misconceptions of him as a bookish academic with dubious political sympathies. In fact, Rossi owes no allegiance to any single party, political or architectural, preferring to pick and chose aspects as he pleases. "How can I be postmodern when I was never modern?" is a favorite Rossian taunt, delivered with the knowledge that both groups claim him as their own. However, he does credit what he calls postmodernism's "unorthodox vision" for casting a more favorable light on his stark esthetic.

"It is strange how I resemble myself," wrote Rossi (a statement as true today as it was when he penned it in 1984), and he might have continued to say how he at times resembles his spiritual mentor, Etienne-Louis Boullée. Rossi admires Boullée's work, where "use and decoration are one." The same might be said of Rossi's work, and, in his case, use and decoration often reveal unexpected human drama. By juxtaposing the simplest architectural forms, Rossi captures many of life's joys, tragedies, and eccentricities. His recent design of the Church of San Carlo alla Barona, for example, uses modest materials—concrete, stone, steel trusses, industrial windows—meant to reveal a Catholic severity that Rossi, himself a Catholic, finds beautiful. The giant columns that connect the chapel with the cloister are made of granite at the base and brick above, as if the congregation ran out of money during construction—an entirely plausible scenario that depicts the local community as bereft, not just of the necessary funds, but also, if its leaders are not vigilant, of a focus for their religious life. For a temporary art gallery in Fukuoka, Japan, Rossi uses classically correct Doric columns to mark the entrance. There is certainly a measure of irony, if not a comment on the lack of permanence in building in today, in his use of the architecture of the ancients in a structure meant to be dismantled after three years. "It's a strange world," Rossi has scrawled across sketches of urban scenes.

Some years ago, Rossi was asked to write an introduction to a catalogue of his buildings. He wrote, "And what of my work, the architecture gathered here: I would have liked to discuss it in detail as I grow ever more involved in the constructions, rising as they do in places so dissimilar and occupying such a great part of my life. I believe I shall describe them one day, when I am old, when the longing for things has been utterly overcome by the desire to tell of them. It is difficult to predict when such a time will come." Rossi's reluctance to discuss his work reflects the view of most great artists, namely that their work should speak for them. In the end, Rossi's strangely silent buildings do exactly that.

Invisible Distances

Aldo Rossi

Prior to visiting the Prince's hunting lodge one day in May, young Werther returns to his hometown. Drawing near, he hails the old, well-known houses set in their gardens, but notes that "...[I] heartily disliked the newer ones, as well as all the other changes that had been made."* Even the old houses where he had once lived made him remember only "the restlessness, the tears, the dullness of mind, the anxiety of heart, that I suffered in that hole." When he goes down to the river, his reflections on his surroundings are transformed into a problem of knowledge: he remembers the long hours spent watching the water and how he followed the faraway current "until I completely lost myself in the contemplation of invisible distances."

Imagining these "invisible distances" leads him to reflect on the natural wisdom of the ancients and on the ambiguity of knowledge. "What is the use of my present knowledge, which I share with any schoolboy, that the earth is round? Man needs only a few clods of earth whereon to enjoy his happiness and even fewer to rest beneath it." Oddly, Werther, with the serene clarity of the suicidal, twice returns to the meaning of life, each time referring to his surroundings and, in a way, to architecture.

He does this the first time when the house of his childhood memories, which he refers to sinisterly as "the den," dissolves into highly personal memories, as if architecture were nothing but pure egotism; the second time is when he reduces the world to a few clods of earth good for two things: love and death. This attitude is apparent from the beginning, when he asserts that he heartily dislikes the changes the city has undergone. In short, Werther seems to annul everything on behalf of the feeling that dominates him—love. At the same time, however, this feeling leads him to view his surroundings and the knowledge of space as deceptions (he does not care whether the earth is round, only a few clods of earth are necessary for love and even fewer for death, and so forth).

It is almost as if the world were but an effort to make us forget that which we cannot possess.

Few visions (not even the famous remark from Loos, where he identifies the tomb and architecture) have reduced the built world to such uselessness. Architecture would amount only to decoration. We know that this is not the case, but his notion of "these few clods" reduces architecture in a way that has always appealed to me. This has also nourished in me what is perhaps an exaggerated and yet still profound aversion to the theories common to major texts on modern architecture in which the architect is presented as artificer and consoler.

Nonetheless, it is a fact that even if we reject the notion of any capacity to console, architecture exists, and as such has its own history and its own becoming, even if this becoming only marginally alters the life

of man. I recently reflected on many of my past observations on architecture when I visited the Ise shrine in Japan. In this virtually uncontaminated place stand two equal and ancient temples. Their antiquity, however, exists exclusively in the constant reconstruction of one of the two temples. Every twenty-five years the earlier temple is definitively destroyed, while the one beside it is completed. The new temple contains only one piece of wood from the earlier one. I believe there are few cases in which the idea of architecture and its construction are repeated in this way and yet at the same time, which evince an indifference toward architecture.

Memories age along with the individual; I do not know if this is just a commonplace saying or an affirmation. In any case, I believe it to be true, and I see this as linked with the recognition of things. That is, things acquire value once they have been recognized, and to "recognize" does not mean to have "lived" them. Recognition in this sense seems to me the essence of the Ise shrine: its ability to be recognized does not lie in the materials, whether new or old, nor in the object in itself, but purely in the image, in an event that, once recognized, is reproduced almost without asking about its meaning. In the western world this may be somewhat related to ritual, but it is totally different from the idea of the fragment, perhaps because the fragment does not presuppose a global image sufficiently strong as to be distinct from its own materiality. I think of the classic "white" stones of humanistic culture, of the cult of the fragment. So this fragment, this eternally new, amazes us, and I use the word "amaze" precisely to mean that which lies outside the norm, but is unitary in itself. Yet there is a nodal point of unity in these things which must be rediscovered; at times it seems to me that this nodal point is growth. In a moment I will explain why I use the word growth, but for now I mean it as a limit and a necessity. By this I mean something like our sadness about a child who fails to grow even though we know that the limit of growth is the loss of childhood. I write and use the word "growth" or "development" because I believe that now I can understand, strangely enough precisely in the domain of architecture, a passage from Quintilian in the *Instituzioni Oratorie* which, even though I was struck by it, I could never grasp. He speaks of a "technics"** of growth and says that it is able to render something so large that it could not permit further growth. ("*Nam et hoc agendi genus est tantum aliquid efficere, ut non possit augeri.*")

These technics of growth, then, are precisely that limit which the artist seizes as a function of some sudden rush of emotion that is perhaps otherwise inexplicable. We can see this in the writings of Boullée as well as in the diary of Pontormo and in many other texts in which artists talk about themselves.

Or this growth partakes of pure technics: as if we possessed a tool capable of measuring it.

Or, again, it is the secret reason we love unfinished works, where growth does not seem (and often is not) a rational choice but the result of some disaster, some breakdown, some abandonment.

When I write about architecture I feel as if I am able to include these things in a general design, and I do not know how much this has to do only with my own architecture. Now it seems to me that that something, perhaps infinitesimal, that always existed between thought and communication, past and present, disappears with increasing persistence. So when I wrote, "It is strange how I resemble myself," it still seems to me that I did not know how to evaluate that something that establishes the difference of differences between the things we do.

Designs change, increasingly resembling one another, and as we work in different places among different people we must step out of ourselves in order to hear the sound of the world. It is still we who hear these sounds, which perhaps increases our interest in what we call art, or architecture, or the technics of design.

But often the world's sounds lead us back to the selfishness of childhood, that of the family. My last design, at least the one now under construction in Japan, was somehow born as a repetition of a design for a gymnasium for Olginate, on Lake Como. It is as if a building on that lake had foreseen the Orient (although the Lombard lake is a site detached from geographical and national reality), but at the same time it is as if Fukuoka constituted the possibility of existing in one of my architectures.

To emerge from our shells in order to listen to the world's sounds, or to those of our century—as in one of Walter Benjamin's most beautiful images—is an aspect of my recent designs. For this reason I am not uncomfortable about seeing them rise in Texas, Japan, or Berlin, or, as in the case of the beautiful Vassivière museum, the most remote island of Europe in the heart of Limousin, the least explored part of France.

But I do not want to talk about my projects here; I would rather describe them meticulously without the drawings. Only a new *école du regard* could spare us the useless details and enable us to examine thoroughly the meaning of the constructions.

What meaning I do not know.

Perhaps, yes, a few clods of earth, and forgetting about architecture and about the technics of design, increasingly fashioning the attempt to make us forget that which we cannot possess. Now it seems to me as if the city Werther revisited, where the house became the den of grief, of tears, of turbulent emotions, has surpassed the sad poetic image and has become the site of everyday life.

I am worried about our cities; it seems to me that everyone who is part of the building trades (engineers, architects, draftsmen, masons, and so forth) is a more or less knowledgeable artificer of interventions into the city; interventions that do not count in the larger system.

I remember once seeing an article suitable for some occasion, I cannot remember where, with the title "What to do about architecture?"

But the answer seems more straightforward than that to me. Stripped of rhetorical and demagogic attributions, it is an art or a profession like any other, and doing things well is a matter of ethics—for example, professional ethics—and that could suffice.

But if by some whimsy or memory I started with the young Werther and the lucidity of the suicidal, I bring this essay to a close with what he said at the outset. Returning to the castle (of which he tells us nothing), he offers some assessments of the people and finally remarks about the prince: "Besides, he admired my intelligence and my talents more than my heart, which is my only pride, and the fountainhead of all—all strength, happiness and misery."

Art, and naturally architecture, perhaps even science, lie on this kind of repetition.

Invisible distances are for us the architecture of the past and present, but above all the future. And the future is not the sound of the trolley's metal wheels on metal tracks in an antiquated Milan, which some of the Futurists saw as progress. Imbeciles always see things at too close range, a way to resolve problems that are already old.

The invisible distances, as the hero I have cited here says, have a passion that upsets everyday logic, so it is not enough to know that the earth is round to feel a scientific or personal emotion.

Perhaps to change the world, only in fragments, to make us forget that which we cannot possess. *Aldo Rossi, Milan, 1989.*

Translated by Diane Ghirardo

Translator's notes

* Johann Wolfgang von Goethe, *The Sorrows of Young Werther*, translated by Elizabeth Mayer and Louise Bogan (New York, 1971), 96–97. In Rossi's original article, the citations are from the Italian translation, which differs in some key respects from the English one. I have therefore translated from the Italian where it was important to the author's interpretation, but elsewhere the quotations are drawn from the standard English translation.

** *Technica* in Italian means a way of doing something, but it is far more comprehensive than mechanical "technique." I have therefore chosen the word "technics" to convey this broader meaning.

PART FOUR

1959
Cultural Center and Theater
Milan, Italy
Thesis for Milan Polytechnic

1960
Urban Renewal along Via Farini
Milan, Italy
With G. Polesello, F. Tentori

1960
Villa at Ronchi
Versilia, Italy
With L. Ferrari
Completed 1960

1961
Peugeot Skyscraper
Buenos Aires, Argentina
With V. Magistretti, G. Polesello
Competition design

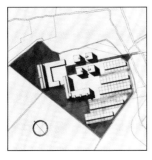

1961
Workers' Housing
Caleppio, Italy
With G. Polesello

1962
Monument to the Resistance
Cuneo, Italy
With G. Polesello, L. Meda
Competition

1962
Country Club
Fagagna, Italy
With G. Polesello

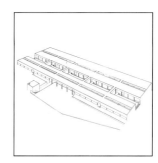

1962
Special School
Monza, Italy
With V. Gavazzeni,
G. Grassi, L. Meda
Competition design

1962
Contemporary History Museum
Milan, Italy
With M. Baffa, L. Meda,
U. Rivolta
Addition and interior design
Completed 1962

1962
Civic Center
Turin, Italy
With G. Polesello, L. Meda
Competition

1964
Iron Bridge and Park Exhibition
Milan, Italy
With L. Meda
XIII Triennale
Completed 1964

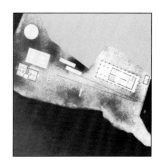

1964
Ticino Sport and Leisure Center
Abbiategrasso, Italy

1964
*Pilotta Square and
Paganini Theater*
Parma, Italy
Invited competition

1965
City Hall Square and Monument
Segrate, Italy
Completed 1965

1966
San Rocco Housing
Monza, Italy
With G. Grassi

1967
Piazza
Sannazzaro de' Burgundi, Italy
Competition

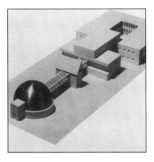

1968
City Hall
Scandicci, Italy
With M. Fortis, M. Scolari
Competition

1968
School at San Sabba
Trieste, Italy
With R. Agosto, G. Grassi,
F. Tentori
Completed 1969

1969
Gallaratese 2
Milan, Italy
Completed 1973

1969
De Amicis Middle School
Broni, Italy
Restoration and addition
Completed 1970

1971
Cemetery of San Cataldo
Modena, Italy
With G. Braghieri
Competition
Awarded First Prize
In construction

1972
City Hall
Muggio, Italy
With G. Braghieri
Competition

1972
Elementary School
Fagnano Olona, Italy
Completed 1976

1973
Single-Family Houses
Broni, Italy
With G. Braghieri
Completed 1973

1973
Villa and Pavilion
Borgo Ticino, Italy
With G. Braghieri
Completed 1973

1973
International Architectural Exhibition XV Triennale
Milan, Italy
With G. Braghieri, F. Raggi
Completed 1973

1974
Bridge
Bellinzona, Switzerland
With G. Braghieri, B. Reichlin, F. Reinhart

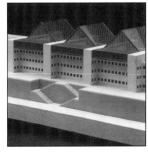

1974
Regional Administrative Center
Trieste, Italy
With G. Braghieri, M. Bosshard
Competition

1974
Student Housing
Trieste, Italy
With G. Braghieri, M. Bosshard, A. Cantafora
Competition

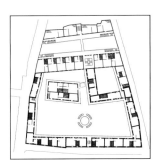

1975
El Corral del Conde
Seville, Spain
With G. Braghieri, A. Cantafora
Addition

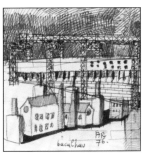

1975
Housing
Setubal, Portugal
With G. Braghieri, M. Bosshard
A. Cantafora, J. Charters,
J. Da Nobrega

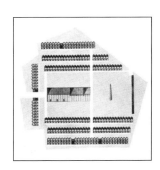

1976
Student Housing
Chieti, Italy
With G. Braghieri, A. Cantafora
Competition

1976
Houses along the Verbindingskanal
Berlin, Germany

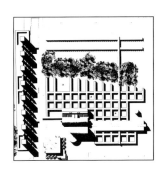

1977
Civic Center
Florence, Italy
With C. Aymonino, G. Braghieri
Competition

1977
Single-Family House
Mozzo, Italy
With A. Pizzigoni
Completed 1979

1977
Roma Interotta
Rome, Italy
With G. Braghieri, M. Bosshard,
A. Cantafora, P. Katzberger

1979
Single-Family Houses
Zandobbio, Italy
With A. Pizzigoni

1979
Secondary School
Broni, Italy
With G. Braghieri
Completed 1980

1979
Civic Center Tower
Pesaro, Italy

1979
Teatro del Mondo
Venice, Italy
Venice Biennale
Completed 1980

1979
A Landmark for Melbourne
Melborne, Australia
With G. Braghieri
Competition

1979
Landesbibliothek
Karlsruhe, Germany
With G. Braghieri, C. Herdel,
C. Stead

1979
Housing
Pegognaga, Italy
With G. Braghieri, COPRAT
Completed 1979

1979
Housing
Goito, Italy
With G. Braghieri, COPRAT
Completed 1979

1980
Biennale Entry Portal
Venice, Italy
Venice Biennale
Completed 1980

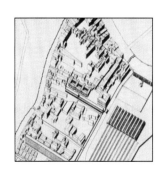

1980
Cannaregio West
Venice, Italy
With G. Dubbini, A. de Poli,
M. Narpozzi
Exposition

1981
Apartment House
Berlin, Germany
With G. Braghieri, C. Stead,
J. Johnson
Invited competition
Awarded First Prize
Completed 1988

1981
Funerary Chapel
Guissano, Italy
With C. Stead
Completed 1987

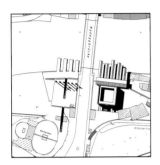

1981
Klösterliareal
Bern, Switzerland
With G. Braghieri, C. Stead
Competition

1981
Idea and Knowledge Exhibition
Milan, Italy
With D. Vitale, L. Meda
XVI Triennale

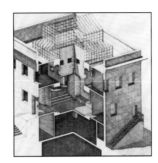

1981
Villa in the Roman Countryside
Rome, Italy
With C. Stead

1982
Zitelle Complex
Venice, Italy
With G. Geronzi, M. Adjmi
Restoration and addition

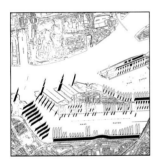

1982
Kop van Zuid Area Project
Rotterdam, Netherlands
With G. Braghieri, F. Reinhart
Competition

1982
Santini and Dominici Shoe Store
Latina, Italy
With G. Braghieri

1982
Interior with Theater
Milan, Italy
With L. Meda
Alcantara Exhibition

1982
Apartment House
Viadana, Italy
With G. Braghieri, A. Gozzi,
A. Medici, C. Castagnoli

1982
Fiera-Catena Area Project
Mantua, Italy
With G. Braghieri, COPRAT
Competition

1982
Palazzo Congressi
Milan, Italy
With M. Adjmi, G. Geronzi

1982
Civic Center
Perugia, Italy
With G. Braghieri, G. Geronzi,
M. Scheurer
Completed 1990

1983
Carlo Felice Theater
Genoa, Italy
With I. Gardella, A. Sibilla,
F. Reinhart
Competition
Awarded First Prize
Completed 1991

1983
Town Hall
Borgoricco, Italy
With M. Zancanella, M. Scheurer
Completed 1988

1983
Apartment House
Berlin, Germany
With G. Braghieri, C. Stead
Completed 1985

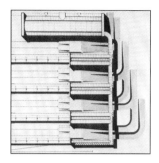

1983
San Cristoforo Train Station
Milan, Italy
With G. Braghieri, M. Oks,
M. Scheurer
In construction

1984
Techint Office Tower
Buenos Aires, Argentina
With G. Braghieri, M. Oks,
M. Scheurer, G. Ciocca
Competition

1984
Casa Aurora
Turin, Italy
With G. Braghieri, G. Ciocca,
F. Marchesotti, M. Scheurer,
L. Uva
Completed 1990

1985
Vialba Low-Cost Housing
Milan, Italy
With G. Braghieri, G. Ciocca,
COPRAT
Completed 1991

1985
Low-Cost Housing
Venice, Italy
With G. Braghieri, G. Ciocca,
G. Da Pozzo, M. Scheurer
Competition

1985
Biennale Entry Portal
Venice, Italy
Venice Biennale
With M. Lena, L. Meda
Completed 1985

1985
Centro Torri Shopping Center
Parma, Italy
With G. Braghieri, M. Baracco,
P. Digiuni, M. Scheurer
Completed 1988

1986
Domestic Theater
Milan, Italy
With M. Scheurer
XVII Triennale
Completed 1986

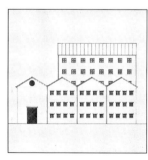

1985
Mixed-Use Restoration
Este, Italy
With M. Adjmi, M. Scheurer
In progress

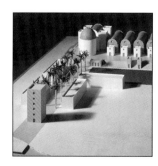

1986
School of Architecture
University of Miami
Coral Gables, Florida
With M. Adjmi
In progress

1986
Secondary School
Cantù, Italy
With G. Da Pozzo
In construction

1986
Bicocca Area Development
Milan, Italy
With A. Balzani, C. Bono,
COPRAT, S. Fera, G. Braghieri,
L. Meda, M. Scheurer, G. Da
Pozzo, D. Muraglia, C. Züber
Invited competition

1986
Alessi Tower
Lake d'Orta, Italy
With G. Da Pozzo

1986
Üsküdar Square
Istanbul, Turkey
With G. Da Pozzo, F. S. Fera,
I. Invernizzi, D. Nava,
M. Scheurer
Competition

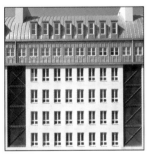

1986
La Villette Housing
Paris, France
With C. Züber, B. Huet
Completed 1991

1986
Stage Sets
Ravenna, Italy
With C. Züber
Completed 1986

1986
Molo San Vicenzo Area Project
Naples, Italy
With S. Fera

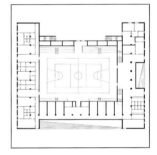

1987
Gymnasium
Olginate, Italy
With G. Da Pozzo
In construction

1987
Hotel Il Palazzo
Fukuoka, Japan
With M. Adjmi
Completed 1989

1987
Monumental Arch
Galveston, Texas
With M. Adjmi
Completed 1990

1987
Lighthouse Theater
Lake Ontario, Toronto, Canada
With M. Adjmi
Completed 1989

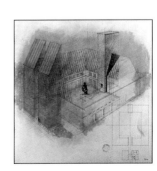

1987
Museum
Marburg, Germany
With M. Scheurer

1988
Museum of German History
Berlin, Germany
With G. Da Pozzo, S. Fera,
I. Invernizzi, D. Nava,
M. Scheurer
International Competition
Awarded First Prize
In progress

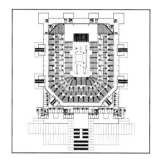

1988
Palazzo dello Sport
Milan, Italy
With B. Agostini, G. Da Pozzo,
F. Gatti, L. Imberti
In progress

1988
Lighthouse
Rotterdam, Netherlands
With U. Barbieri

1988
Duca di Milano Hotel
Milan, Italy
With G. Da Pozzo, M. Scheurer
Restoration and addition
Completed 1991

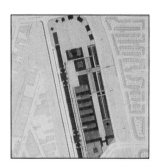

1988
The Hague Area Development
The Hague, Netherlands
With U. Barbieri, M. Scheurer,
R. Schütte

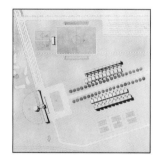

1988
Pisorno Area Development
Tirrenia, Italy
With S. Fera, M. Brandolisio,
L. Vacchelli
In progress

1988
Center for Contemporary Art
Vassivière, France
With S. Fera, X. Fabre
Completed 1991

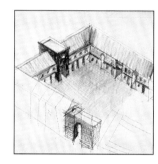

1988
Corte del Chiodo
Garbagnate, Italy
With G. Da Pozzo
In construction

1988
Pocono Pines House
Mount Pocono, Pennsylvania
With M. Adjmi
Completed 1989

1988
Centro Città Commercial Area
Gifu, Japan
With M. Adjmi, T. Horiguchi
In progress

1988
Via Croce Rossa Monument
Milan, Italy
With F. S. Fera, M. Adjmi
Completed 1990

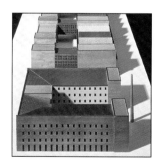

1988
GFT Comune di Settimo Torinese
Turin, Italy
With L. Trazzi
In construction

1988
Lifeguard Tower
Los Angeles, California
With M. Adjmi

1989
Yatai
Nagoya, Japan
With M. Adjmi
Japan Design Expo '89
Completed 1989

1989
Urban Monument
Zaandam, Netherlands
With U. Barbieri
Completed 1990

1988
Art Gallery
Fukuoka, Japan
With M. Adjmi

1989
Restaurant and Beer Hall
Sapporo, Japan
With M. Adjmi, H. Gutfreund
In progress

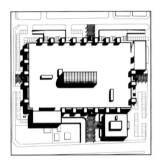

1989
UNY Shopping Center
Nagoya, Japan
With M. Adjmi, T. Horiguchi,
E. Shilliday
In progress

1989
Ambiente Showroom
Tokyo Japan
With M. Adjmi
In construction

1989
International Port and Terminal
Zeebrugge, Belgium
With C. Züber
International invited competition

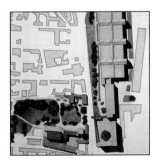

1990
University of Castellanza
Castellanza, Italy
With A. Balzani, M. Brandolisio,
L. Imberti, F. Gatti

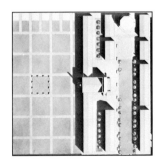

1990
Cemetery
Rozzano, Italy
With G. Da Pozzo, F. S. Fera

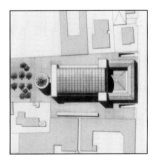

1990
Library
Seregno, Italy
Competition
Awarded First Prize

1990
Mixed-Use Complex
Turin, Italy
With C. Bolognesi, S. Fera,
L. Vacchelli

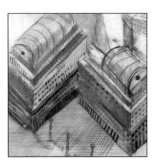

1990
Canary Wharf Office Complex
London, England
With I. Invernizzi, S. Fera,
S. Meda, C. Bolognesi
In construction

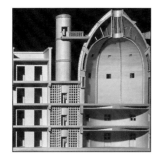

1990
Bonnefanten Museum
Maastricht, Netherlands
With G. Da Pozzo, K. Ho,
U. Barbieri, M. Kocher
In construction

1990
San Carlo alla Barona Church
Milan, Italy
With G. Da Pozzo, F. S. Fera
In progress

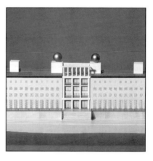

1990
Hotel Ocean
Chikura, Japan
With M. Adjmi, J. Greben
In progress

1990
Asaba Design Studio
Tokyo, Japan
With M. Adjmi, T. Horiguchi,
E. Shilliday
Completed 1991

1990
Lorenteggio Public Housing
Milan, Italy
With D. Nava, G. Da Pozzo
In progress

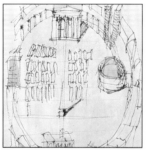

1990
Kentlands
Gaithersberg, Maryland
With M. Adjmi

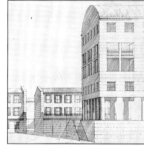

1990
Civic Center
Verbania, Italy
With G. Da Pozzo, M. Kocher
In progress

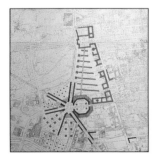

1990
*Potsdamerplatz and
Leipzigerplatz Urban Project*
Berlin, Germany
With M. Scheurer
Competition

1990
Tower and Hotel
Bordeaux, France
With G. Da Pozzo, M. Kocher,
A. Leonardi
Competition

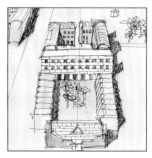

1990
Residential Complex
Città di Castello, Italy
With G. Da Pozzo, C. Dente,
D. Nava
In progress

1991
Villa Alessi
Lake Maggiore, Italy
In construction

1991
Biennale Entry Portal
Venice, Italy
Venice Biennale
With L. Trazzi, M. Kocher
In progress

1991
Palazzo del Cinema
Venice, Italy
With G. Da Pozzo, S. Fera,
L. Meda, M. Scheurer
In progress

1991
Palazzo Congressi
Milan, Italy
With L. Trazzi, M. Scheurer
In progress

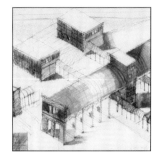

1991
IP Gas Station
Prototype

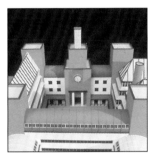

1991
UBS Office Complex
Lugano, Switzerland
With M. Scheurer
Competition

1991
Disney Office Complex
Orlando, Florida
With M. Adjmi, E. Shilliday,
J. Greben
In progress

1991
La Torre del Sole
Makuhari, Japan
With G. Da Pozzo, T. Horiguchi,
Y. Kato, S. Meda
In progress

1991
National Museum Of Scotland
Edinburgh, Scotland
With C. Stead
Competition

1991
City Center
Kuala Lumpur, Malaysia
With M. Adjmi, C. Stead,
L. Trazzi
Competition
In progress

1991
Housing Complex
Bari, Italy
With M. Brandolisio, M. Tadini
In construction

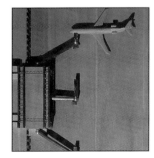

1991
Linate Airport
Milan, Italy
With G. Da Pozzo,
M. Brandolisio, S. Meda,
M. Kocher
In construction

1991
Art Academy
Bronx, New York
With M. Adjmi
In progress

FURNITURE AND PRODUCT DESIGN

1979
Scientific Theater

1979
Capitolo Sofa
With L. Meda

1980
Tea Service
For Alessi

1982
Cassettiera
For Longoni

1982
Armadio Cabina
For Longoni

1982
Teatro Chair
For Unifor

1983
Sedia Chair
For Longoni

1983
Credenza
For Longoni

1984
La Conica Espresso Maker
For Alessi

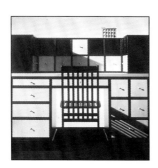

1985
Papyro Writing Desk
For Unifor

1985
Rivielo Table
For Up + Up

1985
Press Filter Coffee Maker
For Alessi

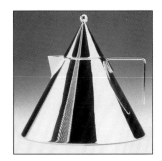

1986
La Conica Water Kettle
For Alessi

1987
Il Momento Watch
For Alessi

1987
Milano Chair
For Molteni & C.

1987
Carteggio
For Molteni & C.

1988
La Cupola Espresso Maker
For Alessi

1988
Sardinian Carpet

1989
Cabine dell'Elba

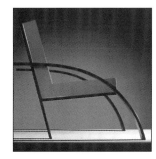

1989
Parigi Lounge Chair
For Unifor

1989
Street Lamp

1990
Jewelry
For Acme

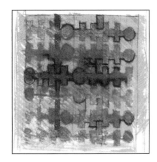

1991
Fabric
For Design Tex

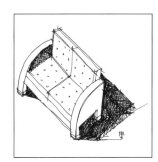

1991
Providence Sofa
For Unifor

BIOGRAPHY

1931

Born 3 May, Milan.

1940

Moves to Lake Como with the outbreak of war.

Attends the school of the Padre Somaschi, then the archiepiscopal college Alessandro Volta in Lecco.

1949

Begins studies at Milan Polytechnic.

1955

Delegate to congress of the International Union of Students, Rome.

Continues studies and begins working with Ernesto Rogers on the architecture magazine *Casabella-Continuità*.

Travels to Prague and the Soviet Union.

1956

Begins working with Ignazio Gardella and Marco Zanuso on various exhibitions, including "Pionieri dell'Aeronautica."

1959

Graduates from Milan Polytechnic.

Joins the Milan editorial staff of *Il Contemporanco*.

1961

Assistant to Ludovico Quaroni at the School of Urban Studies in Arezzo, and to Carlo Aymonino at the Institute of Architecture, University of Venice.

1964

Becomes editor of *Casabella-Continuità*.

1965

Appointed professor at Milan Polytechnic.

1966

Publishes *The Architecture of the City* (first edition) in Italy.

1971

Completes design for the San Cataldo Cemetery competition, the first collaboration with Gianni Braghieri.

1972

Appointed Professor of Design at the Federal Polytechnic of Zurich.

1973

Director of the International Architecture section of the Milan Triennale.

Appointed full professor at the University of Venice.

Makes the film *Ornamento e Delitto*.

1976

Director of the International Seminar at Santiago de Compostela.

Appointed Mellon Professor at the Cornell University School of Architecture, Ithaca, New York.

Visiting professor at the Cooper Union for the Advancement of Science and Art, New York.

1978

Starts association with the Institute for Architecture and Urban Studies, New York.

1979

Elected member of the Academy of San Luca.

1980

Visiting professor at the Yale University School of Architecture, New Haven, Connecticut.

1981

Awarded First Prize in the IBA competition for the development of Block No. 10, between Kochstrasse and Friedrichstrasse, Berlin, Germany.

Publishes *A Scientific Autobiography* (first edition) in America.

1983

Appointed director of the architectural section of the Venice Biennale.

Visiting professor at the Harvard University Graduate School of Design, Cambridge, Massachusetts.

1984

Awarded First Prize in the competition for the Carlo Felice Theater, Genoa, Italy.

1986

Establishes office in New York with Morris Adjmi.

1987

Establishes office in The Hague with Umberto Barbieri.

1988

Nominated Honorary Fellow of the American Institute of Architects.

Awarded First Prize in the design competition for the Museum of German History.

1989

Establishes office in Tokyo with Toyota Horiguchi.

Delivers Walter Gropius Lecture at the Harvard University Graduate School of Design, Cambridge, Massachusetts.

1990

Awarded the Pritzker Prize for Architecture.

1991

American Institute of Architects Honor Award for the design of Hotel Il Palazzo in Fukuoka, Japan.

EXHIBITIONS

1960

"XII Triennale di Milano," Milan, Italy.

1963

"Aspetti dell'arte contemporanea," L'Aquila, Italy.

1967

"Presentazione a Aldo Rossi," Centro Arte viva di Trieste, Italy.

1972

"Milano 70/70" at the Museo Poldi Pezzoli, Milan, Italy.

"Italian Architecture in the Sixties," ETH, Zurich, Switzerland.

1973

"Aldo Rossi—Bauten Projekte," ETH, Zurich, Switzerland and Ecole Polytechnique de Lausanne, France

1974

"Aldo Rossi/Louis Kahn/John Hejduk," University of Stuttgart, Germany.

"Aldo Rossi, Architektur des Rationalismus," IDZ, Berlin, Germany.

1975

"Arquitectura y Rationalismo. Aldo Rossi + 21 Arquitectos Españoles," Palau de la Virreina, Barcelona, Spain.

1976

"Aldo Rossi architetto," Galleria Solferino, Milan, Italy.

"Disegni per un'architettura," Milan, Italy.

"Dortmunder Architekturausstellung," Museum am Ostwall, Dortmund, Germany.

"Europa-America. Centro Storico-suburbio," Venice Biennale, Venice, Italy.

1977

"Architecture I," Leo Castelli Gallery, New York.

"Abraham, Eisenman, Hejduk, Rossi," Cooper Union, New York.

"Assenza/Presenza," Galleria Solferino, Milan, Italy.

1978

"Aldo Rossi in America, 1976–1979," Institute for Architecture and Urban Studies, New York.

"Mostra Progetti per l'area direzionale di Firenze," Florence, Italy.

"I nodi della rappresentazione," Pinacoteca Comunale, Ravenna, Italy.

"Roma Interotta," Rome, Italy.

1979

"Aldo Rossi in America," Ballenford Books, Toronto, Canada.

1980

"Aldo Rossi, Projects: Monuments of Venice," Max Protetch Gallery, New York.

"Autonomous Architecture: 'The Work of Eight Contemporary Architects,'" Fogg Art Museum, Harvard University, Cambridge, Massachusetts.

1981

International Berlin Exhibition (IBA), Berlin, Germany.

1983

"Aldo Rossi, Architecture, Projects, and Drawings," Institute of Contemporary Arts, London, England.

"Opere Recenti," Palazzina dei Giardini, Modena, Italy and Rocca Paolina, Perugia.

1985

"Aldo Rossi—La Conica," Galerie Van Rooy, Amsterdam, Netherlands.

"Aldo Rossi," Arkitektur Museet, Copenhagen, Denmark; Academie van Bouwkurest, Rotterdam, Netherlands; Groningen Museum, Groningen, Netherlands; Museum de Beyerd, Breda, Netherlands; Musée du Château du Ducs de Bretagne, Nantes, France; Arc. En. Reve., Bordeaux, France.

1986

"Aldo Rossi," Cultureel Centrum de Singel, Antwerp, Belgium; Arketektur Museet, Stockholm, Sweden; Ministero di Obras Publicas y Urbanismo, Madrid, Spain.

"Aldo Rossi: Disegni di Architettura, 1967–1985," Galleria Albertina, Turin, Italy.

1987

Collegio Architetti Catalogna, Barcelona, Spain.

Collegio Architetti Balcari, Palma de Mayorca, Spain.

"Aldo Rossi, Architect," York City Art Gallery, York, Great Britain and Royal Institute for British Architects, London, England.

1988

"Aldo Rossi: Other Towers," Gallery for Architecture, Los Angeles, California.

"Aldo Rossi," Architecture Museum, Moscow, USSR.

1989

"Aldo Rossi, USA," Max Protetch Gallery, New York.

"Frammenti," Artium Art Gallery, Fukuoka, Japan.

"Aldo Rossi: Recent Drawings and Projects," Ballenford Books, Toronto, Canada.

"Tessiture Sarde," Deutschen Architekturmuseum, Frankfurt, Germany.

"New School of Architecture Exhibition," University of Miami, Coral Gables, Florida.

"Aldo Rossi, Deutsches Historisches Museum," Galerie für Arkitektur, Berlin, Germany.

1990

"Aldo Rossi: Three Projects in North America," Parish Gallery, Rice University, Houston, Texas.

"Aldo Rossi: Opera Grafica, " Antiquariaat Vlotmans, The Hague, Netherlands.

"The Analogous Landscape," N. No. O Gallery, Dallas, Texas.

1991

"Aldo Rossi par Aldo Rossi," Centre Georges Pompidou, Paris, France.

"Aldo Rossi/Tim Rollins & K.O.S.," Rhona Hoffman Gallery, Chicago, Illinois.

Selected Bibliography

1959

ROGERS, E. N. "L'evoluzione dell'architettura, risposta al custode dei frigidairs." *CBC* 268: 131–132, now in *Editoriali di architettura*. Turin, 1968.

1960

SANTINI, P. C. *Sul progetto per la zona Farini a Milano*. Milan. [Catalogue of the XII Milan Triennale.]

1961

OREFICE, R. "Trucco e galateo di una `Aufklarung' milanese." *Superfici* 1: 44–45.

1962

TENTORI, F. "L'idea di grattacielo." *CBC* 288: 40.

1964

POLESELLO, G. U. "Questa Triennale e l'architettura discoperta." *CBC* 290: 40, 42.

1966

AYMONINO, C. "L'architettura della città." *Rinascita* 27: 21–22.
BULGHERONI, P. Review of *L'architettura della città* in *Città e Società* 6: 108–111.
GRASSI, G. Review of *L'architettura della città* in *Architettura libri* 2/3: 95–106.
POLESELLO, G. U. "Problemi di teoria dell'architettura." *Concorso per la ricostruzione del Teatro Paganini a Parma*, 5, 9. Venice.
ROSSI, ALDO. *L'Architettura della città*. Padua: Marsilio Editori.
SCALVINI, M. L. Review of *L'architettura della città* in *Op. Cit.* 7: 78–83.

1967

GREGOTTI, V. Review of *L'architettura della città* in *Il Verri* 23: 172–173.
SEMERANI, L. *Presentazione a Aldo Rossi*. [Catalogue to the exhibition at the Centro Arte Viva di Trieste.]

1968

TAFURI, M. *Teorie e storia dell'architettura*, passim. Bari.
TENTORI, F. "Un processo al ruolo dell'architetto." [Review of L. Quaroni's *La Torre di Babele*] *Comunità* 153: 136–139.

1969

CORTESI, A. "Un'architettura della città di Parma. Letture morfologiche." *Atti del convegno sul Settecento parmense*, 315–329. Parma.
GREGOTTI, V. *Orientamenti nuovi nell'architettura italiana*. Milan.
LANGE, S. *Problemi di storiografia e progettazione architettonica*, 89. Milan.
PATETTA, L. *Dizionario Enciclopedico di Architettura e Urbanistica*, vol 5. Rome, s.v. "Aldo Rossi." 342–343.

1970

BONFANTI, E. "Elementi e costruzione. Note sull'architettura di Aldo Rossi." *Controspazio* 10: 19–28.
SICA, P. *L'immagine della città da Sparta a Las Vegas*, 208ff. Bari.
TERRANOVA, A. "Storiografia e teoria dell'urbanistica." *Storia dell'arte* 7/8: 306–307.

1971

CID, A. TARRAGO. "Prólogo a la edición española." in *A.R. La arquitectura de la ciudad*, 9–42. Barcelona.
DARDI, C. *Il gioco sapiente*, 48–53. Padua.
SCOLARI, M. "Un contributo per la fondazione di una scienza urbana." *Controspazio* 7/8: 4, 47.

1972

DE SETA, C. Review of *Milano 70/70, un secolo d'arte, vols 1, 2, 3. Op. Cit.* 25: 117–118.
FOLIN, M. *La città capitale*, 15–52. Bari.
NICOLINI, R. "Rendita e creazione di plusvalore nel settore edile in Italia dalla ricostruzione ad oggi." *Controspazio* 8: 52–53.
PORTOGHESI, P. "Città dei vivi, città dei morti." *Controspazio* 10: 2–3.
RAGGI, F. "Alternative per il concetto di monumentalità." *Casabella* 373: 21–26.
REICHLIN, B. and F. REINHART. "Zu einer Ausstellung der Projekte von Aldo Rossi an der ETH, Zurich." *Werk* 4: 182–183.
ZEVI, B. "Una necropoli di asettiche stravaganze." *Cronache di architettura* 7 (Bari): 389.

1973

AA.VV. "Saggi." in *Architettura razionale*, XV Triennale, International Architecture Section, Milan.
AA.VV. Monograph issue on the XVth Triennale, *Controspazio* 6.
Aldo Rossi, John Hejduk. Zurich: Eidgen ossische Technische Hochschule Architekturabteilung. [Catalogue to the exhibition at the Department of Architecture of the ETH Zurich: 3–14 December 1973: Introduction by Colin Rowe.]
BONFANTI, E. AND M. PORTA, *Città, museo e architettura*. Florence.
BONICALZI, R. "Loos, un maestro per i neorazionalisti." *Casabella* 382: 14–15.
BRANZI, A. "Si scopron le tombe." *Casabella* 383: 10–11.
COLQUHOUN, A. "Rational architecture." *Architectural Design* 6: 365–370.
DE ANGELIS, A. "XV Triennale."

Op. Cit. 29: 5–63.
DEGANELLO, P. "1968, XIV Triennale, della contestazione, 1973 XV Triennale, della restaurazione." *Casabella* 385: 30–31.
GERMAN, G. "Denkmalpflege und Städtebau." *Neue Zürcher Zeitung* 68 (11 March): 51.
GRESLERI, G. "E le ossa di Etienne Boullée si voltarono nella tomba ovvero così si muore a Modena." *Parametro* 15: 40–41.
KOENIG, G. K. "Una lettera di Giovanni Klaus Koenig sull'accademismo della cosidetta 'architettura razionale' propugnata dalla XV Triennale." *L'architettura—cronache e storia* 218: 256–257.
MOCCIA, F. D. AND I. FERRARO. "Elementi di una tendenza dell'architettura italian." *Op. Cit.* 29: 36–54.
MONEO, R. *La idea de la arquitectura en Rossi y el cemeterio de Modena*. 3–23. Barcelona.
MOSCHINI, F. "Architettura razionale." *Bolletino della Biblioteca della Facoltà di Architettura di Roma* (December).
RAGGI, F. "15 Triennale 15." *Casabella* 385: 18–19.
RYKWERT, J. "XV Triennale." *Domus* 530: 1–17.
SIOLA, U. "'Materiali' di architettura." *Quaderni dell'istituto di metodologia architettonica*, passim. Naples.
STEINMANN, M. "Architektur," 3–5. Zurich. [Introduction to the catalogue of the exhibition *Aldo Rossi, Bauten, Projekte*.]
TASSI, R. "La linea retta è atea e immortale." *Il Mondo*, 18 October.
ZEVI, B. "Con Piacentini, in nome di Lenin." *L'Espresso*, 14 October.

1974

AA. VV. *Architettura e politica*, edited by Alberto Samonà, 141–171. Bologna.
ANGELETTI, P. "La periferia della grande città: definizione e caratteri." in P. A. et al. *Elementi di costruzione della città moderna—La periferia operaia a Roma negli anni trenta*, 5–7. Rome.
CUOMO, A. "La morte dell'artistico in architettura." *NAC* 12: 18–19.
GERMAN, G. "Städtebau ohne tabula rasa." *Neue Zürcher Zeitung* (5 March): 25.
NICOLINI, R. "Note su Aldo Rossi." *Controspazio* 4: 48–49.
QUETGLAS, J. "Rossi: Dos Construcciónes (Casa Bay, Gallaratese 2)." *Arquitecturas bis* 4: 5–9.

STEINMANN, M. "Das Laubenganghaus." *Archithese* 12: 4–5.

1975

AYMONINO, C. *Il significato della città*. Bari.
CID, S. TARRAGO. "Aldo Rossi y la construcción dialectica de la arquitectura." *Construcción de la Ciudad 2C* 2: 2–7. [Monograph issue dedicated to Aldo Rossi.]
DAL CO, F. AND M. MANIERI ELIA. "La géneration de l'incertitude." *L'architecture d'aujourd'hui* 181: 48–49.
FABBRI, M. *Le ideologie degli urbanisti nel dopoguerra*, 181–187. Bari.
MOSCHINI, F. Review of *Scritti scelti su l'architettura e la città 1956–1972*, in *Bollettino della Biblioteca della Facoltà di Architettura di Roma* (December).
NICOLINI, R. "Oltre la coscienza risentita." *Controspazio* 2: 2–3.
RAY, S. "Pubblicazioni universitarie." *Paese Sera*, 4 July.
SEMERANI, L. "Crisi e continuità della città borghese." *Controspazio* 2: 4–18.
TAFURI, M. "L'architecture dans le Boudoir: the language of criticism and the criticism of language." *Oppositions* 3: 42–46.

1976

CONTESSI, G. *Tra manierismo e classicismo*, 1–12. [Duplicated for the exhibition *Aldo Rossi architetto* at the Galleria Solferino, Milan.]
FRAGO, S. AND MALO DE MOLINA, "Aldo Rossi, Una alternativa progressista para la arquitectura." *Triunfo* 719: 49.
KLOTZ, H. "Architektur auf dem Wege zur Form." *Frankfurter Rundschau* 118.
MONEO, R. "Aldo Rossi: the idea of architecture and the Modena Cemetery." *Oppositions* 5: 1–30.
———. "Arquitectura y Racionalismo." *Construcción de la Ciudad 2C* 8: 21–22.
NICOLINI, R. "Architettura e tipo." *Controspazio* 2: 96–97.
PORTOGHESI, P. "Due tre case che mi vanno a pennello." *Tempo* 16: 96–97.
SAVI, V. "Fortuna de Aldo Rossi." *Construcción de la Ciudad 2C* 5, 6–11. [Monograph issue dedicated to Aldo Rossi.]
SAVI, V. *L'architettura di Aldo Rossi*. Milan: F. Angeli.
STEWART, D. "The expression of ideological function in the architecture of Aldo Rossi." *A + U* 5: 107–111. [Monograph issue on Aldo Rossi.]
TAFURI, M. "Ceci n'est pas une ville." *Lotus International* 13: 10–13.

TAFURI, M. and F. DAL CO. *Architettura contemporanea*, 415–416. Milan.

1977

ARIS, C. MARTI. "Prólogo a la edición castellana." in *Aldo Rossi para una arquitectura de tendencia. Ecritos: 1956–1972*, ix–xv. Barcelona.

AYMONINO, C. "Une architecture de l'optimisme." *L'architecture d'aujourd'hui* 190: 46.

———. *Carlo Aymonino, Aldo Rossi*. Tokyo: A.D.A. Edita.

———. *Housing Complex at the Gallaratese Quarter, Milan, Italy 1969–1974*. Edited and photographed by Yukio Futagawa; Text by Pierluigi Nicolin. Tokyo: A.D.A. Edita Tokyo.

BARILLI, R. "L'architetto diviso in due." *L'Espresso* 1.

CHEMETOV, P., A. KOPP, B. QUEYSANNE, G. GRASSI, AND B. HUET. "Formalisme Réalisme." *L'architecture d'aujourd'hui* 190: 35–36.

IRACE, F. "Modello dell'assenza." *Assenza/Presenza, un'ipotesi di lettura per l'architettura*. Bologna.

PALLAVICINI, R. "Progettare Roma per gioco." *L'Unità* (20 June).

PORTOGHESI, P. "Ancora paura dell'architettura." *Controspazio* 6: 2.

SAVI, V. "Relazione al progetto per il Centro Direzionale di Firenze." *Controspazio* 6: 7–11; and *Parametro* 63: 20–22.

SILVETTI, J. "The beauty of shadows." *Oppositions* 9: 43–61.

1978

CONTESSI, G. "I nodi della rappresentazione." *La tradizione del nuovo* 3: 13–22.

CUOMO, A. "Architettura e negatività." *Controspazio* 4: 42–47.

DAL CO, F. "Criticism and design." *Oppositions* 13: 1–16.

———. "Kritiek en ontwerp." *Kunstgeschiedenis en kritiek* (Nijmegen): 107–142.

DAVIS, D. "Paper Buildings." *Newsweek* 6.2: 54–55.

JENCKS, C. "Irrational rationalism, the rats since 1960." in *Rationalists* edited by D. Sharp, 212–214. London.

KRIER, L. "La reconstruction d'un language collectif," 52. Brussels. [Catalogue of the exhibition *Architecture rationelle*.]

MOSCHINI, F. "Disegni per costruire." *L'architetto* 9: 50–53.

NARPOZZI, MARINO, GIULIO DUBBINI, AND ALDO DE POLI, eds. *Aldo Rossi: Die Venedischen Stadte*. Zurich.

PORTOGHESI, P. "Firenze visitata in sogno." *La Repubblica*, 29 March.

THERMES, L. "Il Nolli, dodici architetti ed una città." *Controspazio* 4: 2–4; republished in *Arquitectura* 214: 8–9.

1979

"The Architecture of the City: An Interview with Aldo Rossi." *Skyline* 2, no. 4 (September): 4–5.

BENINCASA, C. "Aldo Rossi. Galleria Pan/Via del Fiume." *Corriere della Sera*, 9 June, 16.

BONICALZI, R. *Intervista ad Aldo Rossi*. Pescara.

BRENNER, KLAUS THEO. "Die faszination des architektonischen Rituals." *Transparent* 10, nos. 5–6: [4]–25.

"Cemetery in Modena, project, 1979; Architects: Aldo Rossi with Gianni Braghieri." Text in Italian and English. *Lotus International* 25: 62–65.

CUOMO, A. "L'impegno negativo del disegno d'architettura. E ancora possibile progettare?" *L'Avanti*, 17 June, xii.

DAL CO, FRANCESCO. "Ora tutto questo è perduto. Il teatro del Mondo di Aldo Rossi alla Biennale di Venezia [Now This Is Lost: The Theater of the World by Aldo Rossi at the Venice Biennale]." Text in Italian and English. *Lotus International* 25: 66–74.

DUNSTER, D. "Books. *Aldo Rossi: Projects and Drawings, 1962–1979*." *Architectural Design* 8–9: 218–219.

FRAMPTON, KENNETH, ed. *Aldo Rossi in America, 1976–1979*. Introduction by Peter Eisenman. New York: Institute for Architecture and Urban Studies. [Exhibition: 25 March–14 April, 1976; 19 September–30 October 1979.]

KANTZBERGER, P. AND D. STEINER. "Diese ist lange her Beerkungen zu Aldo Rossi." *Um Bau* 1 (December): 18–30.

LAINE, CHRISTIAN K. "The Work of Aldo Rossi." *Crit* 5 (Spring): 22–23. [Address by and interview with Aldo Rossi.]

MINERVINO, F. "Quando il progetto è opera d'arte. I disegni dell'architetto Aldo Rossi." *Corriere della Sera*, 4 July, 9.

MONEO, R. "Le obra reciente de Aldo Rossi: dos reflexiones." *Construcción de la Ciudad 2C* 14: 38–39.

MOSCHINI, FRANCESCO, ed. *Aldo Rossi. Progetti e Disegni. 1962–1979*. [*Aldo Rossi. Projects and Drawings. 1962–1979*]. Italian and English. Florence: Stiav and New York: Rizzoli.

PAGLIERO, A. "L'architetto preferisce ispirarsi a De Chirico." *L'Unità* (8 May): 3.

PORTOGHESI, P. "Recenti progetti di Aldo Rossi: Il Teatro del Mondo." *Controspazio* 5/6 (September–December): 2–27.

"Rossi + Aymonino + Braghieri: Two Projects." Text in Japanese. *A + U* 100 (January): 67–74.

ROSSI, A. "Il prestigio del teatro. Architettura: Il teatrino scientifico." *Gran Bazaar* 2 (May–June): 74–81.

TAFURI, M. "Il teatro della memoria. Disegni e incisioni di Aldo Rossi." *Paese Sera*, 22 April, 18.

VITALE, D. "Ritrovamenti, traslazioni, analogie. Progetti e frammenti di Aldo Rossi ["Inventions, Translations, Analogies: Projects and Fragments by Aldo Rossi]." Text in Italian and English. *Lotus International* 25: 55–61.

1980

AA. VV. "Forum Discussion." *Harvard Architectural Review* 1 (Spring).

DAL CO, FRANCESCO. "Aldo Rossi's Teatro del Mondo." *A + U* 114, no. 3 (March): 3–30.

FILLER, MARTIN. "Rossi Secco and Rossi Dolce." *Art in America* 68, no. 3 (March): 100–108.

FRAMPTON, KENNETH. *Modern Architecture: A Critical History*, 290, 291. London.

GRANDI, M. AND A. PRACCHI. *Milano. Guida all'architettura moderna*, 350–352. Bologna.

KRAFINGER, O. AND D. STEINER. "Protokoll zur Architektur Biennale in Venedig." *Um Bau* 3.

LAHUERTA, J. J. "Personajes de Aldo Rossi." *Carrer de la Ciutat* 12.

LAMPUGNANI, V. MAGNAGHI. "Die Eigenwillge Muse." *Um Bau* 3: 39–53.

LIBESKIND, DANIEL. "Deus ex Machina/Machina ex Deo. Aldo Rossi's Theatre of the World." *Oppositions* 21: 1–23.

MORTON, DAVID. "Italian Rationalism: Rossi and Aymonino: Tendenza." *Progressive Architecture* 61, no. 10 (October): 49–[65].

PLANAS, S. "El teatro del Mondo o el Lenguaje de las cosas mudas." *Carrer de la Ciutat* 12: 5–15.

PORTOGHESI, PAOLO. *Dopo l'architettura moderna*. Bari.

———. "Il Teatro del Mondo." *Controspazio* 5/6.

"Residential Unit in the Gallaratese Quarter, Milan, Italy 1969–70; Architect: Aldo Rossi." *Harvard Architectural Review* 1 (Spring):

210–211, 214–217. [Presented as part of a forum discussion: "Beyond the Modern Movement" (1977).]

SAVI, VITTORIO. "Biennale '79. Reportage dal 'Teatro del Mondo.' Un'architettura galleggiante di A. Rossi e il suo viaggio sulla laguna di Venezia." *Casa Vogue* 102 (January): 94–101.

SEKLER, EDUARD F. "Formalism and the Polemical Use of History: Thoughts on the Recent Rediscovery of Revolutionary Classicism." *Harvard Architecture Review* 1 (Spring): [32]–39.

SEMERANI, L. *Progetti per una città*. Milan.

SILVETTI, JORGE. "On Realism in Architecture." *Harvard Architecture Review* 1 (Spring).

TAFURI, MANFREDO. "L'ephemère est eternel. Aldo Rossi à Venezia." Text in Italian and English. *Domus* 602 (January): 7–11.

———. *La sfera e il labirinto. Avanguardie e architettura da Piranesi agli anni 70*, 330–333. 335–340, 344, 345, 363, 368. Turin.

1981

AIROLDI, R. "I progetti di concorso per Kochstrasse." *Casabella* 471 (July–August): 36–39.

BANDINI, MICHA. "Aldo Rossi." *AA Files* 1, no. 1 (Winter): 106–111.

BERNI, L. "Ampliamento del Cimitero di Modena." *Panorama* 777 (9 March): 37.

BOHNING, I. *Autonome Architektur und Partezipatorisches Bauen. Zwei Architekturkonzepte*. Zurich.

BRAGHIERI, GIANNI, ed. *Aldo Rossi*. Bologna: Zanichelli and Barcelona: Editorial Gustavo Gili.

CIORRA, P. "Né risotto, né post-moderno per la Triennale di Milano." *Il Manifesto*, 16 December, 4–5.

CONFORTI, CLAUDIA. "Il Gallaratese di Aymonino e Rossi, 1967–1972." *Officina Edizioni* (December): 49–64.

DORFLES, GILLO. "On the Waterfront: Casa del Portuale, Naples, 1980; Architect: Aldo Loris Rossi." *Domus* 617 (May): 10–13.

GRAHAM, DAN. "Not Post-Modernism: History as Against Historicism." *Artforum* 20, no. 4 (December): 50–58.

JONES, E. "Review of books. L'Architecture Assassinée or Architecture Abandonnée?" *International Architect* 4, nos. 1–4: 46.

PIZZIGONI, A. "Aldo Rossi. Un'architettura senza aggettivi. Una mostra a Milano." *Bergamo-oggi*, 26 June.

POLIN, G. "Plastici di Aldo Rossi." *Casabella* 472 (September): 5.
PORTOGHESI, PAOLO. "In Germania il migliore è il signor Rossi." *Europeo* 9 (2 March): 73.
———. "Progettare o disegnare?" *Europeo* 27 (6 July): 84–85.
RADICE, B. "Caffettiere Grandi Firme." *Casa Vogue* 125 (December): 212–217.
RIVA, V. AND G. P. SEGALA, "Il concorso per la ricostruzione di Berlino Ovest. Stanotte ho sognato una città." *Europeo* 9 (2 March): 70–73.
ROSSI, ALDO. *A Scientific Autobiography*. Translation by Lawrence Venuti. Postscript by Vincent Scully. Cambridge, MA and London, England: The MIT Press [Oppositions Books].
SANTINI, PIER CARLO. "Dall'Utopia all Realta: La Recente Attivita di Aldo Loris Rossi." Text in Italian and English. *Ottagono* 16, no. 60 (March): 20–27.
STEFANI, A. "Un'idea di teatro—Roma A.A.M./COOP." *Segno* 19 (January–February): 29–30.

1982

"Aldo Rossi and 21 Works." Photographs by Giacinta Manfredi and Maria Ida Biggi. *A + U* (Tokyo) (November) extra edition: 3–232.
"Aldo Rossi and Paolo Portoghesi [inteview]." *AD Architectural Design* 52, nos. 1–2: 13–17.
"Aldo Rossi: Modena Cemetery, Italy, 1971 and 1977." *Architectural Design* 52, no. 5–6: 110–113.
BARLETTA, R. "Panorama d'architettura alla Triennale. L'idea Classica? Rieccola." *Corriere della Sera*, 17 January, 14.
BERNI, L. "Scuola media a Broni [Pavia]." *Panorama* 845 (28 June): 31.
BUCHANAN, PETER. "Aldo Rossi: Silent Monuments." *Architectural Review* 172, no. 1028 (October): 48–[54].
"Capitolo—un divano di due amici: progetto di Luca Meda e Aldo Rossi, Molteni & C." *Rassegna* (9 March): 110–111.
CUOMO, A. "Il piacere della critica del piacere." *Figure* (Rome) 1, no. 1 (May): 94–101.
DE BONIS, A. *Aldo Rossi: Teatro del Mondo*. ed. by M. Brusatin and A. Prandi. Venice: Biblioteca delle Arti I and Cluva (first edition).
DONDA, E. "Rilevazioni su di un luogo analogico." *Il piccolo Hans* 35: 153–175.
DOUMATO, LAMIA. *Aldo Rossi*. Monticello, Illinois: Vance Bibliographies.

HELFENSTEIN, H. "Lombardische Bilder—Zu Zeichnungen von Aldo Rossi." *Archithese* 2: 29–35.
JENCKS, CHARLES. "The Blue of the Sky: Modena Cemetery, 1971 and 1972." *AD Architectural Design* 52, 1–2: 39–41.
JOHNSON, EUGENE J. "What Remains of Man—Aldo Rossi's Modena Cemetery." *Society of Architectural Historians Journal* 41, no. 1 (March): 38–54.
MOSCHINI, FRANCESCO. "Aldo Rossi: La casa della vita [The House of Life: Design for Villa in Roman Countryside]". Text in Italian and English. *Domus* 629 (June): 13–15.
MOSTOLLER, MICHAEL. "Canaletto and Aldo Rossi: The Relationship Between Painting and Architectural Creation." *Modulus*: 78–84.
ODONI, G. "Uno stand e un negozio per Santini & Dominici. Come elementi di un paesaggio urbano." *Casa Vogue* 134 (October): 198–203.
PORTOGHESI, PAOLO. "Quella casa è un personaggio." *Europeo* 40 (4 October): 87.
"Presents of the Past: Revisiting the 1980 Venice Biennale." *Architectural Design* 52, no. 1–2: 1–24.
RAGGI, F. "Colloquio di Modo: com'è vecchia la città. Colloquio con Aldo Rossi sul Sud America, il disegno, la caffettiera, il cinema e l'architettura [interview]" and "La tendenze di Aldo." *Modo* 52 (September): 32–35.
ROSSI, A. AND D. MAZZOLENI. "I live: di I decorate." Text in Italian and English. *Domus* 628 (May): 43–47.
ROSSI, A. *The Architecture of the City* [English edition of *L'architettura della città*]. Translation by Diane Ghirardo and Joan Ockman. Introduction by Peter Eisenman. Cambridge, MA and London, England: The MIT Press. [Oppositions Books].
———. "Modernism's Trajectory: Rossi on Loos." *Skyline* (April): 18–25.
———. "The Tower of Memories." *Domus* 626 (March): 28–29.
SAVI, VITTORIO. "Dalle Triennale di Milano IDEA. Una breve retrospettiva di mostre alla Triennale, dagli anni '30 a oggi. Una visita al più recente allestimento aldorossiano." *Casa Vogue* 129 (April): 204–209, 260–261.
SISTO, M. "Mostre: Sei grandi firme per Alcantara." *Casa Vogue* 133 (September): 384–387.
TAFURI, M. "Architettura italiana

1944–1981." *Storia dell'arte italiana*, part 2, vol. 3 (*Il Novecento*), 541–545. Turin.
TRAHEY, J. "The Drawings of Aldo Rossi." *Fifth Column* 3, no. 1 (Autumn): 33–35.

1983

ABERCROMBIE, Stanley. "Italy: The First Built Parts of a Cemetery Famous Before Building Began." French summary p. 214; Spanish summary, pp. 230, 232. *Architecture: The AIA Journal* 72, no. 8 (August): [162]–167.
Aldo Rossi, special ed. from the *University of Oregon School of Architecture Journal* 12, no. 5 (March).
Aldo Rossi. Architecture, Projects & Drawings. London: Institute of Comtemporary Arts. [Exhibition catalogue: 14 January–20 February 1983.]
CARRARI, G. "Parla Aldo Rossi un solitario…molto 'trainante' [interview]." *Costruire per Abitare* 11 (July–August): 85–87.
DAL CO, F. "L'architettura pervicace. Aldo Rossi e la sorpresa. Appunti su una mostra recente." *Casa Vogue* 144 (September): 350–355.
DAL CO, F. "La macchina modenese di Aldo Rossi. Ostinazione e progetto." *Il Manifesto*, 9 July, 7.
DE POLI, A., N. NARPOZZI, T. ROZE, AND C. COSNEAU, "Aldo Rossi: Théâtre, Ville, Architecture." in *303 Recherches et Créations* (Nantes).
DEL POZZO, "Biennale architettura. I segni del Signor Rossi." *Panorama* 902 no. 11 (1 August): 76–77.
FERRARIS, M. "La città in negativo." *Lotus International* 38: 40.
"La scatola delle costruzioni—La nuova scuola media di Broni." *Lotus International* 37: 67–73.
LUCARELLI, N. "I grandi architetti: la primula Rossi [interview]." *Casaviva* 11, no. 177 (September): 102–109, 252–257.
LUPANO, MARIO AND VITTORIO SAVI, eds. *Aldo Rossi: Opere Recenti*. Modena: Panini. [Exhibition catalogue: Palazzina dei Giardini, Modena from 25 June–5 September 1983 and Rocca Paolina, Perugia in October 1983.]
PASSERI, A. "Aldo Rossi: La Scuola Media di Broni." Text in Italian and English. *Eupalino* 1 (Winter): 8–11.
ROSSI, ALDO. *Aldo Rossi. Selected Writings and Projects*. edited and designed by John O'Regan, et al. London: Architectural Design; Dublin: Gandon Editions.
———. *Il Libro Azzurro: I Miei

Progetti 1981*. Zurich: Jamileh Weber Galerie-Edition.
SAVI, VITTORIO. "Il cimitero aldorossiano: traccia di racconto critico [The Aldorossian Cemetery: Outline of a Critical Account]." *Lotus International* 38: 30–43; in the same issue: "Il cubo e il portico." 36–43.
SCHILLING, R. "Architettura rossiana." *Tages Anzeiger Magazin* 20/21 (May).

1984

"Aldo Rossi's Continuing Exploration of Typology and Morphology." Report on a 5 January 1984 lecture at Harvard University. *GSD News/Harvard University Graduate School of Design* 12, no. 4 (March–April): 7.
"Aldo Rossi's Lecture in Tokyo." Text in Japanese. *A + U* 12, no. 171 (December): 19–30.
"Autonomous Architecture: 'The Work of Eight Contemporary Architects'" *Harvard Architecture Review* 3 (Winter): [93]–153. [An exhibition of architectural drawings, Fogg Art Museum, Harvard University, 2 December 1980–18 January 1981. Exhibitors: Aldo Rossi, O. M. Ungers, Rodolfo Machado and Jorge Silvetti, Diana Agrest and Mario Gandelsonas, Mario Botta, and Peter Eisenman.]
BRONER, KAISA. "Metafyysisen rationalismin arkkitehtuurista." Text in Finnish, French summary, p. 81–84. *Arkkitehti* 5: 24–35. [Interview with Aldo Rossi.]
"Cosa dimostra lo scandalo genovese del Carlo Felice." Text in Italian, English summary p. 572. *Architettura: Cronache e Storia* 30, no. 9 (August–September): 572–573.
CROSET, PIERRE-ALAIN AND GIACOMO POLIN. "Progetto per la ricostruzione del teatro Carlo Felice a Genova." *Casabella* 48, no. 502 (May): 52–63.
D'AMATO, CLAUDIO. "Fifteen Years after the Publication of *The Architecture of the City* by Aldo Rossi: The Contribution of Urban Studies to the Autonomy of Architecture." *Harvard Architecture Review* 3 (Winter): 82–92.
"Dalla storia all'immaginazione. Progetto per il teatro Carlo Felice di Genova [From History to Imagination. Design for Genoa's Carlo Felice theater]." *Lotus International* 42: 12–25.
"Design [European furniture]." *L'Architecture d'aujourd'hui* 236 (December): 91–[102].

FILLER, MARTIN. "Past with a Future." *House and Garden* 156, no. 7 (July): 46–[50].

KRIER, ROB. "Le case di Rauchstrasse: Un quartiere residenziale berlinese [The Rauchstrasse Houses: A Berlin Housing Estate at the Tiergarten]." Text in Italian and English. *Lotus International* 44: 6–27.

MATHEWSON, CASEY. "Over There: Architecture in the Old World." *Crit* 14 (Fall): 22–31.

ROSSI, ALDO AND GIANNI BRAGHIERI. "Un punto di riferimento per la città: edificio per uffice a Buenos Aires [A Landmark for the City: Office Building in Buenos Aires]." Text in Italian and English. Includes technical report by Santiago Calatrava, entitled "Memoria Tecnica." p. 37–39. *Lotus International* 42: 26–39.

ROSSI, ALDO. *Architetture Padane.* Modena: Edizioni Panini.

ROSSI, ALDO. *Tre Città, Perugia, Milano, Mantova.* Texts by Bernard Huet, Patrizia Lombardo. Milan: Electa and New York: Rizzoli.

SPINADEL, LAURA PATRICIA. "Wettbewerb Forellenweg, Salzburg: eine Siedlung der achtziger Jahre?" *Arch Plus* 77 (November): 76–83.

WEISSER, G. "Architettura/Il teatro dell'opera di Genova sarà finalmente ricostruito? Il cuor mi dice che Carlo tornerà Felice." *Europeo* 12 (24 March): 90–93.

"Wohnbau in Berlin: Internationale Bauausstellung Berlin 1984." *Bauforum* 17, no. 104: 10–32.

ZEVI, BRUNO. "Teatro Carlo Felice." *Arch Plus* 75–76 (August): 14–16. [Interview with Daniela Pasti.]

1985

AA. VV. "Progetti." *Progetti Veneziani.* Milan.

"Aldo Rossi." *Architectural Design* 55, no. 3–4: 52–55.

Aldo Rossi, un progetto di Architettura (May) Pescara.

Aldo Rossi. Buildings and Projects. Peter Arnold and Ted Bickford, comp. and ed.; introduction by Vincent Scully; postscript by Rafael Moneo; project descriptions by Mason Andrews. New York: Rizzoli.

"Architetti di tutto il mondo…confrontatevi!" *Marco Polo* (Venice) 18/19.

AULENTI, GAE. "Un punto di vista sull'architettura del teatro." *Casabella* 502: 60–62.

BARBIERI, U. "Aldo Rossi—het geschreven ontwerp." *Wohnen* 2/3: 31–34.

BRAGHIERI, G. AND U. BARBIERI, comps. *Aldo Rossi.* Rotterdam, Groningen, Breda, Nantes, Bordeaux. [Exhibition catalogue.]

CONTESSI, G. *Architetti pittori e pittori architetti, da Giotto all'età contemporanea.* Bari.

EDDY, DAVID HAMILTON. "Authentic City." *RIBA Journal* 92, no. 7 (July): 24–26.

"En plads i Fonti-Veggi-kvarteret i Perugia, Italien, 1982." *Arkitekten* 87, no. 23 (27 December): 525.

"Euro-Communism and Social Realism: Residential Unit at the Gallaratese Quarter, Milan; Aldo Rossi." Text in Japanese. *Toshi Jutaku* 217 (November): [60]–63.

GHIRARDO, DIANE Y. "Mingling the Elements: The Architecture of Aldo Rossi." *L.A. Architect* (February): 6–7.

KOENIG, GIOVANNI KLAUS. "La tana del lonfo: Attenti al dettaglio, che loscarto e breve fra ruggito e raglio." Text in Italian. English summary p. 213. *Ottagono* 20, no. 78 (September): 84–87.

LAROQUE, DIDIER. "Passage a Modene." *L'Architecture d'aujourd'hui* 241 (October): vii–x.

LAWRENCE, RODERICK J. "*The Architecture of the City* Reinterpreted: A Critical Review [book review]." *Design Studies* 6, no. 3 (July 1985): 141–149.

MAGNANI, CARLO AND CARLO TREVISAN. "Il concorso dello IACP di Venezia per Campo di Marte alla Giudecca." Text in Italian and English. *Casabella* 49, no. 518 (November): 4–21.

MANGIN, DAVID. "L'aide memoire." *L'Architecture d'aujourd'hui* 242 (December): v–ix.

MIYAKE, RIICHI. "Tradition, Form and Typology: Riichi Miyake Talks with Aldo Rossi [interview]." *Japan Architect* 60, no. 1 (333) (January): 8–12.

"Nei progetti di Venezia i problemi del mondo." *Corriere della Sera,* 24 August.

"Povera Italia il futuro è tuo." *Rinascita* 31.

ROSSI, ALDO, PETER EISENMAN, KURT W. FORSTER, AND JOHN HEJDUK. "Chamber works par Daniel Libeskind." *Techniques et Architecture* 358 (February–March): 62–67.

ROSSI, ALDO. "Dieci opinioni sul tipo." *Casabella* 509, 510.

———. "The Architecture of the Squares in the Veneto: A Student Thesis." *Architectural Design* 55, no. 5–6: 52–54.

———. "What is to be Done with the Old Cities?" *Architectural Design* 55, no. 5–6: 19–23.

ROZE, THIERRY. "A Nantes, dans le hall du théâtre Graslin, du 6 au 31 mars 1985, Une exposition d'œuvres d'Aldo Rossi [exhibition review]." *AMC* 7 (March): 25.

"Una casa berlinese: 'Villa' a Berlino/Tiergarten." Text in Italian and English. *Domus* 665 (October): 24–25.

VERTONE, S. "L'Italia è imbruttita ma non perduta [conversation with Aldo Rossi]." *Corriere della Sera,* 19 July.

"Zwischen Mies und Memphis: 239 Wohnungen im IBA-Block 189 an der Rauchstrasse in Berlin-Tiergarten." *Bauwelt* 76, no. 31–32 (23 August): 1248–1263.

1986

"Acquarelli, gessetti, penne e matite di Aldo Rossi." *Il Giornale dell'Arte* (February).

APULEO, V. "Se l'architetto dipinge." *Il Messaggero,* 18 February.

BANDINI, M. "L'architetto del silenzio." *Avanti,* 20 February.

BARLETTA, R. "Sogno metafisico di un architetto. Aldo Rossi all'Accademia Albertina di Torino." *Corriere della Sera,* 26 February, v.

BEDARIDA, MARC AND CHRISTIAN DE PORTZAMPARC. "Berlin-Rauchstrasse: Un exercise de style." *AMC* 11 (December): 63–[71].

BETSKY, AARON. "The Mythical Mirror of Aldo Rossi [book review of *Tre Città,* by Aldo Rossi and *Aldo Rossi: Buildings and Projects*]." *Progressive Architecture* 67, no. 1 (January): 159–160.

BOERI, STEFANO. "Alte Architektur für neue Technologien: Wettbewerb zur Umnutzung des Pirelli-Werks 'Bicocca' in Mailand." *Bauwelt* 77, no. 46 (5 December): 1752–1767.

BORTOLON, L. "Sessantotto disegni di Aldo Rossi, un protagonista dell'architettura." *Grazia* 2349 (2 March 1986).

CAPRA, S. "I percorsi segreti: se l'architettura diventa cultura." *La Nuova Venezia,* 2 February.

———. "La città et la memoria." *Giornale di Napoli,* 8 February.

———. "Taccuino d'un architetto: La città memoria collettiva dei popoli." *La Provincia Pavese,* 1 February.

CARAMEL, L. "Aldo Rossi e il progetto surreale." *Il Giornale,* 9 February, 11.

DE PAOLI, E. "Dalla 'grafica' di Carrà alle architetture di Rossi." *L'Informatore del Borgomanerese,* 1 February.

DRAGONI, A. "Rossi, architetto e visionario." *La Stampa,* 5 February.

FILIPPINI, E. "La mano che ricorda. In mostra a Torino i 'disegni di Architettura' di Aldo Rossi." *La Repubblica,* 11 February, 27.

GIACHETTI, F. BERTON. "Tra Mi e To ecco gli architetti artisti, *Il Sole 24 Ore,* 23 February.

GRAVAGNUOLO, B. "Teoria della fantasia: pensare l'architettura." *Il Mattino,* 9 December.

GUALDONI, F. "Aldo Rossi: la casa dipinta." *La Domenica del Corriere,* 15 March.

"Holiday Inn [Nimes, France]." *Architecture Interieure Crée* 209 (December 1985/January 1986): xx–xxi.

"Housing in Berlin, [Tiergarten, West Germany, 1985]." Text in Japanese and English. *A+ U* 3, no. 186 (March): [19]–26.

HUET, BERNARD. "Dopo 'l'esaltazione della ragione.' Aldo Rossi, dalla astrazione razionale alla figurazione emblematica [After 'the glorification of reason.' Aldo Rossi: From Rational Abstraction to Emblematic Representation]." Text in Italian and English. *Lotus International* 48–49: 208–215.

LAVINA, E. SCOTTO. "La poesia dell'architetto." *Il Giornale di Napoli,* 6 December.

LIPMAN, ALAN AND PAWEL SURMA. "Aldo Rossi, Architect, Scientist: A Storm of Silence—An Architecture of Alienation." *Design Studies* 7, no. 2 (April): 58–66.

MARTELLINI, G. "Ma che bel pittore questo architetto!" *Il Gazzettino,* 4 February.

MISTRANGELO. "Larchitettura come un disegno." *Stampa Sera,* 4 February.

MOSCHINI, F. " Poetica della metropoli [interview]." *Rinascita* 28 (19 July).

———. "L'architettura ha un cuore antico. I disgni di Aldo Rossi a Torino." *Rinascita* 7 (22 February): 20.

"Mostra: Aldo Rossi." *Leader* 3 (March).

OLMO, C., ed. *Aldo Rossi. Disegni di Architettura 1967–1985.* Milan. [Exhibition catalogue: 31 January–16 March 1986 Accademia Albertina, Turin.]

PIVETTA, O. "Mie carissime città." *L'Unità,* 27 February.

POLI, F. "L'anima dei luoghi fisici. Le forme di Aldo Rossi." *Il Manifesto,* 11 February, 11.

"Projects: Carlo Felice Theater,

Genoa, Italy, 1982." Text in Japanese and English. *A + U* 1, no. 184 (January): 19–26.

QUINTAVALLE, A. C. "Babele di carta—in mostra i disegni di Aldo Rossi a Torino." *Panorama* 1033, no. 24 (2 February): 12.

ROSSI, ALDO, ERALDO CONSOLASCIO, AND MAX BOSSHARD. *La Costruzione del Territorio: Uno Studio sul Canton Ticino*. 1st ed. Milan: CLUP. [Presentation of Italian edition by Daniele Vitale; introduction by Bruno Reichlin and Fabio Reinhart.]

ROSSI, ALDO. "I progetti per il ponte dell'Accademia alla Biennale Architettura [Designs for the Accademia Bridge at the Biennale Architettura]." Text in Italian and English. *Lotus International* 47: 50–51.

"Terrains du Campo di Marte sur la Giudecca [Venice]." *L'Architecture d'aujourd'hui* 248 (December): 75, 77.

VON BUTTLAR, FLORIAN. "Wurfel und Palazzo: zum IBA-Projekt Rauchstrasse, Wohnen am Tiergarten." *Baumeister* 83, no. 1 (January): 12-29.

ZARDINI, MIRKO. "Il territorio del Canton Ticino: una nuova edilizione italiana [book review]." *Casabella* 50, no. 529 (November): 32.

1987

Aldo Rossi Agenda 1987. Milan: L'Archivolto.

"Aldo Rossi Makes His American Debut [School of Architecture, University of Miami, Florida]." *Architectural Record* 175, no. 6 (May): 67.

Aldo Rossi, Architect. Texts translated into English by Finch Allibone. Introduction by Patrick Harrison. Milan: Electa; London: Architectural Press. [Catalogue of an exhibition held at the York City Art Gallery, 20 November 1987–3 January 1988 and at the Royal Institute of British Architects, 18 February–29 March 1988/exhibition and catalogue organized by Umberto Barbieri and Alberto Ferlenga.]

"Casa Aurora, Torino." *Abitare* 258 (October): 218–[225].

CHRISTIANSEN, JAN AND MICHAEL STEN JOHNSEN. "Arkitektonisk Olympiade." *Arkitekten* 89, no. 23 (23 December): 628–637.

"Competition for Reconstruction of 'Campo di Marte.'" Text in Japanese and English. *Process: Architecture* 75 (October): 134–141.

COOPER, MAURICE. "Aldo Rossi and the Tragic View of Architecture."

Blueprint (London) 42 (November): 22–25.

FERLENGA, ALBERTO, ed. *Aldo Rossi. Architetture, 1959–1987*. Milan: Electa.

"Fragments: A Project for Artforum by Aldo Rossi." *Artforum* 25, no. 9 (May): [103–106].

GABETTI, ROBERTO. "Aldo Rossi: Nuovo edificio per uffici 'Casa Aurora' Torino." Text in Italian and English. *Domus* 684 (June): [38]–49.

"L'architettura dell'angolo: l'ampliamento del GFT di Torino di Aldo Rossi." *Casabella* 51, no. 535 (May): 34–35.

"Neubau: Housing, Rauchstrasse (southern Tiergarten) [West Berlin]." *Architectural Review* 181, no. 1082 (April): 70–73.

PERETTA, G. "Aldo Rossi." *Flash Art* 137 (February–March).

ROSSI, ALDO. "Architektur der Stadt." *Der Architekt* 12 (December): 570–572.

———. "Centro comercial y habitacional 'El Seminario,' Pasto." *PROA* 352 (July 1986): 50–55.

———. "Town Hall, Borgoricco, Italy." *Arkkitehti* 84, no. 3: 58.

TEECCE, A. "I luoghi di Aldo Rossi, *Il Giornale dell'Arte* 39 (November).

1988

"Aldo Rossi: Architetture padane." *Pratt Journal of Architecture* 2: 40–43.

"Aldo Rossi: Casa Aurora and Other Recent Projects." *Architectural Design* 58, no. 1–2: 44–49.

"Aldo Rossi: edificio residenziale, Südliche Friedrichstadt, Berlino." English translation. *Domus* 697 (September): [36]–[45].

"Aldo Rossi: German Historical Museum, Berlin." *Architectural Design* 58, no. 11–12: 92–93.

"Architectenwettbewerb 'Deutsches Historisches Museum' in Berlin. First prize: Aldo Rossi." *Deutsche Bauzeitschrift* 36, no. 8 (August): 1021.

"Architektur der Dekomposition." *Baumeister* 85, no. 5 (May): 46–55.

BARACCO, MAURO AND PAOLO DIGIUNI. "Aldo Rossi: cappella funeraria a Guissano." Text in Italian and English. *Domus* 690 (January): 6–9.

BOGNAR, BOTOND. "Rossi's Ultimate Dilemma?: *Aldo Rossi, Buildings and Projects* [by] Peter Arnell and Ted Bickford, eds. [book review]." *Journal of Architectural Education* 41, no. 2 (Winter): 57–59.

DA PAZZO, GIOVANNI, ET AL. *Aldo Rossi*. Milan: Stampa Nava.

DUNSTER, DAVID. "Aldo Rossi [exhibi-

tion review]." *RIBA Journal* 95, no. 3 (March): 48–49.

FERLENGA, ALBERTO. *Aldo Rossi. Architetture 1959–1987*. French *Aldo Rossi. Architectures 1959–1987*. Milan: Electa Moniteur.

FITOUSSI, BRIGITTE. "Maison du Bonheur." *L'Architecture d'aujourd'hui* 259 (October): 79–80.

HATTON, BRIAN. "'Fellini' at the R.I.B.A. [exhibition review of 'Aldo Rossi' held 23 February–18 March 1988]." *Apollo* 127, no. 314 (May): 354–355.

"IBA: Internationale Bauausstellung Berlin 1987: Urban Villas on Rauchstrasse, Southern Tiergarten, Berlin, 1980–84." *GA Houses* 23 (August): 85–95.

IRACE, FULVIO. "Berlino 1988." Text in Italian and English. *Abitare* 263 (April): 236–256.

———. "Borgoricco (Padova): il nuovo municipio [Borgoricco (Padua): The New Town Hall]." *Abitare* 263 (April): 260–265.

JAEGER, FALK. "Ein mausoleum für die deutsche Geschichte: der Wettbewerb zum Deutschen Historischen Museum Berlin." *Deutsche Bauzeitung* 122, no. 8 (August): 95–97.

KNESL, JOHN. "Postclassical Poesis: Learning from Deconstruction." *Pratt Journal of Architecture* 2: 163–175.

KOEK, RICHARD. "Rossi's Haagse veertellingen: ontwerp voor herbestemming slachtuisterrein." *De Architect* 19, no. 9 (September): 113–117.

LAROQUE, DIDIER. "Aldo Rossi. Un centre d'art en Limousin." *L'Architecture d'aujourd'hui* 258 (September): 72–73.

MAYS, VERNON. "In Progress: Aldo Rossi." *Progressive Architecture* 5 (May): 33–34, 36.

MOOREHEAD, GERALD. "Trolley System Back on Track Following Four-Year Struggle." *Texas Architect* 38, no. 4 (July–August): 12–15.

OLMO, CARLO. "Across the Texts." *Assemblage* 5: [90]–121.

PEPCHINSKI, MARY. "Berlin Win for Aldo Rossi." *Progressive Architecture* 69, no. 8 (August): 25, 28, 30.

PETERS, PAULHANS. "Zur Entschiedung des Wettbewerbs Deutsches Historisches Museum." *Baumeister* 85, no. 7 (July): 10–11.

POSENER, JULIUS. "Geschenkt bekommt Berlin ein Geschichtsmuseum." *Arch Plus* 95 (November–December): 20–21.

"Recent Works of Aldo Rossi." Text in Japanese and English. *A + U* 6, no. 213 (June): [19]–134.

ROMANELLI, MARCO. "Una caffettiera in alluminio alta 28, 5 cm." Text in Italian and English. *Domus* 691 (February): 14–15.

ROSSI, ALDO. "Se guardo questi ultimi progetti: edificio d'abitazione a Kochstrasse, Berlino e centro commerciale a Parma [Looking at These Recent Projects: Housing on Kochstrasse, Berlin and Shopping Center in Parma]." *Lotus International* 56: 6–29.

SCULLY, VINCENT. "Aldo Rossi: Architect of Love and Memory." *Architectural Digest* 45, no. 10 (October): 148, 150, 153.

SPRING, MARTIN. "Rossi's Reasoning [exhibition review]." *Building* 253, no. 9 (26 February): 44–45.

STEIN, KAREN D. "Tempus Rossi: Five Projects in Italy: Aldo Rossi, Studio di Architettura, Architect." *Architectural Record* 176, no. 8 (August): 74–[89].

SWENARTON, MARK. "All About Aldo [Aldo Rossi exhibition review]." *Building Design* 875 (4 March): 10.

VAN GIERSBERGERN, MARIEKE. "Een compositie van fragmenten: Aldo Rossi's ontwerp voor het Deutsches Historisches Museum in Berlijn." *Archis* 9 (September): 8–9.

VON DER DUNK, HERMANN, et al. "Zum Konzept eines Deutschen Historischen Museums." *Bauwelt* 79, no. 28–29 (29 July): 1194–1221.

"Wettbewerb Deutsches Historisches Museum." *Detail* 28, no. 4 (July–August): 364–365.

WILLIAMS, STEPHANIE. "Reconciliation with History: The Future German Historical Museum in Berlin." *Apollo* 128, no. 322 (December): 413–416.

———. "Rossi in Berlin." *Architects' Journal* 187, no. 32 (10 August): 24–27.

WORTMANN, ARTHUR. "L'architettura del mondo: Aldo Rossi's ontwerp voor Den Haag in het licht van zijn internationale optreden." *Archis* 9 (September): 34–39.

ZWOCK, FELIX. "Wohnhaus Kochstrasse, Ecke Wilhelmstrasse in Berlin." *Bauwelt* 79, no. 26 (8 July): 1126–1129.

1989

"4. Premio nazionale IN/ARCH 1989 per un nuovo complesso architettonico [10 awards for new buildings in Italy]." *Architettura: Cronache e Storia* 35, no. 11(409) (November): 792–[800].

Aldo Rossi: Deutsches Historisches

Museum 1989. Berlin: Aedes. [Exhibition August–September 1989. Aedes. Galerie für Architektur.]

"Aldo Rossi Speaks on Architectural Continuity." Report on the Walter Gropius Lecture, given on 15 March 1989. *GSD News/Harvard University Graduate School of Design* 18, no. 1 (Summer): 13.

"Aldo Rossi." English summaries. *L'Architecture d'aujourd'hui* 263 (June): 133–187.

BIANCHETTI, FABRIZIO. "Una casa, una metafora della città [A House: A Metaphor of the Town]." *Frames, Porte & Finestre* 22 (January–March): 46–53.

CASTELLANO, ALDO AND MAURIZIO VITTA, eds. "Il nuovo Portello a Milano: un'esperienza per la città [The New Portello in Milan: An Experience for the City]." *L'Arca* 23 (January): Suppl. [1–128].

COHEN, JEAN-LOUIS. "Aldo Rossi en France, l'incompris intime." Text in French and English. *L'Architecture d'aujourd'hui* 263 (June): 134–135.

DI PIETRANTONIO, GIACINTO. "Aldo Rossi [interview]." *Flash Art International* 149 (November–December): 93–98.

DORSCHNER, JOHN. "Metropolitan Dade County: Miami; 27 città: la gente." *Abitare* 276 (July–August): 134–165.

"Eckhaus in Berlin-Kreuzberg: Wohnhaus mit Bewerbe im Erdgeschoss." *Baumeister* 86, no. 4 (April): 40–43.

"En el corazon de Berlin: museo de la historia alemana." *A & V* 18: 64–69.

FUMAGALLI, PAOLO. "Bestandteile des Entwurfs [book review *Scientific Autobiography*, French translation]." *Werk Bauen + Wohnen* 9 (September): 21.

FUMAGALLI, PAOLO. "Zeichnerische Objektivierung des Stadtraums: Area Fontivegge in Perugia, 1982." *Werk Bauen + Wohnen* 3 (March): 32–43.

JURGENSEN, AXEL. "Om behovet for en arkitekturdebat." *Arkitekten* 91, no. 15 (29 August): 380.

LIOTARD, PASCALE. "Hotel Il Palazzo–Japan." *Pace Interior Architecture* 18 (May): 90–98.

MARCHES, DOMINIQUE. "Le phare et l'aqueduc: Centre d'art contemporain de Vassivière en Limousin." English summary, p. 105; Spanish summary, p. 151. *Techniques et Architecture* 387 (December 1989–January 1990): 102–105.

MICHEL, FLORENCE. "Deux nouveaux musées de France." *Architecture Interieure Crée* 230 (October–November): 26.

NARPOZZI, MARINO. "La tradition et le talent individuel." *L'Architecture d'aujourd'hui* 263 (June): 136–139.

———. "Architektur in der Po-Ebene [Architecture in the Po Basin]." *Daidalos* 32 (15 June): 108–112.

———. "Une architecture pour les musées." *L'Architecture d'aujourd'hui* 263 (June 1989): 184–187.

ROSSI, ALDO. "Introduction to 'Architecture, essai sur l'art,'" *UCLA Architecture Journal* 2: 40–49. [English translation of Rossi's introduction to an Italian edition of Etienne-Louis Boullée's treatise.]

———. "Nuovo Palazzo dello Sport a Milano 1988" and "Per la stazione Croce Rossa a Milano." *Zodiac* 1 (February): 128–[153] and [178]–187.

ROSSI, ALDO AND MORRIS ADJMI. "Lighthouse Theatre in Toronto 1988." *Zodiac* 2 (September): [124]–[133].

SKUDE, FLEMMING. "Raffineret rationalisme: om Aldo Rossis seneste arbejder." *Arkitektur DK* 33, no. 4: 74, 76, 78, 80, 83.

"Una piccola città: Nuevo barrio sobre el viejo matadero de La Haya." English summary, p. 88. *A & V* 19: 70–71.

VAN BERKEL, BEN. "Terminal als landmark: vijf ontwerpen voor Sea Trade Center in Zeebrugge." *Archis* 8 (August): 12–23.

VOGT, ADOLF MAX. "Aldo Rossi, o teorico." *Projeto* 121 (May): 94–96.

1990

"A Milano, monumento-fontana dedicato a Pertini." *L'Industria delle Costruzioni* (September).

"Ad Aldo Rossi il premio Pritzker 1990 [Aldo Rossi Wins the 1990 Pritzker Prize]." *Domus* 717 (June): [20].

"Aldo Rossi opera buffa: Wiederaufbau des Teatro Carlo Felice in Genua." *Bauwelt* (27 July). *Architekten—Aldo Rossi*. 2d enl. ed. Stuttgart: IRB-Verlag.

BRANCH, MARK ALDEN. "Aldo Rossi Wins Pritzker Prize." *Progressive Architecture* 71, no. 5 (May): 23.

CHIRAT, SYLVIE. "Il Palazzo." *Architecture Intérieure Crée* 235 (March): [94]–103.

COHEN, EDIE LEE. "Multiple Talents." *Interior Design* 61, no. 7 (May): [202–209].

"Completata la ricostruzione del Teatro Carlo Felice a Genova."

Casabella 54, no. 570 (July–August): 33.

"Der 'Forellenweg' in Salzburg." *Baumeister* 87, no. 6 (June): 56–62.

DI BATTISTA, NICOLA AND VITTORIO MAGNAGO LAMPUGNANI. "Colloquio con Aldo Rossi [interview]." *Domus* 722 (December): [17]–28.

DOUTRIAUX, EMMANUEL. "Aldo Rossi à Gênes." *L'Architecture d'aujourd'hui* 268 (April): 152–[155].

FRIEDRICH, BARBARA. "Ein haus wie ein dorf." *Architektur & Wohnen* 1 (February–March): 30–38.

FERLENGA, ALBERTO. "The Theaters of the Architect." *Perspecta* 26: 191–202.

FILLER, MARTIN. "Rossi on the Rise." *House & Garden* 162, no. 9 (September): 154–[159], 216.

FREIMAN, ZIVA AND HIROSHI WATANABE. "Report: The Occident Expresed" and "Il Palazzo Hotel, Fukuoka." *Progressive Architecture* (May): 108–117.

GAMBA, R. "A Milano, monumento-fontana dedicato a Pertini." *L'industria delle costruzioni* 24, no. 227 (September): 10.

GARDELLA, IGNAZIO AND ALDO ROSSI. "The Carlo Felice Theatre in Genoa 1983–1990." *Zodiac* 4 (September): [32]–[74].

"Hotel Il Palazzo." *Japan Architect* 65, no. 3 (March): 39–50.

"Hotel Il Palazzo." *Kenchiku Bunka* 45, no. 519 (January): [76–82].

HUBELI, ERNST. "Hot Spots." *Werk, Bauen + Wohnen* 3 (March): 20–23.

"In Giappone, A Fukuoka: Il Palazzo," *Abitare* 286 (June): 148–153.

IRACE, FULVIO. "Rossi dopo Rossi [Rossi versus Rossi]." *Abitare* 286 (June): 154–155, 216.

IVERSEN, ERIK. "Nordjyske Billeder." *Arkitekten* 92, no. 18 (December): 572–573.

JIMENEZ, CARLOS. "El guardian de la memoria: entrevista con Aldo Rossi [interview]." *Arquitectura Viva* 14 (September–October): 38–41.

KILPATRICK, IVAN. "Aldo Rossi." *Arkitekten* 92, no. 16 (November): 514–521.

KUSCH, CLEMENS F. "Verwaltungsgebaude in Perugia." *Deutsche Bauzeitschrift* 38, no. 11 (November): 1544.

"Los soportes de la memoria: edificio 'Casa Aurora,' Turin." *A & V* 21, no. 1: 60–62 [English summary p. 87].

MARCHÉS, DOMINIQUE. "Le phare et l'aqueduc: Centre d'art contempo-

rain de Vassivière en Limousin." *Techniques et architecture* 387 (December 1989/January 1990): 102–105.

MOORHEAD, GERALD. "Rossi Arch Unveiled in Galveston." *Progressive Architecture* 71, no. 4 (April): 29.

NESMITH, LYNN. "Aldo Rossi wins Pritzker Prize." *Architecture: The Magazine of the American Institute of Architects* 79, no. 5 (May): 29.

PARENT, CLAUDE. "Vous avez dit transparence?" *L'Architecture d'aujourd'hui* 269 (June): 24, 26.

PRIORI, GIANCARLO. "Centro commerciale a Parma [Shopping Center in Parma]." *L'Industria delle Costruzioni* 24, no. 221 (March): 16–23.

"Pritzker—Prisen til Aldo Rossi." *Arkitekten* 92, no. 11 (August): 379.

"Raume des alltags: einkaufszentrum in Parma und interieurs in Barcelona." *Werk, Bauen + Wohnen* 6 (June): 54–65.

ROSSI, ALDO. *Architecture, Furniture and Some of My Dogs*. Milan: Unifor–Molteni & C. and New York: Studio di Architettura <distributor>. [Notebook of the exhibition of Aldo Rossi for Unifor in New York, October 1990.]

ROSSI, ALDO AND MORRIS ADJMI. "Il Palazzo, Fukuoka Japon Hotel y Restaurante para JASMAC [Il Palazzo Fukuoka Japan Hotel and Restaurant for JASMAC]." *Composicion Arquitectonica, Art & Architecture* 5 (February): [35]–62.

———. "Nueva Escuela de Arquitectura en la Universidad de Miami Coral Gables Florida [New School of Architecture at the University of Miami Coral Gables, Florida]." *Composicion Arquitectonica, Art & Architecture* 5 (February): [25]–34.

———. "School of Architecture at the University of Miami, Florida." *Zodiac* 3 (April): 170–[189].

SAVI, VITTORIO. "Das neue Teatro Carlo Felice in Genua." *Werk, Bauen + Wohnen* 12 (December): 2–9.

———. "Nuova Teatro Carlo Felice, Genova: Ignazio Gardella, Aldo Rossi." *Domus* 719 (September): [33–49].

"Sistemazione di piazza Cavour e piazza Missori a Milano." *L'Industria delle Costruzioni* 24, no. 227 (September): 66–68.

"Stations chics pour métros de choc." *L'Architecture d'aujourd'hui* 267 (February): 52–53.

STEIN, KAREN D. "Tower of Power: Hotel Il Palazzo, Fukuoka, Japan."

Architectural Record (May): 70–77.
STOLZL, CHRISTOPH. "Nachdenken üeber Deutsches Historisches Museum." *Bauwelt* 81, no. 1 (5 January): 22–27.
TAVERNE, ED. "De bevrijding van de architectuur: wie doorbreekt de wooncocon?" *De Architect* 21, no. 1 (January): 18–21.
THACKARA, JOHN. "Stars and Bars." *Blueprint* (London) 65 (March): 32–39.
"Three unbuilt designs by Aldo Rossi, Barton Myers, and Marco Guzzon." *Ville Giardini* 260 (June): 40–43.
TURNER, DREXEL. "Between Two Seas: Aldo Rossi's Small City in North America." *Zodiac* 3 (April): 190–201.

"Verwaltungsgebäeude in Perugia." *Deutsche Bauzeitschrift* (November).
WELSH, JOHN. "Turning Japanese." *Building Design* 977 (16 March): 24–25.
WORTMANN, ARTHUR. "Een ventiel voor de stad: Aldo Rossi's Teatro Carlo Felice in Genova." *Archis* 10 (October): 36–41.
"Zwei Wohnhauser in Pennsylvania." *Baumeister* 88, no. 2: 56–57.

1991
"Aldo Rossi." GA Document International '91, no. 29 (April): 76–79. Tokyo: A.D.A. Edita.
Aldo Rossi par Aldo Rossi, architecte. Paris: Centres Georges Pompidou. [Exhibition catalogue: 26 June–30 September 1991.]

BRAGHIERI, GIANNI, ed. *Aldo Rossi*. [Spanish and English edition of *Aldo Rossi* (1981)] Barcelona: Editorial Gustavo Gili.
CONFORTI, CLAUDIA. "Teramo: il Premio Terras di Architettura [Teramo: The Tercas Architecture Award]." *Abitare* 297 (June): 163–164.
DEDINI, ANTONELLA AND ANNAMARIA SCEVOLA. "Il grande albergo: la dimora del viaggio [The grand hotel: home of travel]." *Ottagono* 99 (June 1991): [118–146].
Domus 725 (March): [74–80].
FREIMAN, ZIVA. "The Architect of the City." *Progressive Architecture* 72, no. 2 (February): 49–63.
GUNTS, EDWARD. "Disney unveils new town." *Architecture: The AIA*

Journal 80, no. 8 (August): 27.
PIGAFETTA, GIORGIO. "Il Teatro Carlo Felice di Genova, ovvero della sproporzione urbana [The Carlo Felice Opera House in Genoa, or, A Case of Urban Disproportion]." *Abitare* 296 (May): 223–227.
ROSSI, ALDO. "Builings B4 + B5, Canary Wharf, London" and "The Stones of London," *Zodiac* 5 (March): 142–[147].
———. "Invisible Distances." *Via* 11: 84–89.
———. "Ossaria del cimiterio di Bisaccia." *Bauwelt* 82, no. 7/8 (22 February): 329.
STEIN, KAREN D. "Meier, Rossi, Scott Brown and Venturi Add Fabrics to Their Futures." *Architectural Record* (May): 21.

Menachem Adelman

166, 202, 204, 242, 243.

Federico Brunetti

70, 71, 72, 73, 79, 130, 158, 185, 219, 250.

Barbara Burg/Oliver Schuh

Cover, 20, 21, 22, 23, 24, 27, 28, 29, 30, 32, 34, 36 (t), 40, 41, 43, 44, 45, 48, 49, 53, 55, 56, 57, 59 (tl, tr, br), 61, 64, 65, 66, 67, 68, 69, 78, 80, 94, 95, 96, 142, 143, 144, 145, 154, 155, 156 (t).

Marco Buzzoni and Mauro Davoli

52.

Filippo Fortis

210, 258, 261.

Luigi Ghirri

63.

Antonio Martinelli

31, 42, 58.

Ned Matura

2, 83, 85, 112, 114, 149, 152, 153, 164, 176.

Nacása and Partners

101, 103, 104, 106 (tl, bl, br), 160, 170, 174, 175, 206, 207, 244, 245.

Kazuo Natori

100, 106 (tr), 107, 109.

Richard Payne

111.

Uwe Rau

26.

Stefano Topuntoli

50–51, 123, 127, 198.

Etienne Van Sloun and Gregor Ramaekers

299.

Paul Warchol

36 (b), 37, 38, 59 (bl), 76.

All drawings and models courtesy of Studio di Architettura (unless otherwise noted).